The City Authentic

The City Authentic

How the Attention Economy Builds
Urban America

David A. Banks

UNIVERSITY OF CALIFORNIA PRESS

University of California Press
Oakland, California

Library of Congress Cataloging-in-Publication Data

Names: Banks, David A., 1986- author.
Title: The city authentic : how the attention economy
  builds urban America / David A. Banks.
Description: Oakland, California : University of
  California Press, [2023] | Includes bibliographical
  references and index.
Identifiers: LCCN 2022036318 (print) | LCCN 2022036319
  (ebook) | ISBN 9780520383449 (cloth) | ISBN
  9780520383456 (paperback) | ISBN 9780520383470
  (ebook)
Subjects: LCSH: Urbanization—Economic aspects—New
  York (State)—Upstate New York. | City planning—
  Economic aspects—New York (State)—Upstate New
  York. | Social media—New York (State)—Upstate New
  York—Influence. | Authenticity (Philosophy)
Classification: LCC HT384.U62 N38 2028 (print) | LCC
  HT384.U62 (ebook) | DDC 307.1/21609747—dc23/
  eng/20220818
LC record available at https://lccn.loc.gov/2022036318
LC ebook record available at https://lccn.loc
  .gov/2022036319

Manufactured in the United States of America

32 31 30 29 28 27 26 25 24 23
10 9 8 7 6 5 4 3 2 1

Contents

Figures and Tables

Acknowledgments

It takes a village to write a book. Thanks go to Ava Kofman for starting this journey by demystifying some of the process. I also want to thank my students in History and Philosophy of Planning for reading my initial proposal: Andris, Snehal, Katherine, Derek, Zachary, Nora, Aleesha, Emily, Daniel, Ikenna, Jesse, Mark, Gopika, Prachi, Andrew, Nicholas, and Ben. I hope I demystified something by doing that.

Enormous thanks to Niels Hooper, whose email came as if from heaven when I was getting rejections from all sides. He took a risk on my project, and I'll be forever grateful to him. Also to Robin Manley, who shepherded the proposal to acceptance as one of his last acts at UC Press before starting what I expect will be a fulfilling academic career of his own. And of course Michelle Lipinski, who picked up the project once it was accepted, and pinch hitter Enrique Ochoa-Kaup for knocking it out of the park. LeKeisha, Barbara, and everyone else who worked on this, thank you so much.

There's a community of thinkers and writers who have done so much to help me find my voice as a writer and hone my ideas: Nathan Jurgenson, Alexandra Molotkow, Rob Horning, Soraya King, Jenny Davis, PJ Patella-Rey, Jeremy Antley, Stephanie Monohan, and everyone else at *Cyborgology*, Theorizing the Web, and *Real Life Magazine*.

There's also this beautiful community of friends and comrades that I've been honored to fight, love, hope, and drink with: Sean Collins, Ashley Saupp, Adam Pelletier, Jenn Baumstein, David Previtali, Dan

Lyles, Colin Donnaruma, Chris Scully, Emily Robertson, and too many more to list here.

Thank you Zoë Mabry for a lifetime of art: on our childhood books, my walls, my arm, and now my first (grown up) book.

I was blessed with twice the average amount of parents: Connie, Kevin, Roni, and Russell, you gave me life and then taught me what to do with it. Fáelán, Rachel, and Ian (wherever you are) love you.

But most of all Britney Gil, the love of my life and always the first set of eyes on anything I write. I could fill another book describing all the ways you helped me but then I'd *really* be over the word limit so just: thank you.

Abbreviations

ACE   Upstate Alliance for the Creative Economy
BID   Business Improvement District
CDRPC   Capital District Regional Planning Commission
CEG   Center for Economic Growth
CREDC   Capital Region Economic Development Council
EDC   Economic Development Council
IDA   Industrial Development Agency/Authority
PILOT   Payment in Lieu of Taxes

PART ONE

Making the City Authentic

CHAPTER I

Cultural Capital Region

One late afternoon, a few days before Christmas, I was sitting at my kitchen table absentmindedly eating cereal and scrolling through Instagram. I saw the usual fare of earnest bathroom selfies and moody party photos. Between a tastefully arranged bouquet of wildflowers and a dog in a Santa suit was an ad that caught my eye. Figure 1 is a screenshot.

At first, I thought the photo was taken in Troy, where I live, but I quickly realized that neither a three-story brick building nor a church is all that rare. Even though I think of them as unique relics of a bygone era, the reality is that the quirky neighborhoods of today were the alienating, uniform industrial hellscapes of the last century. These buildings could be almost anywhere in North America.

Anywhere, as it turned out, was forty-five minutes northwest in Fulton County, where the Fulton County Industrial Development Agency and the Fulton County Center for Regional Growth were advertising

industrial properties now available in popular towns, such as Gloversville, Johnstown, and Broadalbin, that can be customized to fit your business like a glove. Space is available in historic, grand buildings that feature distinctive architecture, 100 year old brick, and hardwood floors, surrounded by plentiful and free parking. If you need more room, space is now available in mixed-use, multi-story structures, former manufacturing facilities, and textile plants.[1]

The ad for three towns listed in rapid succession followed by the adjective-gilded amenities sounded like it was lifted straight from the

FIGURE 1. An Instagram ad for Fulton County, New York.

sales pitch of Lyle Lanley, the fast-talking salesman that came to Springfield to sell a "genuine, bona fide, electrified six car monorail." A con artist like Lyle Lanley, based closely on Harold Hill from the play (1957) and later hit movie (1962) *The Music Man*, is a familiar figure in times of transition. Whether it's the Eisenhower fifties giving way to the psychedelic sixties, or whatever it is we are living through today, con artistry thrives in uncertain times.

The Simpsons' "Marge vs. the Monorail" and *The Music Man* are rehashes of an ancient story about the outsider who acts as a foil to a sympathetic, but fallible community. It's a story that gives us an opportunity to ruminate on our definitions of good communities and what they need. We get a chance to exercise our suspicion of both salesmen *and* our own desire. Lanley convinces Springfield to buy the monorail by tapping into their fear of being left behind with a threat to take it next door to Shelbyville. The marching band that Harold Hill was selling the fine people of River City, Iowa, in *The Music Man* was meant to save them from the moral panic he had manufactured around the introduction of a new pool table at the local tavern.

These panic-inducing stories of modernity—fading into obscurity or descending into modern depravity—still work. Trump's promises of a border wall deftly used both: a one-two punch of losing in a global economy and stemming the supposed tide of "rapists and murders." City and county officials across the Rust Belt are realizing, just like Trump, that nostalgia for an idealized past and the desire for a dignified future, are a powerful sales strategy.

Are the leaders of Fulton County a bunch of Lyle Lanleys and Harold Hills? They have, at first glance, turned the con job inside out and upside down: unlike Lanley or Hill, who came to town selling something, here we have the town setting out to sell itself to someone else. The product they are selling is both an aesthetic and a business environment: a local government ready to give its antique buildings to an investor for a song.

If these cities think they are running and winning a con game at the expense of businesses, they have, in the parlance of our times, played themselves. Across the world, cities are increasingly strapped for cash. Indeed, even as cities grow to unprecedented sizes, the money needed to keep everything working is drying up.[2] A con game is certainly afoot, and local leaders may be in on it, but the marks in this scheme aren't the out-of-town businesses in the market for a new office; they're the people who need those taxes to pay for schools, roads, and sewers. And as more people move to cities all around the world, this dynamic becomes more important for more people.

This book is about the Capital Region of Upstate New York and its attempts to sell itself to employers, real estate developers, tourists, and potential new residents. And just like any regional label, the geography of what counts as the Capital Region is up for debate. When I asked Rocco Ferraro, the former executive director of the Capital District Regional Planning Council, where to draw the boundary, he declared, "My capital region is the four counties" (by which he meant Albany, Rensselaer, Schenectady, and Saratoga). Empire State Development, the corporation wholly owned by the New York State government and responsible for most economic development, uses a definition that includes four more counties: Greene, Washington, Columbia, and Warren. Fulton County—the self-appointed "final frontier" of the Capital Region sits just to the west of Saratoga County (figure 2). As you may have already noticed in the planning council's title, the geography

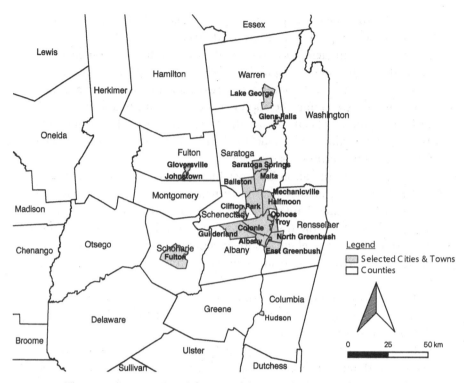

FIGURE 2. There are almost as many definitions of the Capital Region as there are residents. This map has most of the places you need to know about.

around Albany goes by many names: not just Capital Region or Capital District but also the Tech Valley and most recently CapNY. I will mainly be referring to the Capital Region.

We started at the far periphery so let's jump to the center. Albany is the capital of New York State, and in its mid-century heyday, it was home to nearly 135,000 people. As of the last count by the census bureau in 2020, it has a population of 99,224. It hosts several colleges and universities, the area's largest hospital, the State Capitol building, and the state offices that administer one of the largest state budgets in the nation. Many of these offices reside in a massive complex built in the International Modernist style at the behest of Nelson Rockefeller that now bears his name.[3] When the natives want to poke fun at their little city, they call it "Smallbany."

One of the most advertised parts of Albany is Lark Street, whose bounds on a map are Manning Boulevard to the north and Madison

Avenue to the south, but if you asked most people to draw it, they'd probably put the northernmost end at Central Avenue. It is in this third-of-a-mile stretch between Madison and Central that Lark is lined with shops on the ground floor of tastefully restored brownstones. There's a vegan deli, some quirky gift shops that make copious use of the phrase "upcycled," and a few cafes. This is likely why the Lark Street Business Improvement District declares on its website that it is "often called Albany's Village in the City."[4] In all the years I have lived here, I have never heard a living human call it that. I only come across that reference in tourist-oriented sites that are regularly fed copy from organizations like the Lark Street Business Improvement District. Sometimes they're more specific and call it "the Greenwich Village of Albany"[5]—a dated reference for twenty-somethings who are more likely to associate the Manhattan neighborhood with gentrification than bohemian chic.

Walk down the forgotten portion of Lark Street—between Manning and Central—and you will see a very different street. Here many of the buildings are marked with a metal sign with a big red X put up by the city to indicate that they are uninhabitable. The only business north of Central is a cab stand that also serves as paratransit for the disabled. Albany, like any American city, is segregated by race and income. To drive this point home to my students, I take an old map of Albany that bankers used during the era of redlining and let it slowly transition into another map that shows the present racial makeup of each neighborhood. The result is stark: despite over sixty years between the two maps, the Black neighborhoods of today are entirely enclosed within those neighborhoods that banks and insurance companies targeted for disinvestment for most of the twentieth century. This is also the case for Troy and Schenectady.

Schenectady sits to the northwest of Albany, connected by an Amtrak line, highway I-90, and a few state highways. The local transit authority also operates a bus rapid-transit line between the two cities with stops in the small towns and suburban communities that lie in between. All these connections hint at the relationship the two cities had nearly a century ago: Schenectady as an industrial behemoth, played host to both General Electric and the American Locomotive Company (ALCO). Albany served as the government regulator and promoter of these companies' wares. GE now employs about 4,000 people in the area, down from a height of more than 45,000 during World War II.[6] ALCO spent its entire life in Schenectady from 1901 to 1969. At its height, Schenectady had 95,692 people according to the 1930 census. Today it has 66,135.

The prestigious Union College still exists within city limits, and the Proctor's Theater has been kept in pristine condition and regularly hosts traveling productions of Broadway shows. The Golub family, which owns the New England supermarket chain Price Chopper, has kept their headquarters in Schenectady since the chain opened in 1932, and the city has received many philanthropic gifts from them over the years. And of course, no postindustrial town would be complete without a new casino: a Rivers Resort and Casino opened in the winter of 2017 in the old ALCO site thanks to $9 million in state aid.[7] The city also hosts a farmers' market in the street around the city hall on Sundays. From there it's just a few minutes' walk to the Jay Street pedestrian mall, which opened in 2011 as part of a $30 million redevelopment project focused on a neighboring building that now hosts a YMCA.[8] On Jay Street you can get a coffee, an antique lamp, and a tattoo.

Then there's Troy. It will be overrepresented in this book because I live there and know the most about it. I've devoted a whole section to Troy in this chapter as a case study in how small cities go from relative obscurity to social media darling, so I won't say much here except for a few historical details: It used to be a powerful banking and shipping city because of its location at the confluence of the Mohawk and Hudson rivers which marks the easternmost point of the Erie Canal and northernmost point that seafaring ships can navigate the Hudson. At its height in the 1930s 72,763 people called Troy home. Now a little more than 50,000 live in what was once derisively called "Troylet" but is now ironically called "the Troylet" as well as "the New Brooklyn."[9]

The regional approach I'm taking here presents one big challenge: within the three counties that contain these cities (Schenectady's and Albany's respective counties share the names of their biggest cities; Troy is in Rensselaer County), there are also thirty-one towns and villages and many more hamlets and census-designated neighborhoods. Each has its own laws, police department, and elected officials. Within and across these municipal boundaries are Industrial Development Authorities or Agencies (IDAs), Business Improvement Districts (BIDs), chambers of commerce, tourism boards, school districts, state and federal legislative districts, state-managed heritage corridors, neighborhood associations, gangs, cliques, a minor league baseball team, a transit authority, and competing hot dog vendors with rivalrous and dedicated followings.[10] And that's just the three definitely-the-Capital-Region counties. Expand outward and Saratoga Springs, Glens Falls, Hudson, and dozens more counties, cities, towns, villages, and hot dog vendors await you.

All these entities compete with one another for resources and attention. They must scrape together whatever competitive advantage they can find to attract just the right amount of residents, businesses, and tax dollars. Often enough, that means drawing comparisons to neighbors and describing what sets them apart. I was surprised to read on the Fulton County IDA website that "in Schenectady, Saratoga, Albany and Troy, the kind of space we're talking about usually comes at a premium."[11] When I moved to Troy just nine years ago, people were still using "Troylet" sneeringly, and college tour guides warned families against going downtown. Those warnings had always been little more than thinly veiled racism, but when did we become "premium"?

My neighbors and thousands of other people in the Capital Region are asking each other that same question. How did these forgotten backwaters become "historic," "grand," and "distinctive"? Who cares how old our bricks are? Maybe another way to ask all these questions at once is to wonder what exactly is being sold when you sell the character of a place? Not just the amenities or the architecture per se, but how do you put a price tag on the *vibe* of a town? Literally, where does the price tag go? Do you put it on the buildings themselves? On the people who've spent decades building and maintaining the physical and cultural infrastructure of the place? Or is it the land itself that bears the price?

Where to put the price tag or, to put it in a more academic way, where value is stored is one of the central quandaries in *the City Authentic,* a term I use not only to title this book but to describe a set of policies, practices, and ideas that leverage our modern desires for meaning and belonging to drive economic development. Paradoxically, the search for meaning in cities' amenities and landscapes within today's attention economy begets a cynical, postmodern tapestry of symbols, brands, and algorithmically selected aesthetic motifs that are anything but unique or meaningful. Rather, cities are encouraged by governments and businesses to act like reality TV stars and social media influencers— to become cartoons of themselves. Often this means bars that dress themselves up like what used to occupy the building a century ago or festivals that honor a romanticized past with trinkets and twee souvenirs for sale to tourists and new transplants.

A hundred years ago there was a City Beautiful movement. Then, civic leaders used big monuments, new buildings, and the press that followed to attract even more investment and drum up interest in the city. Today the City Authentic uses images of the old, rather than building something new, to grab attention. Civic leaders do this not just because attention is increasingly a precursor to profit, but because people and places mutually shape one another and so much of that shaping happens online and in media, where images are often (though not always) free from the constraints of historical context.

No one uses the term *the City Authentic* yet. I made it up to describe a phenomenon that has only grown since I started writing this book amid the pandemic and its concomitant economic impacts. Despite its ambiguity, *authenticity* has become a watchword in urban planning and economic development. The infinite interpretability of authenticity is fertile, valuable ground for speculation and Lyle Lanley salesmanship. The City Authentic is defined by a nostalgic approach to both building preservation and new construction that foregrounds authenticity and uniqueness over mass production and conformity. However, rather than herald a shift toward slowing growth and bringing economic activity more in line with human needs, the City Authentic gives rise to a ravenous real estate market that mines the delicate patina of history for profit. The City Authentic renders neighborhoods and entire municipalities into brands consumable through not just purchasing or renting real estate but through the conspicuous sharing of artifacts and symbols on social media.

Embedded in the term *City Authentic* is an acknowledgment that authenticity is both crucial to urban redevelopment and nearly infinitely interpretable. In the first quarter of the twenty-first century, I argue, it is the crucial concept that everyone is trying to shoehorn into their development projects. But in the past, other equally interpretable words fit the bill. This next section will go through that history and give us a better idea of where the City Authentic came from.

CITIES OF MOVEMENTS

The history of capitalist urban development is a story of competition for attention and money. This is how we should understand the changes in architectural style, governance, and financing that have defined cities for over two centuries. These changes were brought about through professional reform movements—internecine arguments among elites, not grassroots political campaigns—where powerful people, for both selfish and egalitarian reasons, sought to clean up the city by making it more beautiful or efficient. Above all, these movements sought to reorganize the city for the benefit of wealthy real estate holders, though they are much more complicated—morally and materially—than just that.

The two movements that I want to highlight are the City Beautiful and the City Efficient.[12] With each successive change in urban governance came a new cast of practitioners touting new theories of not only what made for a good city but what society itself should be like. A central thesis of this book is that we are living amid a third great movement of city building called the City Authentic.

The City Beautiful movement of the late nineteenth century was, in a sense, a rebranding of the city itself. Then, cities were dark, dirty, and hectic places to live, and the elites of European cities wanted to shake off the coal soot and dress their workplaces in marble columns and gold leaf. The industrial city of the Victorian era conjured up images captured by Charles Dickens and Emma Lazarus: poor, huddled masses toiling under the ultra-wealthy. The new beautiful city had something for everyone: culture and health for the rabble, security and wealth for the elite.

The historian Peter Hall draws the bounds of the City Beautiful movement as beginning in Napoleon III's Paris in 1853 and ending in Hitler's Berlin. Within these eighty years almost every major city in North America and Europe was fundamentally altered. European cities were rebuilt after and in response to great wars, which meant they had to be both trophies and fortresses, showing the world that they were economically healthy and prepared to defend themselves. Napoleon's Paris, for example, was completely redesigned by Georges-Eugène Haussmann to be both easier to defend and a beautiful model of how rich nations should build their seats of power.

American cites, meanwhile, had a lot to prove. If the United States was to ever dominate the world economy, it would have to build cities that looked worthy of empire. They should be, in the original sense of the word, awesome: physical embodiments of the blood and treasure amassed through conquest. And, because these new buildings were so grand, styled after Greek and Roman temples, they gave an aura of permanence.

Funny then that Daniel Burnham's temporary White City, built for the Chicago World's Fair, is largely considered the first demonstration of the City Beautiful. Washington, D.C., on the other hand, is the quintessential, permanent City Beautiful project. The original district plan was made by the French-born portraitist and friend of George Washington Pierre L'Enfant in 1791 but was never fully executed. The mall and its monuments were half-finished and trampled by the corporate capitalism that had made it rich: grazing animals and even a railroad ran straight across what was supposed to be a four-hundred-foot wide, mile long park from the Capitol building to the Potomac River. The Washington

Monument was financed with the nineteenth-century equivalent of a GoFundMe campaign but little else had been built. Burnham, still dining out on his work in Chicago, led a team of architects and landscape designers tasked by Michigan Senator James McMillan to update the L'Enfant plan and finally put it into action.

According to Hall, Burnham "insisted that they all went to Europe to study the finest urban models, ignoring the obvious irony that many of these had been created by the very tyrannies against which Americans had revolted."[13] The irony was, perhaps, palatable because the contrast that mattered to the ruling class of America was no longer their difference with Europeans but with the native people they were busy slaughtering. It is no coincidence that the business owners of western cities like San Francisco, Kansas City, and Denver were the first to organize and raise funds for their City Beautiful plans. In 1890 the U.S. Census Bureau had announced the closing of the American frontier; having to reckon with the completion of their Manifest Destiny, elites set to the task of graduating their cities from gritty industrial centers to grand cultural capitals. It was also necessary to find new ways to fix capital into urban land now that the frontier could no longer absorb all the money in banks on the East Coast.

It is also not a coincidence that the height of the American City Beautiful movement overlaps perfectly with that era of massive wealth inequality called the Gilded Age. The grand designs of the City Beautiful movement could not have happened without the unchecked power of the ultra-wealthy. While the finished products were and still are beautiful and provide some of the best public spaces in American cities, their construction was anything but a democratic affair. Acres of poor neighborhoods were bulldozed with no compensation given to the displaced. In their place stood grand buildings with quotes about freedom and justice etched in stone above the entrances.

Whereas Daniel Burman was the undisputed central figure of the City Beautiful movement, the City Efficient has a few contenders. One is America's first full-time city planner, Harland Bartholomew. He worked in Newark from 1914 to 1916 before leaving for St. Louis, where he opened a private firm that would go on to prepare comprehensive plans for over five hundred cities.[14] Whereas the City Beautiful built grand public monuments, parks, and buildings and therefore was led by architects and artists, the City Efficient was an exercise in rationalizing and professionally managing the city. Cities were seen as subjects of scientific study and experimentation, rather than artistic design and interpretation. Bartholomew, as an engineer and professional planner, embodies this new orientation. His firm didn't just write plans; it trained city staff in this new, professionalized form of planning, and Bartholomew himself aided in establishing the profession through his participation in federal planning efforts, including the creation of the interstate highway system.[15]

The City Efficient movement had more to do with code than sketches, but there was an architect who warrants mention. Swiss-born architect Charles-Édouard Jeanneret, better known by his nom de plume Le Corbusier, gained popularity with the controversial statement that a house was "a machine to live in." His plans sought to refine architecture down to the efficiency and rational order of industry. Ornamentation was not only extraneous but morally dubious. Buildings were functional things that served a purpose, and to waste time, money, and material on ornament was an inefficiency that took resources away from fulfilling basic needs.[16]

The City Efficient in Le Corbusier's hands felt radically utilitarian, almost communist in its dedication to the maximal distribution of goods and resources to the largest number of people. However, its focus on separation of land uses and obsession with the ultrahigh density of high-rises arranged in super blocks reduced any feeling of humanism. The City Efficient ethos was effectively parodied in Alejandro Jodorowsky's *The Holy Mountain* (1973), where the character Lut, an architect, states: "When we built this multi-family complex, we made a big mistake, we lost money. We gave them small gardens and windows, we installed water, lighting, and heating systems—this was a wrong concept. A man doesn't need a home, all he needs is a shelter." The scene then cuts to a basketball court where a long banquet table has been set up with lavish foods on expensive dinnerware. Aristocrats in tuxedos and ball gowns are gorging on meat as Lut shows them the scale model of what he intends to build: a rack of coffins serviced by water trucks and mobile latrines. The aristocrats applaud.

Burnham, Le Corbusier, Bartholomew, and their respective contemporaries used the latest technologies to finance, build, and manage their cities. The City Beautiful's massive structures would not have been possible without the newly mastered power of steam and the internal combustion engine. Indeed, the technologies that made the millionaires of the Gilded Age—banking, oil, communications, electrification, and mass transportation—were the technologies that made it possible for dozens of cities to undergo massive changes in less than a century.

Carnegie steel, to grab one example, was in the libraries that Andrew Carnegie had built across the country.

Similarly, the City Efficient was built on the Progressive Era's enthusiastic embrace of science as much as new construction technologies like reinforced concrete. The use of the latest technologies not only takes advantage of their new powers and reduced costs, but it also serves to reduce the value of older locations, either through obsolescence or sheer marketing power that encourages us to fetishize the new. Regardless of *how* new technology does it, the effect is the same: "to devalue the capitals employed under inferior technologies or in inferior locations."[17] For Troy that meant its position at the easternmost terminus of the Erie Canal went from vital competitive advantage to historical trivia as soon as the railroad network overtook waterways as the preferred shipping technology of choice. That led to massive investment in neighboring Schenectady (recall, ALCO was based there) and many other cities while Troy lost its pride of place as a shipping and banking hub. Development stopped so suddenly that over a century later, the exterior shots of Julian Fellowes's *The Gilded Age*, a period drama that takes place during the City Beautiful, are filmed in Troy.

The ascendant technologies of their time defined the character and function of the beautiful and efficient cities, and today is no different. Cities are being built to be playgrounds for authentic leisure experiences. What today's cutting-edge technology does exceedingly well is watch, categorize, and record all of life's activity, thus making it more amenable to curation and recombination. Many commentators have remarked how dangerous this has been for culture. Kurt Anderson, writing in *Vanity Fair* in 2012, called this the "first great paradox of contemporary cultural history," explaining that "new technology has reinforced the nostalgic cultural gaze: now that we have instant universal access to every old image and recorded sound, the future has arrived and it's all about dreaming of the past. Our culture's primary M.O. now consists of promiscuously and sometimes compulsively reviving and rejiggering old forms."[18]

To be clear, wistfully romanticizing the past is not unique to the twenty-first century.[19] Designer Wade Graham described nineteenth-century culture as an "ongoing crisis of time: because of the continuous dislocations and traumas of modernity, culture was obsessed with finding the right memories, trying to make sense of, or take refuge from, the present by recovering a golden age, or at least finding a usable past for a guide."[20] Lewis Mumford was more critical, lamenting that the "'era of good feeling' [1815–1825] was an era of bad taste." Architecture of the period, he wrote, was marked by "eclectic experiment, in which all sorts of Egyptian, Byzantine, Gothic, and Arabesque ineptitudes were committed."[21]

What, then, are the consequences of this latest version of nostalgia-obsessed culture and the technology that lets us share it? One, as I will argue extensively in part 2, is that authenticity takes center stage as both a potent tool of self-discovery and a site of value creation. The lab for eclectic experimentation in form, style, and culture has gone from gauche architecture for the nouveaux riches to an inescapable part of the global consumer economy. This is driven by firms' search for new profit centers as the declining rate of profit in older industrial sectors continues apace[22] and the cost of realizing the value contained in data trends falls.

Each successive movement used different techniques to achieve growth. The City Beautiful attracted investment through grand construction projects that signaled their arrival on the world stage and the capital flows that entails. The City Efficient created a standardized regulatory environment to make investment more predictable and transportable, thus making it more enticing to potential corporate employers. The City Authentic is predicated on several technological and financial changes to both real estate markets and media that have given rise to what I call in chapter 4 an upgraded growth machine. Instead of intensifying competition, elites insist on limited coordination such that competition is organized at more profitable scales and geographic dimensions. Telling convincing stories about why a place is unique yet still approachable has lots of commonalities with the tactics used by reality TV producers and social media influencers. While there are some overt relationships between economic development professionals and the worlds of reality TV and online influencers, the reason all three professions have started to look the same is that they share a common goal: to provide a convincing story about authenticity to an increasingly cynical and savvy audience whose attention is divided all the time.

These successive movements—Beautiful, Efficient, and now Authentic—beg an important question: why change the rules of competition? Clearly there was plenty of work left undone, given that there are still ugly and inefficient cities out there. The answer, which I will explore in full detail in the next section, lies in the fact that capitalism needs imbalance and unevenness to sustain its cancer-like growth pattern. Without uneven development, firms and wealthy individuals would not have anything to invest in.

THE FIX IS IN THE LAND

There are a few public intellectuals who like to point out that, at a planetary scale, everything is going fine. The average life expectancy is increasing, as are literacy rates, and the likelihood you'll die in a natural disaster has gone down.[23] This is mostly true. But if we zoom down just a little bit to the continental scale, we find some irregularities and disparities. At the continental level there is a net balance of imports and exports except for Africa, which is plundered at a rate of about 5 percent annually.[24] Go down just a bit further to the national level, and we see that the lion's share of the gains in life expectancy and literacy have come from the modernization of China and the successes of the Soviet Union before that.

Go further down to the level of the city and even Richard Florida, the once unapologetically capitalist soothsayer of economic development, has acknowledged we are in the midst of a "new urban crisis" marked by extreme inequality both within and between cities in the United States.[25] Raquel Rolnik's *Urban Warfare* sounds a similar alarm for the rest of the world, showing that since at least the 1980s American and European finance has built and fueled a "machinery of dispossession."[26] The world does not develop evenly.

Why is there uneven development? Why are some places thriving metropolises and others desolate wastelands? Part of the answer is the uneven distribution of useful things and geographic features. From deep-water ports to avocado trees, some places just have it going on and others don't. But that's not enough to explain continued disparities in an era of global trade. If I can get an Argentinian pepper in an Upstate New York grocery store in February, certainly we have the capacity to smooth out natural inequalities derived from climate and geology. We have boats and planes, computers and drones that can transcend space and shorten the time it takes to move things and people around.

Indeed, the technical capacity might be there to meet most people's needs most of the time, but that is not how global capitalism works. Everyone from Adam Smith to Paul Krugman has puzzled over the issue of uneven development, but with the help of the preeminent Marxist geographer David Harvey, we can make fast work of why the problem persists. In his *The Limits of Capital* Harvey carefully pieces together a case for why uneven development is essential for the overall functioning of capitalism. Equally important are financial crises and natural disasters that clear the land (sometimes literally) for renewed development.

The relevant parts of Harvey's argument go like this: Capitalism is exceedingly good at producing both commodities and profit. In fact, it regularly makes too much, and this overproduction threatens the stability of the whole system. Imagine a brewery making more beer than it can feasibly sell in the short run. It can either hold onto its inventory and sell it slowly over time, or it can find new customers. Any businessperson knows that both options are costly. Warehouse space to store the unsold beer means paying rent and insurance. Add atop that the danger of the beer becoming skunky and undrinkable. New-customer acquisition costs like advertising and finding new distributors have their price too. These costs must be weighed against potential benefits. Selling existing inventory means less money spent on labor brewing new beer, and growing your customer base means potentially expanding the business over the long run.

These sorts of decisions happen at all scales. The biggest firms, however, have many more options at their disposal, including governments that can wage war, colonize, and otherwise significantly alter the conditions of laboring, buying, and selling. Capitalists will go to great lengths to find new markets for their goods because everything they own—even money itself—will become less valuable if they do not. Like great white sharks, markets must keep moving or they will die.

Capitalists never solve the problem of overproduction for good. Instead, they stave it off for a few years or move the consequences around through what Harvey calls a "spatial fix."[27] The spatial fix can take many forms, but a common one is financing the construction of new factories and agricultural projects in poor countries. It's not enough, according to Harvey, to just loan the money; the capitalist must install the "whole package of the capitalist mode of production which includes modes of distribution and consumption."[28]

In the world of international development, that means "modernizing" countries and making sure people sell their labor for cash instead of doing subsistence farming or building local economies closed off from international trade. This not only opens new markets for, say, American corn products, but it also creates a demand for cash to buy products that can be acquired only through wage labor.[29] Often enough this transition is not self-evidently better or more desirable, which is why a series of land "reforms" that dispossess people of their productive farmland is also necessary. These were the kinds of changes brought about by the International Monetary Fund and World Bank in the 1980s and '90s under the banner of structural adjustments.[30]

When the rust belts of North America and Europe were still steel belts, they were the beating heart of capitalist expansion, sending electricity, building materials, and finished consumer goods to the parts of the world that had been identified for spatial fixes. World War II had destroyed much of Europe and Japan, making them excellent candidates for spatial fixes as well. But because the spatial fix never resolves the fundamental problem of capitalist overproduction and market saturation, a series of crises took place (e.g., "stagflation" as well as several recessions) that made the process start all over again. Whereas the American economy of the 1950s, '60s, and '70s was fueled by building suburbs on farmland and skyscrapers in cities and filling them all with appliances, cars, and electronics, the 1980s were marked by a shift to finance and offshoring. Geographically this meant moving factories first to the southern United States, then to Mexico and South America, and finally globally to Bangladesh, the Philippines, and China.

Economic crises and uneven development, despite what CNBC or Econ 101 says, are an absolute necessity for the capitalist mode of production. From the capitalists' point of view, bankrupt cities and rural poverty are potential spatial fixes for a new round of investment. If all cities were on sound financial footing and rural hinterlands were self-sustaining, there would be nowhere to reap profits.

But shouldn't lenders be interested in making loans to reputable, fiscally healthy borrowers? Shouldn't developers want to build only where the economy is stable and predictable? According to Neil Smith, Harvey's student and prominent Marxist geographer in his own right, nothing could be further from the truth. Sure, profits can be made in healthy economies, but the biggest returns can be found where investors buy low and sell high: whether it's decades of disinvestment or an acute disaster, the biggest profits are to be found amid rubble and ruin, not milk and honey. Smith calls the profitable difference between prevailing real estate value and the potential new price the "rent gap."[31]

In Naomi Klein's best-selling book *The Shock Doctrine*, she describes how post-Katrina New Orleans was picked apart by vulture capitalists seeking rent gaps, though she never uses the phrase. The widespread destruction made it the perfect spatial fix for developers looking to privatize services and build on newly bulldozed urban real estate. Klein even starts the book with two particularly gut-wrenching examples of capitalists saying the quiet part loudly:

> Richard Baker, a prominent Republican congressman from this city, had told a group of lobbyists, "We finally cleaned up public housing in New Orleans.

We couldn't do it, but God did." Joseph Canizaro, one of New Orleans' wealthiest developers, had just expressed a similar sentiment: "I think we have a clean sheet to start again. And with that clean sheet we have some very big opportunities."[32]

Baker, Canizaro, and their compatriots may have waited for an act of God, but the story of New York's Capital Region is a slower, more complicated decline connected to the globe-spanning churn of finance and manufacturing. Smith calls this boom-and-bust cycle of urban economies the "see-saw movement of capital."[33] No city is immune from the structural demand of capital to build up, tear down, and start all over again.

Putting all these concepts together, we can say that the American Rust Belt is in a prime position to act as the next spatial fix for global capital. Seven of the top ten zip codes with the most vacant properties are in Rust Belt cities like Gary, Indiana, and Youngstown, Ohio.[34] Poverty in this region—which is typically defined as stretching eastward from the upper Midwest to New England—is more intensely segregated than it is in the rest of the country.[35] That means there are plenty of buildings to spend money on and lots of neighborhoods to gentrify. The see-saw movement of capital is at the bottom and now it's a race to see who can ride it up to the top and realize the biggest rent gaps.

In the Capital Region, a union-dense mix of education, healthcare, and government jobs buoyed the region, keeping it relatively unscathed from the worst of the Great Recession, and the area continues to post low unemployment numbers relative to the Northeast.[36] Still though, 25.4 percent of housing units in the Albany metro area were built before 1939,[37] and its Victorian downtowns have suffered years of neglect. When I arrived in Troy in the summer of 2010, there were many vacant store fronts and dilapidated buildings. Even as I write this, after years of City Authentic policies, there are regular demolitions of buildings beyond saving and many others languish as zombie properties: half alive on some bank's books but half dead because the owner of the building (and its debts) is lost or unreachable.

Capital, sooner or later, needs another fix, and it is up to city leaders to tell the right story at just the right time to attract capitalists' attention. However, with the hard limits of available land and its capacity to absorb the pollution of industry, spatial fixes have turned inward in two respects. First, capitalists are rebuilding the downtowns of Rust Belt cities. This incredibly expensive rehab job is a great way to spend billions of private and public funds. It keeps the shark of capital swimming

while also setting up new opportunities for further investment by raising the profile of the region. That means surrounding suburbs see an
increase in turnover and asking price. The second turn inward is to the
self: changing not only what is hip but how capital finds (or makes) the
next big thing. This double turn suggests that the City Authentic is
much more than a gentrification scheme. It is also the setting for a psy-
chological journey of self-actualization.

The ability to market your city as the "new frontier" of real estate
development that will attract the colonists (and that is indeed what they
are, with all the violent displacement the word implies) is a battle fought
out in public, often online, with ads, hashtags, and write-ups in hip
publications. If social media is a shelf in a store selling real estate, then
each city is clamoring to be the one at eye level with the most enticing
packaging. That means understanding everything from what is trending
on the latest social media platform to the idiosyncratic wealth accumulation strategies of local power elites.

Harvey is clear that against this backdrop of uneven development,
capitalists and the working class will sometimes, temporarily, put aside
their differences for the interest of a region, whether that's a nation or a
single town: "The alliance typically engages in community boosterism
and strives for community or national solidarity as means to defend the
various factional and class interests."[38] Those interests might be as
straightforward as keeping a factory open but, as we will see in the
pages that follow, this collective impulse is increasingly captured by a
relatively new set of professionals whose job it is to manage and promote the brands, aesthetics, and even memes that bolster the cultural
cachet of a place.

A BRIEF HISTORY OF CULTURAL PLANNING

Turning culture and history into money is the jurisdiction of cultural
planning. Outside the profession, few people have heard of it. Perhaps
that is because people find it off-putting to think that something as creative and intimate as "culture" could, in any way, be planned. It feels
like a rude oxymoron. And yet the City Authentic, ironically, owes its
early history to the very idea that it is possible to plan culture.

Cultural planning has its origins in postwar Britain and a relatively
short-lived government appendage called the Greater London Council.
It was at the GLC, specifically its arts subcommittee, that two men,
Geoff Mulgan and Ken Worpole, collected years of research into the

arts and culture industries and eventually put them into a book published in 1986 titled *Saturday Night or Sunday Morning? From Arts to Industry—New Forms of Cultural Policy*.[39] This book is regarded by experts as one of the first texts of cultural planning as economic development strategy. Without Mulgan and Worpole, there would be no authenticity peddling, which is the term I use to describe the myriad techniques, strategies, and business plans whose success relies chiefly on notions of authenticity.

The GLC was established in 1963 with the City Efficient goal of modernizing the administration of a new London rebuilt after World War II. It was responsible for administering essential services like waste disposal and firefighting, but it also had the authority to convene a wide array of subcommittees to study and implement public policy. Control over the GLC was hotly contested between the Tory and Labour parties, but in 1981, in what would be the last election of the GLC, Labour had its best showing since its original founding and used that mandate to embark on a wide range of political programs that were such a hindrance to Margaret Thatcher's regime that she dissolved the GLC entirely in 1985.

It was in this period, between 1981 and 1985, that Mulgan and Worpole did the work that would fill the pages of *Saturday Night or Sunday Morning?* They wrote, "One of the first actions of the new administration was to shift arts funding from its almost hidden position from within the ponderously titled Recreation and Community Services Policy Committee to a space of its own: the Arts and Recreation Committee."[40] It was here, nestled alongside the Ethnic Arts and Sports Sub-Committees that the Community Arts Sub-Committee did its groundbreaking work.

Decades before right-wing American news personality Andrew Breitbart would claim that "politics is downstream from culture,"[41] the GLC wedded culture to its ambitious political programs. Its first report stressed the importance of meeting the cultural interests of the unemployed, youth subcultures (particularly young girls), women's and gay men's groups, and the elderly. This was a self-conscious effort to grab the attention of and become relevant to the marginalized groups that Labour wanted to organize.[42] Mulgan and Worpole recognized that "in any society an important part of oppression is the denial of meanings and identity to the powerless."[43] They theorized: "Within a capitalist society, beset by inequalities of power, the best strategies for survival often involved creating alternative, exclusive realms which reject dominant codes. . . . What makes them effective is that they define an identity through difference."[44]

Mulgan and Worpole spend a considerable amount of ink—two lengthy chapters in their slim volume—lamenting how BBC programing flitted between two extremes: as a broadcaster of boring stuff for rich people and as a "cadet of US television imperialism."[45] Despite a socialist model of state ownership, the British airwaves were stuck in a paternalistic Toryism held over from the 1930s, when John Reith, the first director-general of the Royal Charter BBC, would say things like "Few know what they want and very few what they need."[46] Mulgan and Worpole suggest instead that public radio and television must be used to shore up cultural products that would not find investment in the private marketplace but come from mass audiences, not high society.

Deborah Stevenson, in her 2017 book *Cities of Culture: A Global Perspective,* describes how the GLC's work was embedded in a broader intellectual reinterpretation of culture. The GLC subscribed to an emerging school of leftist thought that saw culture as something that imbued all things with meaning and social structure. It was influenced by the foundational cultural studies scholar Raymond Williams, who expanded the academic definition of culture from discreet creative or artistic artifacts (e.g., a painting or ceremonial dance) to "a general process of intellectual, spiritual and aesthetic development" and "a particular way of life."[47] Stevenson calls this the "anthropological" definition of culture, as opposed to Reith's assumption that high art—the symphony, Renaissance oil paintings, and so on—is synonymous with culture. Instead of foisting the artistic tastes of the aristocracy onto the working class, the GLC set out to make government and the market more responsive and relevant to common people's lives. It soon found that "few [Londoners] thought about the potential of their creative endeavors to generate income or perhaps even become self-sufficient or use their activities to leverage other activities, innovations or sources of funds."[48] The GLC, for example, had a keen interest in town fairs and festivals where working-class people—particularly women—could make money through turning hobbies like baking and embroidery into businesses.

While the anthropological definition is certainly less overtly racist and elitist, it is clear today that this approach can and did open the door for a pernicious kind of cultural commodification—that is, a set of conditions wherein the collective heritage of a neighborhood, city, people, or nation is commodified via tourism or the selling of goods and services, often without their permission.[49] Sometimes this can redound to the benefit of the people whose culture is being commodified, but often just a few well-resourced individuals or firms take the lion's share.

When the Thatcher regime put an end to the GLC in 1985, devolving its authority to more local jurisdictions, the ideas developed by Mulgan and Worpole went international—taking root particularly well in Australia.[50] There, cultural planning was used to Europeanize cities, rather than define them as multicultural bastions of cosmopolitanism. As a result, according to Stevenson, cultural planning in Australia became "highly derivative"[51] of the U.K.'s, and "cultural planning experts with little knowledge of, or connection with, Australia and its towns, cities and cultures have been disproportionately influential."[52] For example, Geoff Mulgan himself was a "thinker in residence" in the southern city of Adelaide in 2007, and at his suggestion the government established a private social enterprise organization called the Australian Centre for Social Innovation (TACSI). TACSI has since gone on to intervene in Australian public policy in a wide range of fields from arts and culture to senior care and wildfire management.

Mulgan would later team up with *The Creative City* author and fellow Brit Charles Landry to build the creative cities network in the 1990s, which helped civic leaders share cultural planning techniques. According to Mulgan, "Many of these ideas moved into the mainstream, popularised and developed by figures like Richard Florida in the US."[53] Landry's *The Creative City* is distinctly cognitive, focusing on how urbanists should think about the city and its inhabitants. In a section titled "The New Thinking," Landry presciently writes, "The city itself is an incredible information source that can lead to sensory overload. That is why attention—the capacity to concentrate, listen and absorb—is increasingly seen as a factor of production like labour, capital and creativity."[54]

Richard Florida popularized creativity-inflected cultural planning with his 2002 mega-hit book *The Rise of the Creative Class*. In the 1990s Florida was a professor at the University of Pittsburgh and watched in horror as several tech companies founded at the university left for Boston or Silicon Valley. He convened his graduate students for a focus group and what he found was that they were bored in Pittsburgh and were willing to spend the extra money to live in a place with more to do.[55]

Florida's solution that would catapult him to stardom was "the three T's": talent, technology, and tolerance. By ensuring a cosmopolitan, tolerant culture, a city could attract the creative talent that growing technology firms needed. Once firms were sufficiently convinced that the talent was already there or future workers would be willing to move, the creative-class theory went, they could be enticed by modest tax abatements or other incentives. Rather than ask if this worked, Jamie Peck, in a 2005 rebuttal to the creative-class thesis, asked a better question: where "did the audience for Florida's arguments come from?"[56]

His answer, which dovetails nicely with Stevenson's observation that Australia imported much of its cultural planning ideas, is that most cities were desperate for new policy tools. Deindustrialization had significantly undermined the typical "smokestack chasing" tactic of luring manufacturers to the city. No city could compete with the growing concentration of manufacturing in China and the Global South. Florida, with the help of Landry, Mulgan, and Worpole had entered an empty market and dominated it quickly. Cultural planning provided a template for luring spatial fixes back to crumbling American and European downtowns.

What survived of the GLC program would eventually return to British shores in the late nineties under the guise of New Labour with direct support from Mulgan, who had become Prime Minister Tony Blair's head of policy. Far from the overtly socialist program of the 1980s, which was expected to maintain a permanent campaigning posture that would "exemplify other parts of the programme—such as commitments to internationalism and disarmament, to the rights of women, ethnic minorities and gay people, to the creation of a fully employed and participative society,"[57] the British people got what author Roger Luckhurst called the "Edenic post-political garden of Cool Britannia."[58] The "third-way" centrist politics of the Blair government attempted to create, in the words of a report issued by a think tank founded by Mulgan and Worpole, "a viable capitalist social order [that would] organize and sustain itself."[59] Today neither Mulgan nor Worpole list *Saturday Night or Sunday Morning?* on their respective websites. Mulgan, in 2010, was alerted to a much-belated review of the book by Deborah Stevenson and called it "ancient history."[60] Blair, far from being a champion of peace and full employment, is remembered for his support of the American war in Iraq and a policy of "backdoor privatization" of British public services.

This history is important for two reasons. First it shows that, from the jump, the constituent programs of the City Authentic were overtly political ones. The role of culture in urban development has always been understood as a reserve of political power whether that be as a means of distraction and subjugation or a rallying cry for liberation. To the extent this early version of cultural planning dealt with notions of the authentic, the GLC sought out long-standing traditions and crafts to build meaningful bonds with marginalized groups and improve their lot in life. This was seen as a vital component of building a base of support among the working class through good-faith interest in preserving culture and small-scale economic development. How contemporary cultural planning deals with authenticity, on the other hand, is best described by the urban sociologist Sharon Zukin:

> To speak of a city being authentic at all may seem absurd. Especially a global capital like New York [or London], neither people nor buildings have a chance to accumulate the patina of age. . . . In fact, all over the world "Manhattanization" signifies everything in a city that is *not* thought to be authentic: high-rise buildings that grow taller every year, dense crowds where no one knows your name, high prices for inferior living conditions, and intense competition to be in style. Lately, though, authenticity has taken on a different meaning that has little to do with origins and a lot to do with style. The concept has migrated from a quality of people to a quality of things, and most recently to a quality of experiences. . . . Viewed through either of these lenses, a city is authentic if it can create the *experience* of origins.[61]

This shift from origins to style means that authenticity itself "becomes a tool of power."[62] Once an experience, a person, or a thing is anointed as "authentic," it takes on a transcendent quality. The experience of origins suggests that the authentic person, object, or event can resist the constant churn of modern society and thus act like a cultural lifeboat in modern waters. This immunity from modernity's changing trends is often packaged as "creativity" because it shows discernment. As Sarah Banet-Weiser puts it in discussing the creative-class thesis, "Through the presentations of indexes and scales, and the slick promotional materials of branders, creativity itself is reified, transformed into an object that is marketed, distributed, and exchanged within the contemporary neoliberal economy."[63]

This brings us to the second reason this history is important. The history of Mulgan and Worpole attests to the fact that cultural planning has an uneasy relationship with the project of human liberation. These men seem to have started off as committed, well-read socialists, only to return to power as lackeys for a centrist government. Florida, too, has an interesting political orientation that he revealed in an interview in the socialist publication *Jacobin*. He started his studies "from a Marxist or neo-Marxian point of view," but then he met the British economist Christopher Freeman and asked him, "'How did you come to Joseph Schumpeter?' And he said, 'Well I was basically a Marxist, but when I wrote stuff about Marx, nobody would publish my articles. When

I substituted the name 'Schumpeter' for 'Marx,' my papers would get published everywhere.'"[64]

Schumpeter, far from being a Marxist, was a suspected Nazi sympathizer[65] and opponent of the New Deal. His coining of the term "creative destruction" has made him a popular citation of neoliberal economists and would therefore explain Freeman's and Florida's adoption for the sake of publication. As Florida explains it, Schumpeter's work is useful to help understand why capitalism, rather than collapsing, "is able to self-revolutionize because it can generate new technologies, new industries." And while Marx may have been good for understanding what happens on the factory floor, "place itself has become the key social and economic organizing unit: where the knowledge workers congregate, where the infrastructure of capitalism is built."[66]

To sum up: the history of cultural planning has been a political project adept at sheepdogging progressive and even Marxist thought toward centrist politics. No one can say for sure what the true intentions of Mulgan, Worpole, Landry, or Florida were, but they all have strikingly similar trajectories: they went from Marxists to something much more conservative. What is unclear is whether cultural planning will invariably lead anyone down the garden path of neoliberalism or if the field can be saved from its best-known practitioners. I suspect that it is unsalvageable, which is why I conclude this book with a proposal for a new economic development strategy that avoids authenticity altogether.

A RUSTED STAR IS BORN

I don't think I would have ever thought to write this book if I hadn't moved to Troy, New York, exactly when I did. I grew up in South Florida and moved to Troy in my early twenties, when it was still a sleepy place with a few good bars, but you had to drive to the suburbs for groceries and everything closed early. Most importantly though, my wife and I could rent a three-bedroom flat for almost half of what our friends in New York City were paying for a single room in a tiny apartment. It felt as though we'd beat the system: we had a nice, walkable downtown with a growing community of young folks surrounding us and we weren't giving the millennial average of 45 percent of our income to our landlord.[67] But then the City Authentic came to town and everything—from the buildings to the city government's website—was reoriented to grab outsiders' attention through the conspicuous deployment of authenticity peddling.

Looking back on the data, it appears as though we arrived just as things were starting to take off. Between 2009 and 2010, the percentage of food service jobs shot up in Troy from 3.79 percent of all jobs in the city to 7.8 percent. That number steadily increased to about 10 percent a decade later.[68] But the real watershed moment was in 2012, when word got out that a wine bar was opening on Second Street. A young couple, Vic Christopher and Heather Levine, had bought a building for $155,000 in the middle of downtown.[69] For nearly a year, butcher paper and hand-painted signs teased passersby with the eventual opening of the Charles F. Lucas Confectionery and Wine Bar. The name was plucked from one of the building's many tenants over the years, a candy shop that had opened in 1863. Had they named the place after the most recent tenant, it would have been called the Troy Insurance Agency and Wine Bar.[70]

The opening of the wine bar had all the drama and anticipation of a small town ready to strike it big. It helped that Christopher was a master salesman fit for the burgeoning Trump era. In 2010 he had been the assistant general manager of the local minor league baseball team (go, ValleyCats!) and ran a blog for them hosted on the local newspaper's website. He had left that job to become Troy's economic development coordinator and was tasked with attracting employers and small businesses with tax incentive schemes, grants, and reports on everything from workforce characteristics to public debt financing. His job with the city ended abruptly after only two years, when "police allegedly discovered Christopher removing items from basement of the city-owned Dauchy Building."[71]

Ever the showman, Christopher was able to turn the coverage of his resignation in April 2012 into an advertisement for his and Levine's wine bar. A short article titled "Troy Economic Development Coordinator Vic Christopher Resigns" included a remarkable line that any brand manager would be proud of: "Christopher is currently in San Francisco, Calif., and is taking tours of Napa Valley, Sonoma and San Francisco on a Vespa to get a better sense of California's olives, cheese and wine so he and his wife Heather can bring back the information to create a world class experience at the old Lucas Confectionary."[72]

The wine bar opened on November 9, 2012, to great fanfare. The reviews were stellar. Under the title "Bohemian Rhapsody," Albany's *Times Union* raved about not just the food but the "space that is less a bar (no hard liquor is served) than an attempt to create a hangout for those who appreciate a luxurious bohemian aesthetic." It went on:

It's trendy but feels like it's been there 200 years rather than two months. It's post-apocalyptic industrial chic, complete with a reinvented-from-salvage interior headlined by a neon Faema steam lever espresso machine. A weighted pulley system shoots handwritten tickets squeakily back to a bare-brick, bare-bones prep space. Artfully restored vintage Troy wood, brick, marble and glass is installed in unexpected ways throughout the building.

Levine and Christopher's wine bar was a runaway success and ended up being the beginning of what local papers would call a "renaissance." They went on to buy several more properties before they divorced, and Heather left the area in 2019. Today, Christopher's Clark House Hospitality umbrella company runs several establishments including a "dive bar" called the Bradley.

The Bradley is a case in the City Authentic worth studying in some depth. It used to be called Bradley's Tavern until Clark House bought it and the place underwent a subtle transformation from a dive bar to a dive-bar-themed bar. To Christopher's credit, lots of people who went to Bradley's Tavern still go to the Bradley but so do much wealthier people. Some parts are cleaned up, but for the most part the bar is preserved in amber from the off-brand jukebox to the Miller High Life sold in seven-ounce pony bottles by Shannon, the longtime bartender that Christopher kept on.

The name change from Bradley's Tavern to the Bradley is indicative of how authenticity works. Old pictures from the 1800s adorn the walls, showing the building at 28 4th Street with a sign over the door that reads College Inn. For forty years it was Dempsey's Pub & Grill, until 1990 when Gary Bradley bought it and renamed the place Bradley's Tavern. Each successive owner gave the place a name that associated it with the proprietor or target customers (such as an inn for college students), but Christopher was the first to name the bar after something in the past rather than the present. When Bradley retired and Christopher bought it, he tweeted, "We decided that Bradley's Tavern is perfect just the way it is. We plan to reopen, with minimal improvements, ASAP."[73] Going from Bradley's Tavern to the Bradley shows how places, people, and things of the past go from active to static—from a real-life person possessing the tavern you frequent to a place that is interesting because it used to be a place like that. Of course, the more material difference is also the consolidation of wealth. Instead of a single person owning one bar, a local celebrity is adding a down-market product to his portfolio of high-end establishments.

What's going on with the Bradley is an old story repeated through time and space. Designer and historian Wade Graham could just as easily be describing entrepreneurs like Vic and Heather when he describes Baron Haussmann's remaking of Paris from 1853 to 1870 as "remaking the city into a museum of its own past, a monument to itself, and indirectly, to those clever enough to live there. The past, recreated or conserved, confers legitimacy on the powers of the present."[74]

The Bradley did, in fact, hold a kind of cultural power. When New York Senator Kristen Gillibrand leased five thousand square feet of office space in downtown Troy for her presidential campaign, the *Wall Street Journal*'s Jimmy Vielkind tweeted, "Hello from The Bradley, a bar around the corner from @SenGillibrand's 2020 headquarters in Troy. Gillibrand was here in the 9 o'clock hour and had a shot of Jack Honey. A dozen people are here now watching her on @colbertlate-show."[75] Being the extremely online buzzkill that I am, I retweeted it and commented, "Get ready for a TON of 'small town authenticity' reporting from people who have no idea that bars like the Bradley are self-consciously exuding the dive bar aesthetic to generate precisely this feeling," to which Christopher replied:

> The Bradley is, and remains authentic for one main reason
> We never raised prices when we took it over
> $3 beers / $5 cocktails
> I wanted to mention that about the pricing, it's why the place continues to be accessible for anyone. That was important to us.[76]

Is this what authenticity means? Rather than ask where to put authenticity's price tag, should we be asking where it is conspicuously absent? But how can something be valuable if it only exists when you don't charge for it? If we take Christopher at his word that keeping the bar "accessible" is an important priority, then we're left with the possibility that authenticity, like a parents' love, is paradoxically infinitely valuable but becomes profane when you seek a numerical value. Attention and broad appeal, prerequisites for such tried-and-true business tactics as making up for low markups with volume, become indispensable. Vielkind would later report, "Troy has become a hipster haven sometimes likened to Brooklyn, and its downtown boosters are excited at the idea that Ms. Gillibrand and her senior aides will be kicking around."[77]

Indeed, even though Christopher had spent weeks in 2012 riding around on a Vespa in Sonoma County, all his properties scream "Brooklyn." By 2014 the local paper ran a story with the titular question "Is Troy the New Brooklyn?" with Christopher and several other business leaders giving an emphatic yes and even ending with the suggestion that Cohoes, the town just across the Hudson, "is the new Troy."[78] By 2018 *New York Magazine*'s real estate section ran a story with the headline "Not the Next Hudson: Newburgh, Catskill, and Troy, Once Downtrodden, Are Hoping Recent Revitalization Doesn't Get Out of Hand." The story, of course, undermines itself instantly. How long does a place stay affordable once a magazine with an audience of East Coast elites advertises to their readers that they can buy "a 1928 house for $12,400 from Troy Community Land Bank" just a few miles away from a coffee shop that an MFA student assures you "really helped pull together this scene"?[79]

And sure, enough rents started to steadily rise and developers from the metroplexes to the south started sniffing around. Shortly after winning a second term in 2018, Troy's mayor Patrick Madden announced that during his first four-year term, the city had attracted "over $500M in private investment from new construction projects and local building permits." To put this in perspective, per capita in 2018, developers invested twice as much as they did in New York City.[80] A large portion of the investment came from larger metros on the coast, from both wealthy individuals and large development companies seeking new markets. Downtown Troy alone has multimillion-dollar-projects by Pennrose from Philadelphia, Hoboken Brownstone from Jersey City, and Bayside Builders from Brooklyn.

From the perspective of a resident—even a well-off one such as myself—living in the City Authentic can range from off-putting to downright dangerous. In January 2022 amid the ongoing pandemic and a particularly frigid winter day, the utility company National Grid was going to shut off electricity to thousands of customers in Troy so that it could do scheduled equipment maintenance. I went to the city's website to try to find more information, and here are the headlines of the news stories I found:

City of Troy Architecture, Streetscapes Featured in HBO's "The Gilded Age"

Statement from Mayor on City's Historic Final Debt Payment to the Troy Municipal Assistance Corporation (MAC)

Mayor: City to Begin Site Preparation Work for Infrastructure Updates at Monument Square Property

Mayor: City's Bond Rating Upgraded by Moody's Investors Services, S&P Global Ratings

These headlines describe the priorities of the City Authentic better than I can, both in what they proclaim and what they ignore. Bragging about being a set piece for a period drama, upgrading your municipal bond ratings, and breaking ground on new development are more important than conveying up-to-date crucial information about utility maintenance.

By now I hope you have both a working definition of the City Authentic and a sense of what it feels like to witness its full expression. One person's life experience is not enough to base a theory on, however, so in addition to what I have witnessed firsthand, I have drawn information from other sources. I conducted interviews with professionals in the fields of economic development, cultural planning, media, and real estate. I knew some of them quite well, while others were referred to me for this project. I asked questions that ranged in and out of their respective areas of expertise, because how a developer thinks about authenticity or the way a content creator thinks about urban development is crucial in a multidisciplinary study such as this one.

I also dug deep into the archives of state and local offices and read planning documents, budgets, and speech transcripts that show institutions' animating concerns and ultimate goals. And because plans, budgets, and speeches are meant to persuade readers as much as inform them, I also used them as guides for further research in the business press and industry databases.

Finally, a note of warning about my extensive use of local print media. The *Times Union* and *Albany Business Review* are excellent publications with talented reporters. They are also subject to the same financial pressures as any other American regional publication: they too are caught up in authenticity peddling, not to mention even more insidious forces that I have yet to introduce, including the thirst games and the upgraded growth machine. All of which is to say I treat people and news outlets the same way: as imperfect beings with their own perspectives, interests, and priorities. You should do the same.

In the next chapter, we will zoom out to the regional level and see how the City Authentic incites much broader, structural changes to government and the economy.

CHAPTER 2

Upscale Upstate

Getting to a point where you can develop your own thing—
that is the story of this place, right? That's always been the
story of this place. You go back to even Prohibition days,
when everything was shut the fuck down, you had mother-
fuckers out here making hard cider and shit! That is what
this place is and that's not the story they told.

—Patrick Harris, co-founder and co-owner of the media co-op
Collective Effort

If you went to the movies in the fall of 1986, you probably went to go
see *Back to the Future*. Maybe *Blue Velvet* if you were the more serious,
cerebral type. Others would have munched popcorn while watching
Population: 1, the story of a defense contractor who survives the nuclear
apocalypse and spends the rest of his solitary life learning about the history of his extinct species through musical numbers. But if you were a
true connoisseur of musical film, you would have attended the New
York Film Festival to watch the coach from *Revenge of the Nerds* belt
out Talking Heads songs with a Texas drawl.

   True Stories, directed by and co-starring David Byrne, was John
Goodman's first leading role, and while it was never a commercial success, it deserves attention now more than ever. The movie is set in the
fictional town of Virgil, Texas, which is holding a Celebration of Special-
ness in honor of its sesquicentennial anniversary. Byrne filled the movie
with characters inspired from stories he read in the tabloid *Weekly World
News*, which is why there is a faith healer (played by the blues legend
Roebuck "Pops" Staples), a married couple who haven't spoken directly
to each other for years, and a millionaire who refuses to get out of bed.
Byrne is the film's narrator, who frequently breaches the fourth wall,
speaking directly to the audience before jumping back into the movie.

Much to the chagrin of everyone around me, *True Stories* is one of my favorite movies of all time. A self-aware pop musical from the eighties is, admittedly, a hard sell. But perhaps the biggest reason I can never find anyone to watch it with me is explained by Byrne himself in a 2018 *Rolling Stones* interview commemorating the film's Criterion Collection release: the movie, he realizes now, "was taken to be ironic and critical, a New Yorker looking down his nose at the simple wacky people in the heartland, which is not what I intended. To that extent, if that's what came across, that would mean it would be a failure."[1]

When I showed this movie to a very dear friend who grew up in Texas, he hated it to the point that he seemed offended that I'd shown it to him. He saw the movie just as Byrne describes: an elitist laughing at the little people in flyover country. I was taken aback, because I saw it as a deeply earnest portrayal of people making culture within mass consumerism, creating personal meaning out of an assemblage of brands and commodities. Or as Byrne says in the movie as he walks through a mall: "People here are inventing their own system of beliefs. They're creating it, doing it, selling it, making it up as they go along."

As the camera pans past the anchor stores of this brand-new mall, Byrne explains that modern consumers are agnostic as to whether they do their shopping in "a funky old building downtown or a clean modern place like this." From the position of 1986, it was already obvious that this agnosticism was really a choice to let Main Street die off. None of the mom-and-pop stores could compete with the efficiency, low prices, and selection of the department stores and corporate chains. What was unclear at the time, however, was whether the mall would be enough to fulfill the role of Main Street: the center of local social and economic activity. *True Stories* suggests that the mall and postwar suburbia was a sufficient compromise position to satisfy a growing number of highly mobile middle-class entrepreneurs that were forming the center of a brand-new economy. This is all laid out very explicitly in my favorite scene, where Byrne has dinner with the Culvers, a prominent family in Virgil.

After some polite conversation, Earl, the patriarch, extols the virtues of the town's main employer, a fictionalized version of Texas Instruments named Varicorp. "Let me show you what I think is going on," Mr. Culver declares before starting what sounds like an incantation: "Mainframe. Microprocessor. Semiconductor." As he says this, he brings his hands up into a sort of benediction. His children, Larry and Linda, start cheering him on. Earl is playing with the food now, using the dinner as a makeshift model town. He explains that middle-class families used to rely on the single income earned at a big company or in the public sector. But in the early eighties, scientists and engineers left these big institutions to make their own businesses. "Our way of business has been based in the past," he says as he picks up the lobster and spins it around like a toy plane. "We have to keep these guys in Virgil, even if they do leave Varicorp." He rolls cherry tomatoes down a string-bean highway. "They don't work for money anymore, or for a place in heaven, which was a big motivating factor once upon a time, believe you me. They're working and inventing because they like it!" Asparagus, which had represented "the workplace with its goods" at the beginning of the monologue, is thrown in the air and lands all over the table. "Economics has become a spiritual thing. I must admit it frightens me a bit. They don't seem to understand the difference between working and not working. It's all become part of one's life." The music that has been playing this whole time begins to crescendo as Mr. Culver addresses his children: "Linda, Larry, there's no concept of weekends anymore!" Fade to black.

True Stories is one of those pieces of culture that are haunted by their own critique: throughout the film Byrne is pointing to a change in the American landscape where postindustrial work can be done anywhere, and so places like Virgil must invent completely new reasons for people to stay. As you may have already guessed, small towns will turn to services, mass consumption, and cultural amenities as a new source of both tax revenue and a reason for existing. But in so doing, the town must fight to both understand what makes these mobile wage earners tick and what will keep them in the town's borders. A New Yorker can't tell this story because, in the eyes of everyone else, big cities are immune to this sort of problem. New York is the exporter of culture and the center of finance. If anything, it caused this! Now you're just laughing at the little people trying to understand this new future you've thrust upon them.

But what we will see in this chapter is that New York, both the city and the state, were eaten alive by these forces just as much as anywhere else. Indeed, Byrne was in the perfect place to make *True Stories* as a sort of clarion call to remain vigilant about the impending brandification of ourselves and our hometowns. This happened to New York City before it happened to small Texas towns. Sure, the banks and ad executives were physically closer, maybe even down the road, but that doesn't matter much if you're priced out of your neighborhood just the same. In fact, in a cruel twist of fate, the punk bar CBGB, which was central to the scene that launched the Talking Heads along with Blondie, Patti Smith, and the Ramones, was kicked out by its landlord in 2006 after its rent went up to a whopping $19,000 a month.[2]

The demise of CBGB was possible, in part, because of the forces Byrne had put in the mouth of Earl Culver: the Bowery's gritty punk bars had made the Lower East Side iconic. Economics had become a spiritual thing, and what was once clearly a space of play and artistic expression is now decidedly branded work: CBGB has been transformed into an ethereal brand that lends nostalgic credentials to an iHeartRadio station and a bar lounge at the Newark International Airport.[3] The bar's famous awning is a museum piece in the Rock & Roll Hall of Fame, and the storefront now hosts a Patagonia store. *True Stories* wasn't an ironic joke; it was a warning.

We've already watched Troy transform from a down-on-its-luck college town to a rusted rising star of postindustrial chic. Now we will focus on the Capital Region at large and see *how* the landscape changed with the introduction of managed inter-city competition and branding. Crucially, we'll see that many of the phenomena described by Byrne and more explicitly theorized by the urban sociologist Sharon Zukin are not simply *exported* from New York City but refined and even reinvented in smaller, more obscure cities.

SETTING THE CITY ON FIRE

"When it comes to low-income housing, it's not just a public housing authorities' responsibility. Okay? It's everyone's responsibility." So says Rocco Ferraro (who everyone calls Rocky), the principal planner for the Capital District Regional Planning Commission (CDRPC) from 1985 to 2000. After a relatively brief stint in the private sector, he returned and served as its executive director from 2002 to 2016. In that role, Rocky was responsible for playing matchmaker across private and public institutions: facilitating meetings, providing data, and generally coordinating the economy of the region.

I first met Rocky when we were office mates at the University at Albany Department of Geography and Planning. We were both adjunct professors, a profession I had just started and one that he had been practicing since 1996. We shared a small, windowless office stuffed with filing cabinets that we never opened and two bare desks. He had grown up in New Jersey, but he would make frequent pilgrimages beginning in his early teens across the Hudson to go see his beloved Mets play at

Shea Stadium: "My friends and I went to the City all the time, but some of those neighborhoods you wouldn't ever want to go to. Brooklyn, you know—my dad said, 'You don't go to Brooklyn.' And when going to Mets games, I always took the 7 subway directly from Port Authority to Shea Stadium and did not get off at any of the stops in between. Okay, fast forward to the present. Due to gentrification, I couldn't afford to live in some of those neighborhoods today, in particular in Brooklyn!"

Neither living in Saratoga County nor the intense gentrification of some of the neighborhoods in New York City has stopped Rocky from his Mets ritual: "I still do the same thing I did sixty years ago: drive to the Port Authority, park there, get my slice of pizza at the pizza place at Port Authority, and take the 7 to Shea—well, it's not called Shea anymore, of course, but, you know."[4] Rocky, like me, is a transplant to the Capital Region, and part of his job for many years was to get new people to make the same decision we did. I asked him what it takes to get people to move to the area, and his response was not entirely surprising:

> Cultural attractions that the region has to offer—the Richard Florida creative-class strategy. It is extremely important in order to attract and retain young people in the Capital Region. We have an advantage here that many other regions do not have: we have a large number of educational institutions in the four counties, public and private universities, that bring students to the Capital Region to study. We need to retain them here after graduation, and we have had some success.

You will recall from chapter 1 that Florida's creative-class theory is essentially an answer to the dilemma posed by Mr. Culver: if people don't stay at the same employer for very long, then chasing big employers is less important than making sure your city is a nice place to live and caters to the tastes of high earners. This sounds like a win-win scenario: city officials get to be the elected equivalent of weekend dad—the fun, laid-back, would-be authority figure—while also presiding over an economic renaissance. No hard conversations about raising taxes and reducing services, just a rising tide of artisanal mayonnaise shops selling their wares to web developers and architects. Except that doesn't always pan out. By 2017 Florida wrote what amounted to a book-length mea culpa called *The New Urban Crisis*, where he admitted that he had abetted the rise of a "winner-take-all urbanism" where "a few big winners capture a disproportionate share of the spoils of innovation and economic growth, while many more places stagnate or fall further behind."[5] This growing inequality is seen between cities—big cities see massive gains in population and investment at the expense of smaller ones—and within cities as neighborhoods bifurcate into wealthy enclaves and poor ghettos.

I knew all this when I was speaking to Rocky. I had even written a book review of *The New Urban Crisis* when it came out, noting how Florida was obviously cribbing "materialist accounts of capitalist crisis in order to try to render it amenable to incremental reform rather than a more radical reorganization."[6] So when Rocky told me that Florida's creative-class thesis was a key to attracting new residents, you might expect that I flew off the handle. Instead, all I said was, "You got me!"

"Right, okay," Rocky replied with the sort of gratified grin of a man whose theory was just proven correct. "What made you stay here?"

Now I was forced to admit the cringe-worthy truth: he was right. All the things I have described so far in this book—growing up in suburban South Florida, the cool old buildings, the affordability—all of it had contributed to me putting down roots. "Right. Exactly. Exactly," Rocky said, nodding emphatically. The creative-class thesis described me to a tee. And to some degree it always was going to. Countless cities had rebuilt themselves to attract people like me: a white, overeducated guy who wants to try the new slider place with a great tap selection.

But who lost so I could win my fun downtown? Here Rocky was less enthusiastic and that's why he was telling me it's everyone's responsibility to make sure housing is affordable. Since his retirement from the Regional Planning Commission, in addition to teaching (he's a student favorite) and serving as treasurer to the Saratoga County Prosperity Partnership, he is also president of a nonprofit development company called Saratoga Affordable Housing Group (SAHG) Inc. It is in this capacity that he sees how the hospitality and restaurant business is reliant on affordable housing. Restaurant owners—some of whom are fellow founders of the SAHG—he argues, recognize the importance of affordable housing because of the wages. He tells me that while there are always going to be benefits from increasing rents, restaurateurs know that their "workforce needs affordable housing, and that we could work with the parts of the small business community that understands. They are advocates as well."

Many business owners are renters themselves, leasing the space where they set up shop, and it is this fact that often leads to the degradation of a neighborhood once it becomes gentrified. Real estate prices get so high that only corporate tenants can afford the rents. In this way, land speculation destroys the very thing that instigates it in the first place. That's why CBGB is an airport bar, and the building it used to occupy is a pricey clothing store. The urban sociologist Sharon Zukin describes this contradiction: "The more 'local' the neighborhood's character seems to be, . . . the more it attracts media attention; and the more media attention it gets, the greater the risk that it will become a cultural 'destination': local character will become more expensive, give way to standardization, and disappear."[7]

Capitalists have always struggled with the balance between cheap labor and valuable land because expensive land makes everything that sits on top of it more expensive too, including workers' labor. In his 2019 book *Capital City* Samuel Stein writes, "Since the industrial revolution took hold, cities had been governed by the political party that could best bridge the divide between the needs of industrial capital and its workforce."[8] Often that meant placating factory owners who wanted cheap land to build even bigger factories on and a working class that wanted their paychecks to go as far as possible. The working classes and their bosses tenuously agreed that cheap rent was in both their interests. But, as Stein puts it, "With the flight of manufacturing from cities, real estate and finance became the remaining major urban power bloc and the key to rebuilding local economies."[9] Today the finance, insurance, and real estate (or FIRE) industries prevail over all others as the primary political force in cities. Add to this the approximately 42 percent of Capital Region residents who own their home[10] and want to see its value go up as well.

For better or worse, Rocky's pilgrimages to Mets games are not the only ongoing connection between the Capital Region and New York City, and so any depiction of the former would be incomplete without at least a mention of the latter. The connections between the New York City metro area and the Capital Region include not only the FIRE sectors but also government, innovation, and culture. In her latest book, *The Innovation Complex*, Sharon Zukin declares that in the early 2000s, New York City "leaders and their economic development advisers had been all abuzz about 'creative cities,'" but they switched tactics after the Great Recession; "under pressure to repair a 'damaged economy' they were talking about innovation clusters."[11] This "'next act' of global capitalism"[12] is marked by rapacious competition among governments and cozy relationships among elected officials, financiers, and tech company executives.

Winner-take-all urbanism is evident in how the Capital Region positions itself economically and culturally. New York City's superstar status is assured by what Florida calls "the clustering force." Cities bring industries together—finance in New York City, show business in Los Angeles—but they also bring together people who want to be where the action is and get jobs in multinational firms that are almost exclusively located in the biggest cities.[13] Everything from venture capital to artists are found in abundance in big cities, and their presence begets more of themselves in geographically defined clusters. Big cities' ability to attract capital helps them drive economic growth, but it also drives inequality. Florida calls this a fundamental contradiction of contemporary capitalism: "The more things cluster in space, the more expensive land gets; the more expensive land gets, the higher housing prices become, and the more certain things get pushed out."[14] The result is a division of "the world's cities into winners and losers, but ensures that the winner cities become unaffordable for all but the most advantaged."[15]

Zukin drills deeper into this phenomenon. What usually gets branded as "innovation" in the biotech and information technology space is really an outgrowth of high-risk speculation in the FIRE industries, which acts as a "speculative base for an ecosystem of interrelated businesses, meetups, and training programs that makes the new economy come alive."[16] Cities must also create pipelines that scale up small startups into profitable enterprises. Business incubators, coworking facilities, and boot camps perform these functions by providing venues to prototype, network, and develop new skills. Also central to this new economy is media, both social and traditional, from hosting the likes of Meta and Snapchat in Midtown Manhattan to Netflix, Disney, Amazon, and a dozen movie studios both creating and marketing content in the city. The result is a very high-profile set of brands and companies whose C-suite executives join hands with politicians to announce the return of high-paying jobs to burnt-out warehouse districts. The reality, however, is that these companies hire relatively few people and lavish even fewer with long contracts and high pay—all of which is built on the unstable foundation of venture capital and an ouroboros of hype.

The Innovation Complex, while being endemic to the biggest cities in the world, is by no means disconnected from smaller cities, which find niches that play to their competitive advantages. The Capital Region cannot compete head-to-head with New York City when it comes to venture capital or clusters of media companies. It can, however, do what Rocky is saying: offer a low-cost alternative for someone who wants an urban lifestyle and a business that could use some well-educated employees.

That is why the Capital Region's Regional Economic Development Council—a forum of governor-appointed business leaders and institutional bureaucrats—has identified "key regional clusters" that play to the strengths of the region's medical and educational facilities. In its 2019 progress report, it crowed that "the Life Sciences Cluster's employment has increased by 7.2 percent over the past year. Capital Region firms and institutions received 6 percent more in National Institutes of Health funding, and local colleges and universities invested 2 percent more on life sciences R&D. . . . The National Center for Science and Engineering Statistics has identified the Albany-Schenectady-Troy metropolitan statistical area (MSA) as one of only 47 MSAs where businesses spend more than $1 billion annually on R&D."[17]

As Rocky says, the region's leaders have a difficult task in front of them. They must seize a moment where lots of people are moving out of big cities and convince them to check the place out and stay. Unfortunately for the Capital Region, even as the pandemic has forced companies to allow a record number of their employees to work from home, New York City's talent clustering is likely to persist. Zukin is told by the founder of a data analytics startup that while "we can pick amazing engineers wherever they live," the sales and marketing teams have to be in the city because they are "able to knock on the door of major media companies and get in-person meetings."[18]

Mark Castiglione, who took over the executive directorship of CDRPC after Rocky, is also skeptical about whether the pandemic will have a lasting impact: "Whether or not that fundamentally changes the composition of the region remains to be seen; I think there are some questions about the degree to which remote work is going to continue to be a component of our work lives and whether or not that's going to have an impact on where people choose to live."

Clearly there are some very contradictory forces at play here, because while middle-class professionals tend to stay at companies for a shorter amount of time than their forebearers and it is *technically* easier than ever to do most jobs from anywhere, the reality is they are staying put. A 2020 Harvard study found that about half as many people move today as they did in the 1970s. The most mobile age cohorts of twenty-year-olds saw the most significant drops too: nearly 40 percent of twenty– to twenty-four-year-olds in 1976 had moved within the last year compared to less than 25 percent in 2016. Twenty-five– to twenty-nine-year-olds went from approximately 33 percent to 24 percent over the same period.[19] The main reason for both moving and not moving, the report speculates, is the cost of housing and the rise of the dual-earner household. We move less because it is expensive and it is harder for two people to find new jobs than for one person. But when we do move, it's to outrun the increasing cost of housing.[20]

Forty percent of people who moved in 2018 said they did so because of housing-related reasons, and most moves were within counties, suggesting people were moving to a more affordable area of the same metro region. As moves get longer, however, the main reason switches to job-related reasons. It's important to put this in perspective though: 65 percent of moves were within the same county and only 14 percent were across state lines.[21]

What does all this mean for the Capital Region? First, it means that while none of its constituent cities are going head-to-head with New York City or Boston for every new corporate East Coast office, it is in the running for the odd satellite office and high-earner, work-from-home types. It also means that to grow the region, leaders must hold onto their competitive advantage of a relatively cheap cost of living while also encouraging all the land speculation that ultimately undermines it. We know this is happening because, as I mentioned in the first chapter, even *developers* are looking to the Capital Region for land that they can afford to develop.

For the remainder of this chapter, I will be focusing on the decade between 2010 and 2020 for two reasons. First, the data I want to compare from the American Community Survey (a more frequent sampling of the U.S. population conducted by the Census Bureau) matches best in this decade. Before 2010, some important jurisdictional lines moved, complicating comparisons. Second, having lived here since 2010, I've witnessed firsthand a transformation of the area that, if it didn't start that year, certainly had a dramatic inflection point around that time. Between the rise of Andrew Cuomo and his Economic Development Council system, the development and maturation of smartphone technology, and national postrecession economic trends, I feel safe in assuming that whatever I want to know about the City Authentic can be found within this time frame. To the extent possible, I will also factor in the impact of the COVID-19 pandemic, whose full implications are still ongoing.

THE THIRST GAMES

When I was in college in 2007, my friends and I danced to Soulja Boy's "Crank That." It is perhaps because of people like me, who danced to it after a six pack of Bacardi Raz, that the song and Soulja Boy's career is not considered artistically remarkable despite its commercial success and cultural ubiquity. The track "She Thirsty" off the same album, while never having enjoyed the Billboard status of "Crank That," has nonetheless been influential to the lexicon by mainstreaming the idea that *thirsty* is synonymous with demanding of affection and attention.

Thinking of the desire for attention as something akin to the need for water highlights two important characteristics of the attention economy. First, it promises that, like our need for water, our desire for attention can never be truly and definitively slaked; it can only be temporarily abated. Second, it introduces attention as having liquid-like qualities. In this way Soulja Boy echoes sociologist Zygmunt Bauman's 2000 book *Liquid Modernity*, which argues that success and power in a consumer society are both defined by and confer the means of getting around. Put simply, the richer you are, the more resources and tools you have at your disposal to be anywhere or stop anyone from getting near you. This power further increases your ability to access even more wealth and power. Bauman uses liquidity as a metaphor to describe the centrality of movement, transformation, and flexibility in the economy and society.

In another book, co-authored with Leonidas Donskis in 2013, titled *Moral Blindness: The Loss of Sensitivity in Liquid Modernity*, Bauman also posited that "the updated version of Descartes's Cogito is 'I am seen, therefore I am'—and that the more people who see me, the more I am." This quote alludes to the fact that success is predicated on one's ability to project one's brand and have it seen by millions. President Trump is the perfect example of successfully navigating liquid modernity: he is physically near impossible to approach but can easily and instantly project his brand/identity/self onto millions of screens around the world in such a way that largely redounds to his benefit.

When we hear the phrase "attention economy," we tend to associate it with social media companies, but the truth of the matter is that attracting the attention of potential employers and grant-making foundations is just as important and common as seeking YouTube subscribers.

Cities must play what can accurately be called the thirst games: a free-for-all, mercenary fight where city governments pay consultants to write proposals that are inscrutable to laypeople but slick enough to catch the eye of the appointed judges. The problem with this process, beyond its obvious lack of democratic accountability and transparency, is the perverse incentives that focus on obtaining a single influx of cash for a handful of pet projects instead of building and improving necessary services that require (and sometimes provide) recurring revenue to city coffers.

There are all sorts of thirst games across the world. Chinese urban planners, for example, have gone from humble managers of urban form to savvy marketers of "placemaking" schemes. Local governments, in consultation with well-paid experts from domestic private agencies, compete against each other to win new entitlements doled out by the central government for things like manufacturing centers, information technology clusters, and tourism.[22] The result has been meteoric growth coupled with an ever-present danger of outpacing the ability of labor to follow capital. That means city officials have indulged in less-than-legal maneuvers to entice developers to build without a clear plan for how to get people to live and work in what is being built. This kind of behavior contributed to a severe bond-market instability in late 2021, where the Chinese developer Evergrande threatened to bring down the global economy.[23]

For my tax money, though, there's no better thirst game than the one set up in 2011 by Governor Andrew Cuomo. His administration "established 10 Regional Councils to develop long-term strategic plans for economic growth for their regions. The Councils are public-private partnerships made up of local experts and stakeholders from business, academia, local government, and non-governmental organizations,"[24] appointed by the governor, who serve two-year terms that can be renewed indefinitely.[25] These Economic Development Councils (EDCs) are housed within Empire State Development, an umbrella organization for two of the state's public benefit corporations devoted to economic development. Each EDC has a geographic jurisdiction spanning multiple counties. The Capital Region's EDC (CREDC) includes Albany, Rensselaer, Warren, Greene, Washington, Saratoga, Schenectady, and Columbia counties.

These competitions set up by the EDCs have been derisively called "the hunger games" in the media,[26] but I think "thirst" is a more accurate descriptor because, as Soulja Boy teaches us, *thirst* can also refer to a desperate desire to be recognized.[27] To be thirsty is to use every tool at your disposal to be seen, usually by a particular someone for a particular purpose. And as Bauman reminds us, this effect compounds such that the more influential you become, the further your image can be projected and the higher the likelihood that your image might reach people who are difficult to access.

But how do you know what kind of image to project? To get someone's attention, you need to know what they like, and the EDCs tells potential applicants what they want through progress reports, plans, and other documents published on their website and in public meetings with the press and the public. For example, one of the strategies listed in a 2011 planning document was the establishment of a Capital Region Media Coalition, which would

> increase awareness about economic development programs in the Region, engage the general public and business community, and promote the Region to internal and external audiences. The Media Coalition will employ a variety of tactics to develop and disseminate messages to brand the Region, engage the community in ongoing economic development efforts, and raise awareness of positive changes in the Region. For example, the Media Coalition produced a thirty-second public service announcement that encouraged people to submit Consolidated Funding Applications.[28]

The particulars of the Consolidated Funding Application (CFA) system are taken up in chapter 5; all you need to know for now is that this is the form the regional EDCs use to accept requests for funding. While individual CFA submissions are not publicly available, some key information on funded projects is released and it is easy to infer from their titles and short descriptions how they fit into the Strategic Plan. For example, in the second round of funding, the Greene County Council on the Arts won $150,000 for a CFA application aiming to "create a cultural tourism corridor that connects Greene County's historic communities traveling east to west along the Rip Van Winkle trail on Route 23A."[29] In the same year, the Greenway Heritage Conservancy received $90,000 to "promote access to the Hudson River and tourism in the Hudson River Valley and its National Heritage Area."[30] Both applications clearly fit into a wider project of raising awareness of the region's cultural and natural heritage and boosting tourism.

Firms within an EDC's jurisdiction look to their reports to see what kinds of projects are likely to be funded. In turn, an EDC points to rankings and even the governor's office itself to show how it is performing in comparison to other EDCs. The EDCs' annual progress reports follow the same general outline: they begin with an ego-stroking letter from the cochairs to the then-governor in the third person (e.g., "Governor Cuomo recognized that our economy cannot thrive by the success of individual businesses or sectors, and knew that bringing our regions back economically would require the synergy of people working together and sharing ideas"[31]), followed by an update on the region's accomplishments, usually described in terms of rankings (e.g., "The region has continued GE's rich tradition of innovation, prompting U.S.

News & World Report to name Albany the third best place in the nation to find a job in technology. ZipRecruiter also named Albany the fourth fastest-growth tech market in the nation, and Forbes named the Albany-Schenectady-Troy metro area the nation's seventh most thriving manufacturing facility"[32]). Or this from the progress report two years later: "Earlier this year the area jumped up 11 slots on U.S. News & World Report's 'Best Cities to Live' rankings to 28th. The area ranked 10th on ZipRecruiter's list of the 'Hottest Cities for Jobs' and 21st on WalletHub's 'Most Educated Cities in America.'"[33]

And so on. Then comes a series of reports and updates on priorities and identified issues from either the council itself or other state agencies. The 2019 report, for example, has sections on the lack of affordable childcare, low unemployment, workforce development (especially among veterans), the progress of particularly high-profile previously funded projects, business loans to minority- and women-owned businesses, and the state of the region's innovation complex.

Some of the reports appear to be inflated, as if to show more is being planned than is actually the case. The 2019 report lists several workgroups cochaired by CREDC members and made up of community leaders outside the committee. One of these was Mark Castiglione, executive director of the Capital District Regional Planning Commission. When I asked him what went on in the placemaking working group, he told me, "I think I volunteered to be on that committee but I'm not sure if we ever met."

That certainly doesn't mean he was unfamiliar with the way the CREDC works. Before he took the role as executive director of the CDRPC, Castiglione had worked for the state helping set up the EDC system. "What was interesting to me," he told me, "is that they're all like different families that all have different dynamics and different priorities based on who is the loudest voice in the room or whatever priorities are." That may not sound like a resounding endorsement, but he thinks they are an important component of regional economic development:

> I kept coming back to: What's the null hypothesis? What would you be missing out on? And, I think, for all their challenges, getting those people in the same room has been very helpful in terms of helping to at least getting out there: What are the significant projects for the region? And having that be a conversation, rather than a one-on-one or sort of a backroom deal. It hasn't overcome completely the competitive nature of economic development. That continues to be a challenge, but you know, again, that's the nature of how we

broke ourselves up into counties, but I think there has been a benefit to bringing those people in the same room together. Some could say that that's just consolidating the power of the power elites, but others could say that you've definitely done things to expose people to a cross section of regional priorities that they would not otherwise be exposed to.[34]

This last point about competition, division among the counties and cities, and the inability of leaders in the region to work together came up many times in my interviews. Rocky Ferraro agrees with his successor that the CREDC has "been extremely successful in bringing together the different stakeholder interests in the region, literally around the same table . . . and to brainstorm how to strategically move forward as a region." Rocky, like Castiglione, was never on the CREDC but played a support role for a time as the cochair of the metrics working group, which established the metrics that would be used to evaluate the success of the programs. Rocky described intraregional competition with that in mind:

It's just a reality that I'm representing my community—say, the City of Albany. That's my priority, and as much as I want to see positive things happen in the City of Troy and the City of Schenectady insomuch as they are connected by the metrics [that my community members will judge me with], so yes, I respect a regional perspective, but it has to be balanced in terms of my priorities, which is to represent the interests of my local government. . . . That being said, you know, the [county-specific] economic development agencies—the metrics in terms of financial support for that organization or for the executive director to continue is primarily based on what have you done for this community, the county employing you. . . . When it comes down to "Okay, decision being made: should this entity be located in Albany County, Rensselaer County, Saratoga, or Schenectady County?" I'm going to do all I can to have them located in the county that I'm employed/working in and that I'm responsible for. So that's where you get that intra-regional competition coming into play amongst the different communities in our region.[35]

Shelby Schneider, the president of a county-specific economic development agency called the Saratoga County Prosperity Partnership, answered my question about intergovernmental competition with a question of her own: "How many cities do you see sharing services?" The answer is not much. My city of Troy has one of the better examples. It built a water reservoir in the late nineteenth century and has since been using it to sell water to nearby municipalities, raking in millions of dollars in wholesale water contracts but also saving those cities the trouble and expense of running their own water departments. That's rare though, and many cities compete to attract services and employers even though it would benefit everyone if they worked together. Schneider tells me to

> look at the major employers in our region. . . . We have a state capital. You have a ton of public jobs. They're secure; they pay benefits generally better than private sector employers; and they stabilize the region. When we had the recession in 2008, besides the fact that GlobalFoundries [a major chip manufacturer] started construction in 2009 and we had this boom of construction jobs and so many hotels were built because we had so many extended stay, there was so much demand because we were using our regional workforce. The recession, for the most part, really kind of skipped over this region.[36]

The sense I got from these interviews and my own experience in the region and my understanding of municipal governance is the following: despite the obvious benefits of cooperation, cities and counties have few opportunities to cooperate. Everyone knows this, including state and corporate leaders who use this fact to induce a race to the bottom for everything from property taxes to the build quality of an apartment complex. Big box retail stores have always sought to build just outside population centers on unincorporated land where construction and taxes are cheaper, and Amazon famously pitted every city in North America against each other when it was contemplating where to build its secondary headquarters in 2018. Big cities like Chicago and New York City prostrated themselves in the hopes of getting the smallest taste of Amazon's thousands of high-paid managers and signature office towers. It was eventually decided that it would be built in Crystal City, thanks to Arlington County and the State of Virginia's promises of $800 million worth of incentives.[37] Thousands of these sorts of deals, at proportionately similar scales for cities and towns of much smaller sizes, happen every year.

But what the people I spoke to worry about more, it would seem, is that if the Capital Region's cities and counties compete *against* each other, they cannot compete *together* to land another big fish like GlobalFoundries and attract a more educated, affluent workforce. This is, at least in part, why one of the "metro" projects listed in the 2019 progress report was a rehash of the 2011 Media Coalition but was now called the Capital Region Branding Initiative:

> As part of its affiliation with ACE [upstate Alliance for the Creative Economy], CEG [Center for Economic Growth] is seeking to create a regional identity effort to help drive economic development and attract talent to the

Capital Region. This strategy aims to market and brand the Capital Region as a "metro region" with more than 1 million residents, positioning the region as a Top 50 player with distinct competitive advantages, including strategic location, educational assets, cultural vibrancy, innovation, recreational opportunities, affordability and livability. This initiative will attract individuals back to the region, increase the availability of highly skilled talent within our growth industries, help diversify talent, retain local graduates and provide local businesses with tools to help recruit new employees.[38]

This chapter will conclude with a deep dive into how this regional branding initiative panned out, but before we get there, I want to step back and look at how the region has transformed since the CREDC's inception and what new challenges arise when a largely rural region tries to become a single authentic city.

DOWNTOWN IN CHAINS

Earlier in the chapter I quoted Sharon Zukin, who says that attention to a neighborhood eventually gives way to increased patronage of establishments but often enough falls to real estate speculation.[39] The result is an ironic twist of fate: the very thing that made the area popular to begin with is diluted by corporatization. "The desire for authentic urban experience" she explains, "began as a reaction to the urban crisis of the 1960s."[40] As governments fueled white flight to the suburbs and corporations followed suit—first to the suburbs, then the low-tax, low-union-density American South and West, then overseas—cities had to find a way to compete with the suburbs on quality of life. Through the seventies, city blocks were bulldozed in favor of new-construction shopping malls (nearly every city in the Capital Region has an example of this) and waterfront districts.

By the eighties, as *True Stories* depicted, malls were outcompeting downtowns for daily shopping needs. The only way to stem the tide of disinvestment was, by the turn of the century, to start embracing Mulgan and Worpole's depoliticized cultural planning strategies. Instead of creating a site of working-class political and economic independence, Zukin says urban leaders were busy "reinventing the city, turning its pervasive image of decay into an emotionally and aesthetically satisfying, and sometimes even cool and glamorous, lifestyle."[41] Eventually, however, things came to a head when demand for limited urban real estate outstripped the supply. This spurred both activism and financial speculation. Activists and organizers forced several questions: Who should own downtown? What is best for a regional economy? Should big corporations with their access to global markets bring cheap goods to the city center or should more expensive, slower local consumer markets be allowed to develop?

Despite the best efforts of committed housing activists, much of the energy in this arena was absorbed into bourgeois consumer activism. A fetish for the gritty and the obscure was transmuted into delectable luxury goods. All the better if such goods were sold near the places that they were associated with: "elevated" soul food from Harlem and limited-edition IPAs at Brooklyn Brewery's Williamsburg location. Those who wanted a modern grocery store and a cheap blouse found themselves in an impossible position: cave to big box stores with their low wages and cookie-cutter style or try to preserve the local shopping streets. The latter employ more people and are in many cases able to carry more items that serve the specific needs of the neighborhood, but they were quickly losing access to suppliers who feared that if they didn't sell on the terms of Wal-Mart (and now Amazon), they would be locked out of major markets altogether. Zukin concludes, "Together, capital investment and consumer culture encouraged both city governments and city dwellers to think they could have it all: a postindustrial revolution with no human costs, both a corporate city and a new urban village."[42]

Why can't we have it all? The answers lie in the cost of rent and the nature of attention. These are the forces that smashed CBGB to pieces, so they can certainly destroy your favorite dive bar too. In this section we will focus on commercial real estate, but it will become clear that as the shopping goes, so goes the housing.

Both workers and their bosses have a material interest in cheap rent, as we established earlier. Workers want to spend less of their hard-earned money on housing, and bosses want to spend less on workers' wages and land for factories and warehouses. This has been the case for at least as long as urban industrial capitalism has been around. Like their manufacturing forebears, owners of restaurants, bars, and entertainment venues have a vested interest in keeping rents cheap. I pulled real estate data on the four core Capital Region counties—Albany, Rensselaer, Saratoga, and Schenectady—and looked at how many businesses in the restaurant, bar, amusement, and recreational services rent or own their property. Out of 898 establishments, 37 percent (326 locations) owned their property. That means the other 63 percent were subject to the whims of rent increases. Of those 326 owner-occupied locations, I could not identify a single Starbucks, McDonald's, or other chain restaurant. Only one, an off-track betting establishment, was a subsidiary of a larger company (in this case, one wholly owned by the state). None of them were minority owned, and 14 were women owned.[43]

The reasons for this last bit are straightforward: owning a piece of property requires access to significant credit, as well as a lot of money up front. The history of banking in this country means that white people—and more specifically, white men—are most likely to have access to these resources. But why then are all chain stores in rented storefronts? The answer is that they are the only ones that can afford the high rents of the most sought-after locations and have the staff of lawyers and accountants that can sign lease agreements on good terms quickly. Moreover, valuable land is more likely to be used as permanent capital to be leased out to those that can afford it, rather than owned by people who want to do something productive with it.

To make this clearer, consider two hypothetical entrepreneurial scenarios. First is Cody, a recent college graduate with a business degree who wants to borrow his father's money to finance a contract to bring a new fast-casual restaurant brand to Schenectady. There is an outparcel available to lease in a strip mall managed by a large retail management firm, and so he goes to a bank to make up the difference for the initial startup costs. They see he is well capitalized with family money and the restaurant chain has a very straightforward business plan that shows one of their restaurants making good money in a location very similar to the one Cody wants to open in Schenectady. Everyone is happy and soon the lease is signed, and Schenectady has a new place to eat a slightly different kind of sandwich.

The second entrepreneur is Gabriella. She has worked as a server for five years and wants to open a vegan burger restaurant in a vacant building near her apartment in Cohoes. She goes to apply for a business loan to buy the building, but she hasn't saved anything on a server's salary and a multiunit building requires at least 20 percent down in New York State. She doesn't have family money to borrow from, and while her business plan is sound, there's no proof that it will work in such a competitive market. Even though the building is dirt cheap and in a great location, she can't get financing to buy it, let alone renovate it to turn it into a restaurant. She turns to the seller, an out-of-town property owner who inherited the building in the nineties and asks if he would be willing to let her lease to own. He tells her no because he wants to hold out for a good offer. Apparently, downtowns are popular again. No one gets vegan burgers, and Gabriella keeps waiting tables.

Note not only the sad realities of the representative identities here but the role of institutions in conservatively seeking profit. While one wing of the FIRE industry may play fast and loose with billions of dollars—investing it in cryptocurrencies bought on margin calls, Poké-mon card futures, or whatever else becomes the asset du jour—these bets are offset by very conservative money lending to businesses and individuals. These investments are easier to make when a fast-casual dining company can show that its franchisee has chosen to build an identical restaurant in a location that looks like every other location in suburban America. This is a predictable formula with relatively low risk. Gabriella's idea, on the other hand, requires that a loan officer agree that there's a market for vegan burgers. Then the building renova-tion must go smoothly—no surprise problems with the old building's foundation—and while the downtown is starting to get attention, it might not be enough to get the foot traffic needed for a successful res-taurant. After all, wasn't the building abandoned for years? Surely it must be a bad location.

I asked Shelby Schneider what she thought about these hypotheticals, and she gave me a real story that combines them both. "Nafeesa Koslik: she opened Nani's Kitchen in Ballston Spa. She worked in hospitality and tourism, managed hotels for many years. . . . She was like, 'I got laid off. I've had all this time. I've always thought about this. Why not now?' And I'm like, 'Why not!"

Koslik was featured in the *Saratoga Business Journal* in December 2020, one of the worst months in New York for the pandemic: "The building, which she is renting, needed some renovations, including new grease traps in the kitchen, a new floor and removal of the bar in the dining room, and some general painting and sprucing up. Her husband and children pitched in to get the work done. The family also helps out, as needed, with the restaurant business. In addition, there are two employees."[44]

It takes a family to bootstrap the business, and sure enough, there are some expensive renovations needed in this rented storefront. The barri-ers for a Gabriella are significant challenges for Nafeesa but are reduced to hurdles for Codys. They not only have the staff and data to convince a bank that their development will work, but they can also weather downturns in the market and, crucially, afford to rent in-demand spaces. This is the pivotal factor in the contradiction described by Zukin. As rent prices go up, the Gabriellas and Nafeesas of the world are priced out, and maybe even a few Codys too. All that's left are corporations that can lease from one another and drive the cost of rent further up because—did you hear?—a new Whole Foods is coming to town!

Corporate restaurant chains have either embedded real estate strategies into their core business models (McDonald's famously became a real estate manager for their franchisees) or farmed these out to the FIRE industry. Owning very few tangible assets, except for some intellectual property on a name-brand chicken sandwich or a recognizable logo, rose to prominence in the 1990s, the same time frame as the return of the downtown. This was well documented in Naomi Klein's first book, *No Logo*. Instead of making things, Klein argued, corporations shifted resources to managing their brands. Your Nike shoes might have slightly better build quality than some discount brand, but the difference in price is dictated by the status of the brand itself, not the actual product. Superbrands like Apple, Coca-Cola, Starbucks, and MAC cosmetics don't invest in researching and developing new products so much as they find new ways of cultivating a brand that customers want to be associated with. Instead of producers of things, the biggest companies in the world have become stewards of valuable symbols.

It should be no surprise then, that cities themselves got into this game—paying close attention to their reputation and cultivating a brand of their own. For big cities like New York City, Paris, or São Paulo, this means seeking out world-renowned architects to build grand signature buildings and cultivating world-class institutions in art, technology, or commerce. But in places like the Capital Region, something slightly different happens. According to Zukin, smaller cities "compete for a place on the global cultural circuit by developing art fairs, film festivals, and even parades in which painted fiberglass cows or bison or moose, depending on a city's chosen symbol, are installed on the streets as public art."[45]

This is precisely what the Capital Region has done. Each city has a farmers' market, each on different days of the week so as not to compete with one another and let the same farmers sell in each one. There's the Tulip Festival in Albany; Troy is in the midst of planning a SXSW-inspired music festival; and Saratoga has its racetrack. Separately, each city and town attracts regional tourist dollars and encourages weekend outings at local venues.

These events hit the sweet spot of approachable, unique, and relatively cheap to execute. They are perfect for the visiting parents, busy families, and weekend tourists looking for low-stakes entertainment. But what about the big dollars? How has the Capital Region fared in

TABLE 1 POPULATION CHANGES IN CAPITAL REGION COUNTIES AND MAJOR CITIES COMPARED TO NEW YORK CITY BOROUGHS AND NEW YORK STATE, 2010–2020

	Pop. 2010	Pop. 2020	Change	Change %
Saratoga County	219,607	235,509	15,902	7.24%
Schenectady County	154,727	158,061	3,334	2.15%
Albany County	304,204	314,848	10,644	3.50%
Rensselaer County	159,429	161,130	1,701	1.07%
Total counties	837,967	869,548	31,581	3.77%
Troy	50,129	51,401	1,272	2.54%
Schenectady (city)	66,135	67,047	912	1.38%
Albany (city)	97,856	99,224	1,368	1.40%
Saratoga Springs	26,586	28,491	1,905	7.17%
Total cities	240,706	246,163	5,457	2.27%
Bronx Borough	1,385,108	1,472,654	87,546	6.32%
Brooklyn Borough	2,504,700	2,736,074	231,374	9.24%
Manhattan Borough	1,585,873	1,694,251	108,378	6.83%
Queens Borough	2,230,364	2,405,464	175,100	7.85%
Staten Island Borough	468,730	495,747	27,017	5.76%
New York State	19,378,096	20,201,249	823,153	4.25%

SOURCES: U.S. Census Bureau, "Total Population, 2010," *Social Explorer Tables*, https://www.socialexplorer.com/data/CENSUS2020/metadata?ds=SE&table=T002. U.S. Census Bureau, "Total Population, 2020," *Social Explorer Tables*, https://www.socialexplorer.com/data/CENSUS2020/metadata?ds=SE&table=T002.

attracting permanent residents and big employers and growing the cities themselves? This is what the economic developers I spoke to use as their measuring stick, so we should see how they are doing.

I WANNA BE WHERE THE PEOPLE ARE

It's about time we ask the big question: Does the City Authentic regime work? Are exposed brick walls and small-city pride enough to convince a Brooklynite to move to Saratoga Springs? If your success is defined by an increase in population, then the short answer is no. From 2010 to 2020, the four main counties of the Capital Region—Rensselaer, Albany, Schenectady, and Saratoga—saw only modest population increases of 1.07 percent, 3.5 percent, 2.15 percent, and 7.24 percent respectively. Together, the four Capital Region counties added 31,581 people between 2010 and 2020.[46] At the city level over the same time frame, Troy, Albany, Schenectady, and Saratoga Springs had low

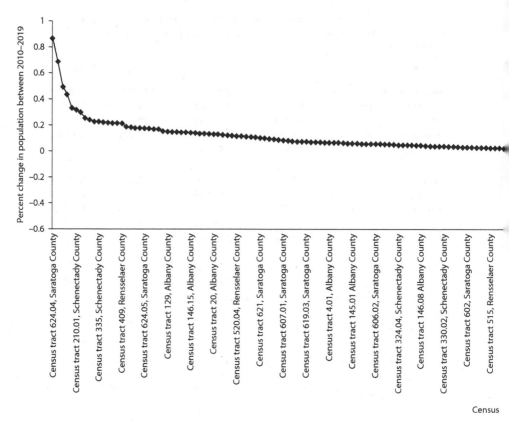

FIGURE 3. Percentage change in population between 2010 and 2019 within Albany, Rensselaer, Saratoga, and Schenectady Counties, by census tract. Source: U.S. Census.

numbers too: 2.54 percent, 1.40 percent, 1.38 percent, and 7.17 percent respectively.[47]

As the answer gets longer, however, it becomes much more complicated. If we compare the Capital Region to New York City and New York State, as I do in table 1, we see that Saratoga County and the city of Saratoga Springs beat Staten Island, the Bronx, and the statewide increase in population. But when we compare the cities and counties of the Capital Region, it becomes clear that the major cities—where the funky old buildings containing restaurants and shops are—are not where most of the growth is. Except for Troy and Rensselaer, the major cities grew less than their host counties.

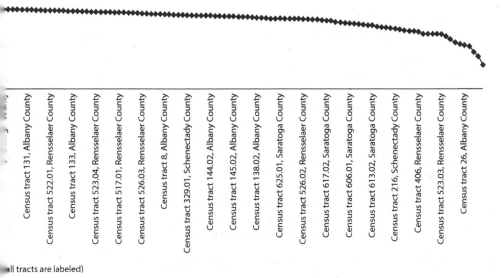

Census tract 131, Albany County
Census tract 522.01, Rensselaer County
Census tract 133, Albany County
Census tract 523.04, Rensselaer County
Census tract 517.01, Rensselaer County
Census tract 526.03, Rensselaer County
Census tract 8, Albany County
Census tract 329.01, Schenectady County
Census tract 144.02, Albany County
Census tract 145.02, Albany County
Census tract 138.02, Albany County
Census tract 625.01, Saratoga County
Census tract 526.02, Rensselaer County
Census tract 617.02, Saratoga County
Census tract 606.01, Saratoga County
Census tract 613.02, Saratoga County
Census tract 216, Schenectady County
Census tract 406, Rensselaer County
Census tract 523.03, Rensselaer County
Census tract 26, Albany County

ll tracts are labeled)

Within the four Capital Region counties there are 243 census tracts. Figure 3 plots the percent change in population between 2010 and 2020 for every tract. The takeaway is that most tracts barely changed and only a handful grew as much as 75 percent or shrunk by as much as 39 percent. The average percentage change is 4.2 percent, almost identical to the statewide increase over the same time frame. Tracts that lost population averaged a loss of 3.9 percent, with a median of 2.75 percent. Tracts that gained population averaged a 9 percent increase, but the median was only 6.11 percent. As the average and median of a set of numbers move apart, it means that the amounts are skewed. So we can infer that the increases in population are enjoyed by a fairly small

TABLE 2   KEY FIGURES FOR CAPITAL REGION POPULATION CHANGES AT CENSUS-TRACT LEVEL

Albany County	
Number of census tracts	85
% of tracts with increase in population	60%
Highest % increase in population (Tract 11)	56.20%
Rensselaer County	
Number of census tracts	48
% of tracts with increase in population	73%
Highest % increase in population (Tract 523.01)	24.63%
Saratoga County	
Number of census tracts	65
% of tracts with increase in population	72%
Highest % increase in population (Tract 624.04)	75.61%
Schenectady County	
Number of census tracts	45
% of tracts with increase in population	58%
Highest % increase in population (Tract 335)	27.34%
Number of Capital Region tracts with increasing population	149
Number of Capital Region tracts with decreasing population	93
Average % change of population for all Capital Region tracts	4.20%
Average % increase of population for all tracts that gained population	9%
Average % decrease of population for all tracts that lost population	–3.90%
Median % increase of population for all tracts that gained population	6.11%
Median % decrease of population for all tracts that lost population	–2.75%
Number of census tracts with no change	1
Population of the most populous census tract as of 2020 (Tract 136.04)	7,198
Average population of a Capital Region census tract in 2020	3,578
Median population of a Capital Region census tract in 2020	3,440
Average % increase in population for 10 most populous tracts as of 2020	13.54%
Average % decrease in population for 10 least populous tracts as of 2020	–5.46%

SOURCE: U.S. Census Bureau, "Total Population, 2020," *Social Explorer Tables*, https://www.socialexplorer.com/data/CENSUS2020/metadata?ds=SE&table=T002.

minority of census tracts while losses are more evenly distributed. Table 2 summarizes these and other figures.

What should we make of these numbers? First, these are relatively small numbers. Adding a single new apartment complex of two hundred units, assuming an average occupancy of 1.5 people per unit, to the average census tract would increase its population by 8 percent, which is just one point short of the average increase for all census tracts that had an increase at all. Then again, figure 4 shows that there is no discernible correlation between the size of the population in 2020 and the percentage change in the population between 2010 and 2020, which means those high-percentage-change tracts are not the result of a sparsely populated region adding only a few homes. In fact, the highest percentage increases come from tracts around the middle of the distribution: the ones with between 3,000 and 4,000 people per tract.

Unfortunately, as I write this, there is incomplete data on population in the Capital Region. The COVID-19 pandemic slowed data collection while seemingly speeding up migration to the area. We'll reckon with that later in the chapter. For now, though, this means if we want to dig deeper into the data, we'll have to rely on different data sets where some borders of census tracts change, so we will have to zoom out again to the county, city, and metro region.

Where are the new people coming from? Table 3 shows the percentage change in people who reported moving to their current rented residence from different counties, states, and countries. All cities and counties reported an increase in residents who moved from one New York State county to another, which can mean new people coming into the Capital Region but it could also mean people moved between its constituent counties. What is remarkable is that across the whole metropolitan region there was a 35 percent increase in people moving from another state, especially to the cities and Saratoga County, which has some of the wealthiest and newest suburbs in the area.

The Census Bureau also tracks how many people say they walk to work, and the percentages in the four cities is fairly high. In Troy and Albany, it is particularly high, at 9.18 percent and 10.61 percent respectively. For the whole region it's 3.5 percent. That's in contrast to 6.14 percent in New York State and 2.67 percent nationally.[48] This suggests that many people are actually using the downtown as a place to live and work and aren't just visiting it as a playground on Friday nights. Part of this high figure can be attributed to income (people who would rather

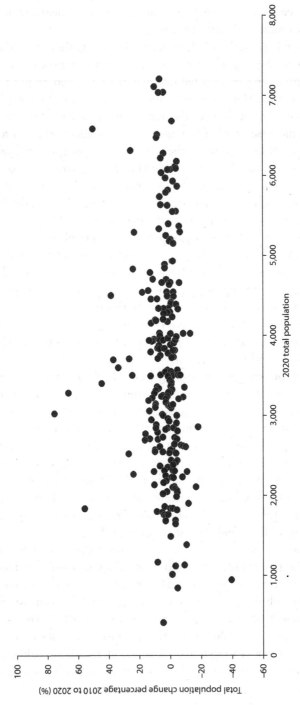

FIGURE 4. Percentage change in total population between 2010 and 2020 within Albany, Rensselaer, Saratoga, and Schenectady Counties, by census tract. Source: U.S. Census.

TABLE 3 GEOGRAPHICAL MOBILITY IN CAPITAL REGION COUNTIES AND MAJOR CITIES IN THE PAST YEAR FOR CURRENT RESIDENCE, PERCENTAGE CHANGE, 2010–2019

	Capital Region cities					Capital Region counties					Albany-Troy-Schenectady metro area
	City of Albany	City of Troy	City of Saratoga Springs	City of Schenectady	Total of all cities	Albany County	Rensselaer County	Saratoga County	Schenectady County	Total of all counties	
Population 1 year and over in households in the United States	−0.1%	−3.6%	1.5%	1.3%	−0.3%	1.3%	1.3%	5.5%	1.5%	2.1%	1.90%
Householder lived in renter-occupied housing unit	3.7%	7.7%	25.8%	8.0%	7.2%	8.9%	8.9%	16.4%	12.4%	10.9%	10.8%
Same house 1 year ago	11.0%	11.3%	19.2%	10.2%	11.4%	15.1%	15.1%	18.6%	15.7%	14.3%	14.2%
Moved within same county	−18.8%	−5.0%	0.8%	−7.1%	−11.8%	−8.9%	−8.9%	−20.2%	−5.9%	−8.7%	−8.5%
Moved from different county within same state	18.7%	8.4%	97.8%	4.6%	16.7%	2.8%	2.8%	26.8%	10.9%	12.2%	12.4%
Moved from different state	−24.2%	38.4%	108.1%	49.2%	26.2%	−12.7%	−12.7%	93.0%	26.4%	35.6%	35.8%
Moved from abroad	−15.1%	−33.6%	39.7%	−20.8%	−14.3%	9.0%	9.0%	−2.9%	4.2%	8.6%	8.6%

SOURCES: U.S. Census Bureau, "Geographical Mobility in the Past Year for Current Residence in the United States (Renter-Occupied Housing Units), 2010," Social Explorer Tables, https://www.socialexplorer.com/data/ACS2010_5yr/metadata?ds=SE&table=A08002B. U.S. Census Bureau, "Geographical Mobility in the Past Year for Current Residence in the United States (Renter-Occupied Housing Units), 2019," Social Explorer Tables, https://www.socialexplorer.com/data/ACS2019_5yr/metadata?ds=SE&table=A08002B.

commute more comfortably but cannot afford it), but in general it appears as though living in a walkable downtown is more than just an aesthetic choice for a lot of people.

We would also expect a fully functioning creative-class strategy to increase the region's population of young, highly educated professionals, and that appears to have happened too. The industry changes outlined in table 4 are telling as well, with increases across the four counties in many "white collar" industries (e.g., the strange agglomeration of Professional, Scientific, and Management, and Administrative and Waste Management Services that the Census Bureau tracks, as well as Educational Services, and Health Care and Social Assistance) and in its attendant service sector (e.g. Arts, Entertainment, and Recreation, and Accommodation and Food Services). Manufacturing went up 29.5 percent in Saratoga County, but it was mostly flat everywhere else.

Within the major cities, we see something similar from 2009 to 2019. The age ranges the creative-class hypothesis would predict to go up— younger childless people as well as 65+ empty nesters seeking smaller apartments—posted big gains across the board (see table 5). Meanwhile, age brackets 34–64 and under 18, which would mainly include families, went down cumulatively in cities and counties. Startlingly, households making over $200,000 more than doubled in the counties and cities. In fact, every household making above $100,000 had strong double-digit percentage increases, while all other income brackets either decreased or made very modest increases.[49] Given that the net increase in population was modest, we can assume a lot of what we are seeing here is replacement of existing residents by newer, wealthier, more educated ones.

So far all of this sounds like classic creative-class gentrification. But there are complications. Of the fifteen census blocks with the greatest increase in population in the Capital Region, the one with the highest increase in gross median rent was Block 1 of Census Tract 135.08: a sparsely populated suburban neighborhood in Albany County off Highway 87.[50] Halfmoon, Malta, and Saratoga Springs, along with the suburban town of Brunswick in Rensselaer County, were the only Capital Region municipalities to make it to New York State's list of fastest-growing towns or cities list.[51]

What is bringing people to the Saratoga County suburbs are not, as the creative-class thesis would suggest, the quaint downtowns. The most likely answer is GlobalFoundries, a semiconductor manufacturer owned by the Emirate of Abu Dhabi that set up shop in Malta, a town

TABLE 4   PERCENTAGE CHANGE IN EDUCATIONAL ATTAINMENT AND EMPLOYMENT INDUSTRIES IN THE CAPITAL REGION COUNTIES, 2009–2019

	Albany County	Rensselaer County	Saratoga County	Schenectady County	All counties combined
Change in education of total population 25 years and over	7.8%	6.4%	9.9%	5.0%	7.6%
Less than high school	-8.2%	-24.0%	-24.7%	-1.4%	-14.6%
High school graduate or more (includes equivalency)	9.5%	10.3%	13.2%	5.8%	10.0%
Some college or more	18.2%	19.6%	22.6%	10.1%	18.2%
Bachelor's degree or more	23.2%	28.9%	33.4%	15.4%	25.7%
Master's degree or more	25.3%	26.9%	35.9%	7.3%	25.3%
Professional school degree or more	22.1%	16.1%	32.2%	-3.8%	19.0%
Doctorate degree	26.9%	17.9%	52.5%	5.2%	27.2%
Change in industries of total employed civilian population 16 years and over	6.7%	2.7%	6.7%	2.6%	5.2%
Agriculture, Forestry, Fishing and Hunting, and Mining	-33.9%	-24.1%	10.9%	-16.8%	-13.3%
Construction	-5.6%	4.3%	-3.3%	-7.4%	-3.0%
Manufacturing	3.8%	2.5%	29.5%	-3.0%	11.0%
Wholesale Trade	-10.3%	-21.9%	-23.2%	-9.6%	-16.7%
Retail Trade	2.1%	-11.8%	7.7%	1.5%	0.8%
Transportation and Warehousing, and Utilities	-15.2%	47.0%	-11.9%	33.7%	5.0%
Information	-5.6%	-27.6%	-20.5%	-24.6%	-17.5%
Finance and Insurance, and Real Estate and Rental and Leasing	4.8%	-7.8%	-12.0%	-5.1%	-3.8%
Professional, Scientific, and Management, and Administrative and Waste Management Services	34.7%	21.3%	27.0%	7.3%	25.1%
Educational Services, and Health Care and Social Assistance	7.0%	3.2%	10.7%	8.3%	7.4%
Arts, Entertainment, and Recreation, and Accommodation and Food Services	24.6%	10.2%	16.3%	22.0%	19.1%
Other Services, Except Public Administration	21.7%	9.1%	2.2%	-7.4%	8.3%
Public Administration	-4.7%	-2.3%	-8.7%	-10.0%	-5.9%

SOURCES: U.S. Census Bureau, "Highest Educational Attainment for Population 25 Years and Over, 2009," *Social Explorer Tables*, https://www.socialexplorer.com/data/ACS2009_5yr /metadata?ds=SE&table=A12002. U.S. Census Bureau "Industry by Occupation for Employed Civilian Population 16 Years and Over, 2009," *Social Explorer Tables*, https://www.socialexplorer .com/data/ACS2009_5yr/metadata?ds=SE&table=A17004. U.S. Census Bureau, "Highest Educational Attainment for Population 25 Years and Over, 2019," *Social Explorer Tables*, https://www .socialexplorer.com/data/ACS2019_5yr/metadata?ds=SE&table=A12002. U.S. Census Bureau, "Industry by Occupation for Employed Civilian Population 16 Years and Over, 2019," *Social Explorer Tables*, https://www.socialexplorer.com/data/ACS2019_5yr/metadata?ds=SE&table=A17004.

TABLE 5   HOUSEHOLD INCOME AND AGE RANGES OF RESIDENTS IN THE
CAPITAL REGION COUNTIES AND PERCENTAGE CHANGE, 2010 AND 2019

	2010		2019		Change
Total households	333,150		340,154		2.1%
Less than $10,000	19,299	5.8%	15,213	4.5%	−21.2%
$10,000 to $14,999	16,320	4.9%	13,297	3.9%	−18.5%
$15,000 to $19,999	14,810	4.4%	13,081	3.8%	−11.7%
$20,000 to $24,999	17,347	5.2%	13,140	3.9%	−24.3%
$25,000 to $29,999	15,764	4.7%	12,694	3.7%	−19.5%
$30,000 to $34,999	15,730	4.7%	14,557	4.3%	−7.5%
$35,000 to $39,999	15,308	4.6%	11,986	3.5%	−21.7%
$40,000 to $44,999	15,063	4.5%	13,406	3.9%	−11.0%
$45,000 to $49,999	14,127	4.2%	12,882	3.8%	−8.8%
$50,000 to $59,999	27,395	8.2%	24,800	7.3%	−9.5%
$60,000 to $74,999	35,752	10.7%	31,800	9.3%	−11.1%
$75,000 to $99,999	47,560	14.3%	46,810	13.8%	−1.6%
$100,000 to $124,999	32,264	9.7%	37,400	11.0%	15.9%
$125,000 to $149,999	17,727	5.3%	25,446	7.5%	43.5%
$150,000 to $199,999	16,973	5.1%	28,389	8.3%	67.3%
$200,000 or More	11,711	3.5%	25,253	7.4%	115.6%
Total population	833,193		849,514		2.0%
Under 18 years	183,112	22.0%	167,944	19.8%	−8.3%
18 to 34 years	189,240	22.7%	204,697	24.1%	8.2%
35 to 64 years	346,202	41.6%	333,629	39.3%	−3.6%
65 and over	114,639	13.8%	143,244	16.9%	25.0%

SOURCES: U.S. Census Bureau, "Household Income (In 2010 Inflation Adjusted Dollars)," *Social Explorer Tables: ACS 2010 (5-Year Estimates)*, https://www.socialexplorer.com/data/ACS2010_5yr/metadata?ds=SE&table=A14001. U.S. Census Bureau, "Household Income (In 2019 Inflation Adjusted Dollars)," *Social Explorer Tables: ACS 2019 (5-Year Estimates)*, https://www.socialexplorer.com/data/ACS2019_5yr/metadata?ds=SE&table=A14001. U.S. Census Bureau, "Age (Short Version), 2010," *Social Explorer Tables: ACS 2010 (5-Year Estimates)*, https://www.socialexplorer.com/data/ACS2010_5yr/metadata?ds=SE&table=B01001. U.S. Census Bureau, "Age (Short Version), 2019," *Social Explorer Tables: ACS 2019 (5-Year Estimates)*, https://www.socialexplorer.com/data/ACS2019_5yr/metadata?ds=SE&table=B01001.

in Saratoga County just northeast of the county's top-performing census tract. The facility opened in 2009 and in April 2021 moved its headquarters there from Silicon Valley.[52] We also see the effect of that in table 4's occupation statistics. I find this bit interesting because while GF is certainly the kind of company a creative-class playbook would tell you to seek out, it means that manufacturing is what really changes a region, not the kind of white-collar office work typically associated with Floridian gentrification schemes.

One thing that I had expected but did not see was an increase in White people in the cities. Instead, across all four cities there was a total net *decrease* in White residents of 7.4 percent, from 67.4 percent to 62.3 percent of the population. Asian Americans increased their share of the population from 4 percent to 6 percent and Black residents went from 20.5 percent to 21.2 percent. Income for Black households went up 19.6 percent over the decade, compared to 33.3 percent and 31.1 percent for White and Asian households respectively.[53] These changes are happening in the urban neighborhoods and suburbs, however; the demographics of downtown core neighborhoods remained largely the same over the decade.[54] This reflects earlier work by Nevarez and Simons, who rightly point out that immigration in the American "regional context" is understudied but appears essential to understanding demographics in the twenty-first century.[55]

To summarize then, there are clear signs of the Richard Florida creative-class development program at work at nearly every level: county, city, and neighborhood. The employment sectors with the biggest gains were professional management and service industry jobs. The percentage of people with advanced degrees increased fast enough to suggest that these are new people, not existing residents who earned advanced degrees. And while there was a modest net increase in overall population of 31,581, there were many more people coming and going within the span of a few years. The data paints a picture of a highly mobile professional strata that maintained a remarkably steady equilibrium. There did seem to be some displacement within neighborhoods, but the overall picture was one of increasing racial diversification, even as income distributions bifurcated to the ends of the spectrum. That is, these cities are becoming more cosmopolitan, and with that increasing urbanism comes increasing inequality. And yet, the biggest gains in population have actually been in the suburbs, thanks in some part to a good old-fashioned, labor-intensive manufacturing facility, not necessarily graphic design or some other distinctly creative-class job.

A SOLID RETURN ON INVESTMENT

Let's ask the question again, this time slightly differently: Does the City Authentic regime work? Are $8 pour-over coffees and proximity to camping grounds enough to convince a Manhattan socialite to buy a new home in Schenectady? If you define success in terms of real estate values and rents, then the answer is a resounding yes.

	Capital Region counties					Capital Region cities				
	Albany County	Rensselaer County	Saratoga County	Schenectady County	Total change (all counties)	Albany city, Albany County	Troy city, Rensselaer County	Saratoga Springs city, Saratoga County	Schenectady city, Schenectady County	Total change (all county subdivisions)
Renter-occupied housing units with cash rent, gross rent change	8.0%	10.2%	16.7%	3.1%	9.3%	3.3%	6.8%	24.0%	1.0%	5.3%
Less than $300	-20.8%	-35.1%	-23.6%	18.7%	-17.9%	-20.8%	-45.1%	-36.9%	8.4%	-22.6%
$300 to $599	-42.2%	-45.4%	-48.8%	-56.0%	-46.3%	-47.4%	-51.2%	-53.3%	-47.6%	-48.9%
$600 to $799	-41.6%	-36.4%	-49.5%	-42.5%	-42.0%	-45.1%	-39.1%	-75.3%	-40.9%	-44.7%
$800 to $999	-3.3%	17.2%	-25.6%	11.2%	-2.9%	16.4%	18.3%	-24.6%	25.0%	15.5%
$1,000 to $1,249	35.5%	88.8%	53.5%	63.7%	50.5%	49.2%	136.9%	43.7%	49.6%	63.9%
$1,250 to $1,499	142.8%	63.6%	260.9%	127.2%	145.8%	94.5%	136.1%	1,064.2%	93.1%	149.2%
$1,500 to $1,999	227.7%	292.5%	238.5%	162.3%	233.7%	191.3%	965.8%	155.5%	113.9%	215.0%
$2,000 or more	189.2%	250.6%	225.5%	189.0%	209.8%	66.7%	274.7%	194.6%	197.1%	148.3%
Median gross rent change	19.5%	24.9%	30.7%	19.8%	22.3%	18.8%	28.2%	53.0%	16.2%	22.0%

SOURCES: U.S. Census Bureau, "Median Gross Rent, 2010," *Social Explorer Tables: ACS 2010 (5-Year Estimates)*, https://www.socialexplorer.com/data/ACS2010_5yr /metadata?ds=SE&table=A18009. U.S. Census Bureau, "Median Gross Rent, 2019," *Social Explorer Tables: ACS 2019 (5-Year Estimates)*, https://www.socialexplorer.com/data /ACS2019_5yr/metadata?ds=SE&table=A18009.

Let's start with an obvious one: the cost of rent. As you can see in table 6, the median rent across the Capital Region went up about 22 percent in the cities and counties. Availability of rental housing that cost less than $800 a month saw double-digit decreases while anything over $1,500 saw *triple*-digit increases. Saratoga Springs saw an astounding 1,064 percent increase in rentals going for $1,250–$1,499. Troy also saw a nearly 1,000 percent increase in housing units renting between $1,500 and $2,000. Saratoga Springs saw the biggest change overall, with a 53 percent increase in median rent.[56]

Now the next logical question is whether anyone can *afford* these rents. New York State overall has some of the worst rates of housing affordability in the country.[57] The percentage of cost-burdened households—those that spend more than 30 percent of their income on rent or mortgage payments—is between 38 and 53 percent in the major cities (see table 7). Most of the Capital Region cities hover just below the statewide averages.

Achieving slightly better rates than New York State's baseline affordability is faint praise, and even that might be going away. A woman from Boston told the *Albany Business Review* in 2019 that she "saw an opportunity to get a solid return on investment by purchasing older apartments in [the Warren County city of] Glens Falls, acquiring nearly 60 apartments in 18 months." A local real estate agent put this buying spree into context: "From 2009 and 2015, buyers spent approximately $10 million purchasing multifamily housing in the city. Over the past two years [2018–2019], nearly $22 million in transactions have occurred."[58]

And yet, the mix of renting versus owning has remained virtually unchanged in the Capital Region for two decades. In 2000, 64 percent of homes were owned and 36 percent were rented. In 2019, ownership had actually fallen by half a percent.[59] The rapid increase in buying and selling is not an indication of renters saving enough money to become owners, it is an ownership class buying and selling among one another, driving up the cost of rent in the process.

The action isn't all at the top of the market. Remember that the fastest growing municipalities in the region are in middle-class suburban towns like Brunswick, Halfmoon, and Malta (median household income in these areas is mostly $65,888–$90,877),[60] where cheap cookie-cutter townhouses abound and taxes are relatively low.[61] In fact, if we take the fifteen census tract blocks that grew the most in terms of population between 2010 and 2019, we see a 100 percent increase in families with

TABLE 7   PERCENTAGE OF RENTERS CONSIDERED COST-BURDENED IN THE FOUR
MAJOR CAPITAL REGION CITIES AND RALEIGH, NC, THREE DATE RANGES

	2005–2009	2010–2015	2015–2019
Albany	53%	53%	53%
Saratoga Springs	45%	41%	38%
Schenectady	46%	52%	48%
Troy	46%	51%	46%
Raleigh, NC	47%	48%	44%

SOURCES: U.S. Census Bureau, "Percent of Renters Who Are Burdened," PolicyMap (based on *American Community Survey 2005-2009 [5-Year Estimates]*). U.S. Census Bureau, "Percent of Renters Who Are Burdened," PolicyMap (based on *American Community Survey 2010-2015 [5-Year Estimates]*). U.S. Census Bureau, "Percent of Renters Who Are Burdened," PolicyMap (based on *American Community Survey 2015-2019 [5-Year Estimates]*).

income below the poverty line and a 186 percent increase in female-led households with a related child at or below the poverty level.[62] Median gross rent in the same areas went up 32 percent.[63] Median gross rent as a percentage of household income went up an average of 13 percent in the nine blocks where data existed.[64] At the same time, however, the percentage of households across all four cities and counties with income below $49,000 went down, while households making more than $200,000 more than doubled.[65] Since cost-burdened households weren't going down at the same rate as incomes per household were going up, we can assume one or both of the following were at play: a generous portion of the increase in high-earning households moved here, rather than the same people becoming better off, and rents increased to the extent that they negated increases in wages.

The Capital District Regional Planning Commission (CDRPC) has kept a close eye on these figures and has written several reports comparing the region to similarly sized ones. One such report, published in 2016, compared the Capital Region to fourteen other similarly sized capital cities throughout the country and other cities in upstate New York.[66] This report is useful not only for the data it contains but also because it shows us how economic development professionals and planners conceptualize the Capital Region and its peers. It shows us what indicators they find important and what kinds of cities they consider to be peers. Unfortunately, the data covers 2005 through 2014, which doesn't line up with what we have been using thus far, but there are some useful observations in the report that give context to what we are seeing.

Two similarities across cities immediately stand out. First, renters that spent more than 30 percent of their income on rent all hovered around or just below the 40 percent range for both years, except for Rochester, where percentages stayed above 50 percent. The same was true for homeowners who all saw a little less than 30 percent of households cost-burdened in 2014. The Great Recession and the lopsided recovery impacted all these cities where cost burdens increased across the board (except for Little Rock, Arkansas) from 2005 to 2009.[67] Second, the distribution of jobs by industry were fairly consistent as well. Educational Services and Healthcare and Retail Trade were consistently the two biggest employment sectors in all cities and collectively accounted for 36 percent of all employment across the peer cities.[68]

This is quite incredible. Cities with radically different histories and prevailing policy frameworks—from Salt Lake City to Baton Rouge—all have affordability problems, and the mix of employment sectors are roughly the same as well. It suggests a robust economic phenomenon that is immune to the efforts of localities' housing authorities or federal affordable housing programs. This becomes even more incredible when you look at how these cities differ. Raleigh, for example, blows every other city out of the water with 11,647 residential building permits between 2010 and 2014. Salt Lake City comes in a distant second at 5,318, yet their construction sectors' percentages of overall employment are within a few points of each other. Madison has nearly twice as many college-educated residents as Baton Rouge, and yet their rent-burdened rates are within half a point of one another at around 47 percent.[69] In 2019, after all that building, the percentage of cost-burdened renters in Raleigh was 44.47 percent.[70] That puts it in the middle of the pack of Capital Region cities. For homeowners, Raleigh fares a bit better, though as table 7 shows, the cities in the Capital Region actually improved more over time than Raleigh.

Now think back to all the promises every politician has ever made: that growth creates construction jobs or that run-down cities and towns just need some training centers so that coal miners or assembly plant workers can meet the demands of the new, innovation-based economy. This data would suggest those claims are misleading at best. A city can literally double the amount of building permits it issues and college-educated workers it attracts but very little will change.

The CDRPC report doesn't comment on this, instead opting to describe how the Capital Region competes with its peers in terms of readily available metrics. There is no analysis across metrics to assess whether strategies to increase high tech jobs or building permits can be expected to increase quality-of-life indicators for residents.

To summarize the numbers in the Capital Region: Rents have increased dramatically, with some places seeing the median rent more than double. The percentage of cost-burdened households has gone up too, even for homeowners. Purchasing frequency is anecdotally going up, though the ratio of owning to renting has not moved substantially since 2000, which suggests property owners are selling to one another, not to first-time home buyers.

Nonetheless, economic development marches on, seeking new investments and attracting as many new residents as possible. When I first started writing this book, the pandemic had only just begun and no one knew how long it would last. In a very early draft, I had written that the City Authentic was extremely vulnerable to economic downturns. After all, eating out and buying custom throw pillows are some of the first things you cut from your budget when money dries up. But what happened amid the pandemic was a bit more complicated. Many restaurants were crushed, and many lives and livelihoods were lost, but it seems as though the Capital Region will come out on the other side fulfilling the goals local elites had always sought to achieve. The pandemic had enough of an impact on the region that it deserves close review, so let's turn to that now.

IMPACT OF THE PANDEMIC

When COVID-19 struck and decimated New York City in the winter of 2020, killing over thirty thousand people, it seemed as though the Capital Region was poised for a massive influx of new residents. Many wanted to flee the city, and so we can look at these plague years as a test of whether people would move to the Capital Region cities that once existed only in their Instagram feeds.

In 2021, when change-of-address data started coming in from the post office, *Times Union* reporters Kenneth C. Crowe and Leigh Hornbeck wrote that it finally gave something to "support the tales of downstate residents turning up to buy homes, rent apartments or Airbnbs, move back with family or ride out the pandemic in weekend or summer residences."[71] The post office data revealed a massive migration from the city to the Capital Region: "Rensselaer County had a 787 percent increase in address changes from New York City in 2020, compared to 2019. Saratoga County was next at 518 percent followed by Schenectady

County at 152 percent and Albany County at 126 percent."[72] The towns that were already doing well prior to the pandemic continued to post the most gains: Saratoga Springs and Halfmoon added about three thousand new residents each, and Malta gained about half that.

According to the real estate firm CBRE, "Nearly all urban centers saw an increase in move-outs. Nationally, urban centers had 15% more move-outs in 2020 than in 2019. . . . The biggest cohort of this urban outflow [was] affluent young adults who are well-educated, childless and can work remotely."[73] That report identified Hudson, New York, a small city of 6,235 in Columbia County just south of Rensselaer, as the biggest beneficiary of fleeing New Yorkers. Kingston, even further south, in Ulster County, with a population of 23,070, was the second biggest.

In April 2020, Tracey Boomhower, president of the Columbia Greene Northern Dutchess Multiple Listing Service, told HudsonValley360, "The minute a house goes on the market it already has 20 showings."[74] An hour north in the Capital Region, the real estate market was also exploding. Residential real estate sales from the top twenty-five firms in the region saw a 19 percent increase in sales from the previous year.[75] Dan Davies, owner and broker at Davies-Davies Real Estate, speculated in the pages of the *Albany Business Review* that the increases were directly caused by the rich fleeing the city: "People found Lake George and the Adirondacks who used to go other places, they fell in love with it. I think Lake George and Lake Placid have jumped forward [in expected housing prices] 10 years."[76] The median sale price in the region rose 7 percent in 2020 from the previous year.[77] The US Post Office estimated that three hundred thousand people had fled New York City, mostly for wealthy zip codes.[78]

Mark Eagan, CEO of the Capital Region Chamber of Commerce and the Center for Economic Growth, used two different buildings renovated by Redburn Development to describe the changes since COVID began: "When they opened up their first building in downtown [Albany] probably about two years ago—it's called the Knick—there's a little over 100 units in that building, and they literally had one person that was from New York City move into that. Their most recent building opened up was Kenmore, [which] I think was around 40 percent of the people from New York City."[79]

It makes sense to look at Redburn's properties to gauge interest in the Capital Region because it sells the area as much as the properties themselves. The developer operates liveindowntownalbany.com, which lists all the buildings and off-site parking garages it owns and operates. In

2021, it was advertising studio apartments starting at $850 in the Kenmore but most are over a thousand. All buildings advertise access to a common lounge that all residents can use, a single utility bill managed by the company that is called "All-In Living," and discounts to local businesses (from axe throwing to dog walking services) if you show them your key fob. The website for the River Street Lofts, a Redburn building in Troy, even linked to a 2013 *New York Daily News* article about Troy that assures the reader, "with an abundance of affordable studios, shops and homes in grand turn-of-the-century buildings, artisans, restaurateurs, and other creative types are helping resurrect this venerable old town just north of Albany." It gives plenty of column space to Vic Christopher and Heather LeVine's wine bar and the president of First Columbia Development, who calls Downtown Troy "one of the best-kept secrets of the Capital District."[80]

Developers are certainly no stranger to marketing the places where they own property, but to bring in the money, capital, and attention the region needs, they have to build something bigger. What they need is a cohesive, integrated strategy that will transform the region from a constellation of small towns into a decentralized city of a million people.

BULLSHIT, NY

In the horror film *Scare Me* (2020), Fred Banks (no relation) meets Fanny, who says she is on a writing retreat before appending "hashtag escape Brooklyn." Such a hashtag does exist, and its contents include quaint cabins (which just so happen to be the setting of the movie) along with farms, exquisite food, fishing, and a *lot* of real estate agents' listings. Megan Brenn-White, the head of the Upstate Curious Team at Keller Williams Hudson Valley North, runs the @upstatecurious Instagram account with over forty-two thousand followers. Her immaculately curated account has many videos of home walk-throughs for new listings, but that's maybe two-thirds of the posts. The other third is filled with roadside farm stands, nature trails, and a lot of pizza. A post with two pizzas and a cocktail reads:

> I got zero pics of the charming interior of the huge, equally charming beer garden-style outdoor seating area at @thedaleny in @visitmountaindale, BUT it's only cause my cocktail was soooo good and none of us could stop talking about the delicious sourdough pizzas and burrata-tomato plate we'd ordered.

Check their insta for live music and specials and be sure to visit soon—maybe during the Second Saturdays events coming up from May through October with a market and street fair?!

(PS The Dale—and the other great shops and restaurants in Mountaindale—are 15 mins away from our new lakefront listing in Rock Hill ;)[81]

Hashtag escapebrooklyn draws a big circle around Brooklyn, often encompassing the entire Capital Region but regularly capturing the counties to the south like Sullivan, where Mountain Dale is situated. (I've seen buttons with the tagline "You take Brooklyn, I'll take Troy.") Josh Ruben, the writer, director, and co-star of *Scare Me* lives in Ulster County, to the east of Sullivan, and told *MEL Magazine* that he added that little "hashtag escape Brooklyn" to "jab at that culture, but I feel like I can do that because I'm a small-town boy from the area that's now turning into the East Coast's alt-Hamptons. It's really just a treat for me. It's an artisan inside joke for no one."[82] Ruben has more company than he realizes, because the escape-Brooklyn ethos is not just a hashtag on Instagram, it is the name of a whole business that publishes travel guides and write-ups of cute restaurants and shops and advertises real estate listings.

"*And North, Escape Brooklyn, Design Sponge, The Shop Keepers.* Those were the main blogs at the time that were beginning to pay attention to new businesses of this type popping up on Upstate NY." That's Caroline Corrigan. For four years her giftshop, the Fort Orange General Store in Albany, was the only Capital Region entry in *Escape Brooklyn* until Saratoga Springs got a whole travel guide at the end of 2019. Corrigan reached out to these blogs to drive business to her store, which sold gifts and unique items from the region. "We knew if they wrote about us or posted about us on Instagram, it would help get the word out. I think those posts made an impact for sure, especially with folks from out of town or the Hudson Valley area." Instagram, too, "was a huge way of how we, like, got people. I attribute a lot of its success [to Instagram]."[83]

Corrigan, along with her business partner, closed the Fort Orange General Store in 2016 to pursue other projects, but Instagram remains a big part of her work life. "I wouldn't have so many of my clients without it. I think I get 90 percent of my [illustration and design] work from people who find me on Instagram." Even though most of her clients still come from the social networking platform, the brick-and-mortar store caused her to spend "more time obsessing over Instagram. If you're a business in a brick and mortar and you sell food or coffee or your shop sells clothes or something, like yeah, you need it. Gotta be on there."

Cities of any size and their constitutive neighborhoods must now use social media—just as they used to use blogs, message boards, travel magazines, and regional newspapers—to build a buzz and brand. Williamsburg, Brooklyn, in the nineties relied on restaurant and gallery reviews to attract Manhattan money before the attention went national and then international. It was only through this media attention that, as Zukin writes, "Williamsburg crystallized into an identifiable local product for global cultural consumption: authentic Brooklyn cool."[84]

Big cities and their neighborhoods are physically and culturally closer to the media than smaller cities, and so the Capital Region has had to work a bit harder to get attention. The May 2019 cover story of the *Albany Business Review* asked "What is Albany's brand?" The illustration that went along with the article was of a grocery store shelf with different boxes with city names on them. Nestled among Boston, Nashville, Austin, and Columbus was Albany in a box slightly bigger than the rest. The lede explained the illustration to anyone who hadn't caught on: "Are we the Capital Region, Capital District, Albany, Tech Valley, or Tri-City Area? Business and creative leaders say a regional brand is a good first step to attract more investment."

The Capital Region is not the first place to describe the need for city branding this explicitly. In the wake of a 2015 episode of Roman Mars's popular podcast *99% Invisible*, where he decried the terrible state of American city-flag design, fans of the show who lived in cities with ugly flags started campaigns to make new ones. This kicked off a flurry of initiatives and competitions across the country to update municipal flags, and the conversations that ensued showed just how closely aesthetics, brands, economics, and politics have grown.

In Milwaukee, local graphic designer Steve Kodis took it upon himself to set up a competition, assuming a grateful local government would throw out the confusing mishmash of outdated symbols on their old flag for whatever won. Fellow graphic designer Robert Lenz won the competition, but the city council refused to adopt the flag, citing a lack of democratic participation in the online poll. This led to the Milwaukee Arts Board conducting its own city-approved competition, but it never made a decision. Board member Polly Morris, in an interview with a local paper, cut to the chase: "It strikes [us] that this process is fundamentally not an aesthetic process; it's a political process."[85] About a flag design competition in Rochester, Minnesota, council member Nick Campion told the *Post Bulletin*, "I look at [a new flag] as unifying the brand of Rochester. . . . It's something we can use to sell ourselves collaboratively."[86]

Similar fights broke out in nearly a hundred other cities between 2015 and 2017. In his overview of these efforts, the flag expert[87] Ted Kaye (who is heavily cited in Mars's program) reported that "the kind of person who might initiate the process" would usually be "a media figure, often a designer or an activist, and sometimes an elected official."[88] In just about every case, choosing a new flag caused controversy, leading to a success rate of about 50 percent. The cities that couldn't seem to pick a new flag, according to Kaye, failed because of "a lack of political groundwork, with minor exceptions."[89]

If Milwaukee is indicative of these failures, then the "political groundwork" for a successful flag adoption needs to bridge both economic and racial gaps in cities. Robert Lenz's design for a new Milwaukee flag, titled "Sunrise over a Lake," is a rising white sun on a yellow field with two shades of blue beneath. Many saw the white sun, meant to symbolize unity, as a poor choice for one of the most racially segregated cities in the United States. Additionally, the whole vibe of the flag came off "as a hipster's flag, a sort of private label for millennial creatives—the polar opposite of what was intended."[90]

As far as I can tell, none of the cities or towns in the New York Capital Region took part in this conflagration,[91] but I bring it up for two reasons. First, it shows that city branding is on everyone's mind, not just those in the Capital Region. City governments take their time on these things because, as the Rochester, Minnesota, council member put it, they can be a great branding opportunity. Second, the flag competitions bring into stark relief a cultural division that was already boiling beneath the surface in Rust Belt revival narratives. That division is best summarized by a Facebook commenter on a KOMU-8 News article about Columbia, Missouri's flag redesign: "No need for city flag. We're Americans; therefore, the flag of our great country should be enough. USA flag!!!!! ▬▬"[92]

This comment points to another level of competition. Beyond the competitions between cities and nations, there is a competition within us for meaning and belonging. For many people, nationalism fulfills the desire to be part of something bigger, and so the American flag does the trick. This Facebook commenter is right in that if you feel being an American deeply informs your identity, a city flag is redundant.

But for a certain set of people—those hipster cosmopolitans who listen to podcasts and have a lot of opinions about design—identifying with the city may be equally if not more important. More importantly though, cities are melting pots, and so it may not be the case that a city dweller is even an American citizen.[93] Therefore, what binds people together in urban centers are the things they choose for themselves—sports teams, social clubs, and so on—and the city itself. That is why Maureen Sager, the executive director of the Upstate Alliance for the Creative Economy (ACE), told the *Albany Business Review*'s Liz Young, "We need to create something that's bigger than a tagline or a logo. We need to create an identity that feels real to us."[94]

Achieving this would be difficult and expensive. That is why Sager was just one of 250 business leaders who gathered in the historic Troy Music Hall to hash out a regional brand identity. Six hundred thousand dollars in cash and services had been donated by several organizations, including a property developer, a local health insurance provider, and two marketing firms. The challenge was succinctly described by Ellen Sax from MVP Healthcare: "We're competing against the Austins and North and South Carolina and Nashville. . . . We're competing against all these different communities that have been developing their identities and that's what we need to do so that we can attract top talent."[95]

Granted, these are replies given to a business reporter in a public setting—which means they're canned responses meant to convey to the world that the Capital Region is setting up the cultural infrastructure for the creative class. That's all the better for our purposes because what these quotes also show is that marketers realize that people are suspicious of marketing and want to feel something authentic when making the decision to move.

Corrigan, who—like me—came here to get an education and stayed, told Young that selling a city isn't all that different from two restaurants "where one has tin ceilings, great music and nice furniture, and the other has cheap chairs and fluorescent lighting. 'Even if the food is identical, you're going to want to stay at the place that looks nicer. . . . The big lesson that I think is sometimes overlooked is investing in the visual experience for a visitor or a customer is so valuable.'"[96]

When I spoke to Corrigan, she struck a different tone with me than the one she had in the article: "You know, there's a part of me that's not even sure it makes sense to advertise cities because it always feels so forced or almost like if you need to advertise for it and like something is wrong with it." She tells me a story about an ad that seemed to fail but then made her think:

> I remember seeing this ad for Rensselaer County on I-90 that read something like "The secret is out!" with a picture of a mountain, and it just made no sense to me. The county is pretty diverse. What are we talking about? Troy? East Greenbush? Avril Park? What is this mountain? What is this secret? Maybe it was just a terrible ad. But, you know, it made me think also: who advertises a county? No one is like repping their county. I mean, maybe like Orange County, California, but it was terrible. Now, I do think that the way that people find out about a city could be through Instagram, and social media in general has a lot of weight in this.[97]

Corrigan was an art student in Albany but had grown up in Hicksville on Long Island. College friends who grew up near Albany told her to steer clear of the "Troylet," but after being invited to a gallery show and enjoying some free wine, she walked around town. "I'm like, 'This place is so beautiful.' Like, 'What, this is the Troylet?' I just couldn't believe how nice it was. And then, you know, eventually I started sticking around." She's suspicious that stuff like this still happens and thinks that social media has now taken the place of box-wine serendipity: "You know, going to this cool event here or there—I don't know if anyone discovers places so organically like that anymore. It's more like you heard about it from someone on Instagram."

Not to leave anything to chance and undeterred by the pandemic, Sager and ACE—which since the *Albany Business Review* article has become affiliated with a larger organization called the Center for Economic Growth (CEG)—moved forward with the branding project. In April 2021, they launched the brand that would unite the over one hundred cities, towns, municipalities, industrial development authorities, and chambers of commerce. It was a brand that would be so powerful, so relatable that creatives from Nashville to Asheville would know it by name. New York's Capital Region would now be called CapNY.

"I like it! I . . . um . . . I don't . . . I have to be honest. I don't love CapNY because it's not compelling in my mind." Real estate broker Michael Field and insurance agent Ryan Hanley are speaking to Katie Newcombe, the chief economic development officer at CEG, for their *Capital Region Business Podcast* about the CapNY campaign.

"Be honest! Be honest!" Newcombe urges.

Hanley pivots to a positive: "I love the [web]site though. The stories, the imagery, I really like the site. I think this site does give a more real . . . almost—I don't mean this in the negative connotation in any way—almost gritty kind of real feel to what it is to live here."

"Yes! Yes!" Newcombe replies. "There's an authenticity to it, right?! There's an honesty to it."

"Oh, 100 percent," says Hanley. "We're not trying to be anyone but who we are and then you gotta tell those stories about who we are."

The three of them are now feeding off each other's excitement about the website and the promise of the CapNY brand. The hosts express the familiar frustration over the fact that the constituent cities, towns, and counties are reticent to cooperate and in fact compete with one another for attention. The result is a disconnected feel to the region. Hanley points out that "Albany and the Catskills, they're right next to each other, [but] you don't see that connection made very often."[98]

The website—I have to be honest as well—does not strike me as gritty. The site follows the best design practices of the time: big photos and punchy text laid out on contrasting fields of color. The site has a slick, Vimeo-hosted video where smiling denim and flannel-clad workers restring guitars, pour farm-to-table cider, and hold baskets of baguettes as a man's voice intones, "New York's Capital Region, where one million people, twenty-four higher educational institutions, thousands of acres of parks and trails, over a hundred arts and cultural institutions, an abundance of farms and farm-to-table restaurants, over one hundred breweries, distilleries, cideries, and wineries. New York's Capital Region. Together, we're capable of anything." The generic, upbeat music stretches this ungrammatical script to a little over a minute. Above the video, the site reads:

> Start your day with a bike ride across the Hudson. Grab an espresso at your favorite cafe. Work your job—Fortune 500 pharma, freelance web developer, loan officer at a community-based bank, baker, organic farmer . . . Next it's local brews and an open mic. Go home to water your garden, tweak your latest game designs (yeah, you've kind of got a side hustle), watch the last of the sunset from your porch.
>
> Room to breathe. Dream big. Live large.
> CapNY. CAPable of aNYthing.

Poking around the site one finds pages devoted to things like affordability, diversity and inclusion, and daycations. The top of that page reads, "Jaw-dropping food, scenery, stays. Yeah, we got that."

In a story about buying your first house in CapNY, the site reads, "Many CapNY millennials are finding great single family properties with mortgage payments that are lower than what they were paying in rent."[99] The article interviews a young couple who bought their first house to build a family in. Tatiana, ("the 25-year-old Founder of Home Aesthetic and Real Estate Investor") is quoted as saying, "We got approved for $250,000, which was interesting because at the time I only made $13.50 an hour. That just shows how easy and affordable it is."[100] Other stories on the website include "5 Millennials on Buying Investment Properties" and "Moving Upstate: Miami Transplant Tony Quezada."

That last one caught my attention—would I see myself in Tony's story? In a way, yes. His adjustment to the seasons was highly relatable, but this part about affordability was so interesting that it's worth quoting in full:

> The salary-to-cost-of-living ratio is a key comparison factor here. The Miami economy is dominated by lower-wage tourism and hospitality. This leads to a lower living wage overall. It's no surprise the average, working-class individual experiences a range of financial difficulties. From purchasing a home to achieving financial independence and freedom, it's harder in Miami.
>
> The Capital Region's lower cost of living and higher living wage was conducive to me improving my financial situation, making home ownership a short-term reality. As a result, I did not sacrifice my standard of living nor quality of life. I was still able to indulge in restaurant delicacies and consume material goods at my desire. And I could have all of this with less of an impact on my cashflow.[101]

A couple of things: First, it's a little strange for something written in the first person to have a byline from someone else. This is certainly not an *authentic* way of speaking to your audience. It also doesn't help that there are phrases that sound like they came out of a Federal Reserve report (e.g., "I was still able to . . . consume material goods at my desire"). More substantively though, these claims about affordability and economic stability are questionable. Using the Longitudinal Employer-Household Dynamics dataset provided by the Census Bureau, we can see that the percentage of jobs in food service, accommodations, entertainment, arts, and recreation in Miami, Florida, is not substantially larger than that in the Capital Region (table 8).[102]

The affordability claims, however, are accurate. Only 12 percent of homes in Miami–Dade County would be considered affordable for a four-person family making the area median income, compared to between 29 percent (Saratoga County) and 61 percent (Schenectady

TABLE 8   PREVALENCE OF TWO INDUSTRY GROUPS ACROSS MAJOR CAPITAL
REGION CITIES AND THE CITY OF MIAMI, FL, 2015–2019

	% of jobs in Accommodation and Food Service	% of jobs in Arts, Entertainment, and Recreation
Albany	8.53	2.19
Saratoga Springs	9.7	4.60
Schenectady	7.36	2.52
Troy	8.15	2.68
Miami, FL	10.76	2.34

SOURCES: Percent Arts, Entertainment, and Recreation Industries employment, 2016-2020, for the City of Miami, FL; Troy, NY; Albany, NY; Schenectady, NY; Saratoga Spring, NY, PolicyMap (based on data from U.S. Census Bureau), https://www.policymap.com. Percent Accommodation and Food Service employment, 2016-2020, for the City of Miami, FL; Troy, NY; Albany, NY; Schenectady, NY; Saratoga Spring, NY, PolicyMap (based on data from U.S. Census Bureau), https://www.policymap.com.

County) in the Capital Region.[103] The reason, as we saw earlier in the chapter, is that affordability is a function not only of income. It is also determined by real estate market speculation driven by global finance and the desires of the ultra-wealthy to park their wealth in investment properties like condos and, increasingly, of pension funds that buy entire housing developments to flip into rentals.[104] This unrelenting push toward growth, what we'll learn in chapter 4 is called "the growth machine," is what drives up prices more than anything else.

Avoiding the uncomfortable conversation of global wealth accumulation and inequality is understandable, even advisable, for a regional branding campaign. But as you read on and find out Tony "found a job he loves" at Goldman Sachs, the rest of the story begins to feel different. Again, while no one is expecting hard-hitting journalism or advanced political economy in their advertorial, it's not a stretch to say that CapNY has a perspective that is friendly to capital and less interested in improving the lives of the poor. *Gritty* is a pliable word, but using it to describe a Goldman Sachs associate buying a house in the suburbs just doesn't make sense.

"What they meant was Black," says Pat Harris, co-founder of Collective Effort, an entirely Black-owned and operated media co-op based in Troy. "There's a ton of color all over that site. It's one of the things I respect about it. Y'all did your due diligence. You found a fair representation of what up here looks like."[105] Harris is right, the site builders clearly went out of their way to show a wide range of people and include multiple stories about women- and Black-owned businesses. Tony from

Miami is Hispanic, and Tatiana—the real estate investor who got a $250,000 loan for a home—is Black.

Collective Effort has worked with global brands like Puma and Under Armour, and CEG approached them to help with what would become the CapNY project. Harris describes the early meetings they had with the CEG team, who had yet to hone in on a brand but already wanted content. Collective Effort told them, "We can tell any story. You need a story, a foundation." They showed up at the Collective Effort office about a year later with an idea they called "all Caps," with messaging around exuberance and living life out loud. "It looked nice; the creative was beautiful," says Harris, but the message was all wrong. "We were just like, 'You ever heard of "no cap"?' So it's a thing that we all say in the Black community. It's very popular; most people say it. It means 'no bullshit.' [*Cap*] means lies. So you just made a campaign that said y'all full of shit."

The CEG folks took it well. They were, in fact and to their credit, appreciative that the Collective Effort team was willing to do this translation work, and a few weeks later the team came back with several new ideas focused on community. They bought the work but what came out at the end was the tagline "CapNY. CAPable of aNYthing." So while they had been taught what *cap* meant, they couldn't shake it, though they did tone it down a bit.

What frustrates Harris more than anything is not the insistence on the use of *cap* but the loss of access and creating a community with those that are already there. "They were serving the wrong audience," he says.

> They were serving the financiers, right? They were serving the people that put up money for this campaign and trying to make them happy, and what makes them happy is bringing talent up here that they can hire and will eventually pay for one of those expensive-ass lofts—that is their idea of what regional success looks like. That's their whole thing, but that's the failure too, because no one gives a fuck about that. That's not what this place is! This place is about folks like us that have literally been here and just keep grinding it out, doing stuff and trying things and fucking making awesome relationships.[106]

In the blog post announcing the launch of the campaign, Maureen Sager included a note at the bottom that read:

> ACE is aware of the inadvertent problems that can occur when a region takes its eye off of the people who live here, and focuses its efforts on attracting and courting outsiders. This was made clear by consultant Meredith

Powell during our "Lessons from Austin" event in 2019. Meredith said something that sticks in our heads to this day—"Dance with who brung ya." In other words, don't forget the residents who made the region great in the first place.[107]

"You talk to Maureen now. That's all she talks about," says Harris. "All that came from us. Like that literally came from us from being like, 'This campaign isn't about us here. It is about everyone else and why the Capital Region would be great for you in Boston or you in New York or you in, you know, somewhere in Canada.'"

While Harris disagrees with the direction CapNY took, Collective Effort's contributions are still visible on the site, and individuals at CEG seemed to genuinely take these issues to heart even if the organization is clearly focused on drawing people from outside the region. Collective Effort is featured on the CapNY site as one of "5 Companies with Unique Social Missions."[108] Fellow Collective Effort founder Jamel Mosley was even invited to be a panelist alongside CapNY producer Gabby Fisher and others at a CEG-sponsored event that I attended in July 2021. Mosley told the story about "no cap" to a crowd of about fifty young creatives. What followed was a surprisingly frank conversation about economic development moderated by Jeff Buell, a principal of Redburn Development. "You caught something that would have been a disaster," Buell said to Mosley.

Buell, who'd worked for the City of Troy in 2005 and worked on a citywide branding campaign, remarked that he saw something in the CapNY campaign that he had seen "come up over and over again: the genuine opportunity to make a change." The rest of the panel agreed emphatically. In a place like New York City, experimentation is frequent but expensive and very difficult to get noticed. In the Capital Region, however, experimenting with a totally new menu in your restaurant, having a dance party in the rain, or some other quirky event can fail miserably and not completely sink you. And with the power of social media, they argued, the reach can still be there if you're savvy enough.

There seemed to be a consensus in the room that day that growth, hometown pride, and creative experimentation were all connected in a frustrating but ultimately rewarding web of relationships. You want to show off your city and be protective of its authentic character, but you also know that more people joining you is inevitable and with it comes change. That change is good, it's inherent to a city, but it is something that must be managed and cultivated.

For now, though, I'm going to leave the last word to Pat Harris, who captures something we would be foolish to forget. While he's not against new people coming to the Capital Region, he is steadfast in believing "that's not the only way you create jobs. You don't just create jobs by begging people to come here, you know? Oh, we're a million strong? Yes, we're a fucking million strong. Now imagine if you made those million even stronger."[109]

PART TWO

Theorizing the City Authentic

CHAPTER 3

What Is Authenticity?

I'm going to describe a selection of Instagram posts that share a hashtag. Let's see if you can guess what that hashtag is. The first one: A young, bearded man wearing sunglasses and a straw hat sits on the shoulder of a country highway. In the bokeh-blurred background is what seems to be his road-trip van crowned with an overstuffed luggage rack. He is taking a selfie, but you are not looking at the selfie photo; you are looking at a photo of him taking a selfie with a big, open-mouthed smile. Next to him sits a cow licking his face.

In the second, a woman is staring out of a street-facing barred window. The photo is taken from the angle of someone sitting next to her. She is staring at something left of frame which, judging by the lighting, is probably the sunset. Her thin frame is juxtaposed by the masculine vices she is holding: a lit cigar in her left hand and in the right, a hard, amber-colored drink in a crystal-cut rocks glass.

And the third post, this time a short video: A large balcony to the left suggests a mansion just off frame. In the center is a woman dressed in a form-fitting, ankle-length, sand-colored dress and matching wide-brimmed hat. She is standing on a large swing suspended from the limb of a banyan tree. As the six-second video progresses, she swings smoothly to the right with her left arm cocked like she's doing the Egyptian. But in her outstretched palm must be food because a giraffe bends its enormous neck and eats out of it.

These three posts have very little in common and yet they share the popular hashtag #liveauthentic. These posts, along with another thirty million or so similarly tagged photos and videos, are a mélange of wide-eyed young people, angular close-ups of exquisite objects, and heavily edited sunset photography. "There was a time in the beginning of the Fort Orange General Store days that people started using hashtags on Instagram." Caroline Corrigan is telling me a story. "There's this one that my friend and I used to make fun of so much that was just like #liveauthentic." When she says this, I almost jump out of my chair. My research had already brought me to this postmodern parade of symbols and photos, and the fact that a real store owner felt the need to use this hashtag confirmed my theory that these were more than eye candy. They had economic impact. Fellow store owners would tell Caroline, "Oh, these are the hashtags that we use, #liveauthentic." She says, "I was just like, 'What? I just can't . . . I just can't tell you that shopping at [my] store is the key to living authentic!" She starts mimicking looking at her phone. "I used to sit back and would see that it was always just white people having picnics in fields. It just felt very wrong to me, but I did use it, yeah."

I asked every single person I interviewed for this book "What is authenticity?" I have arranged the responses in order from the most objective and identifiable to the existential:

> What you like may not be what I like . . . so what our region has to offer is the full range of quality-of-life opportunities to satisfy almost any type of desire. . . . So maybe that's how we're unique—authentic, if you will—[in] that we do offer a range of opportunities to enhance one's quality of life.[1]

> Authenticity is that quality of originality that reminds you of where you are. It's a sense of place that is not like other places, complete with its own mix of quirks, gems, grit, beauty, tragedies, and treasures.[2]

> I would say authenticity is, you know, being real and honest and . . . not changing, you know, to, you know, fit what others think you should be.[3]

> Reflecting something accurately. I lived in the Midwest till I was thirteen. Then I moved to Colorado, and then I moved to Brooklyn, and then I married my husband, who's British, and I worked in all these international countries, and who I am now is a reflection of all of those things. [Authenticity is] not trying to hide any of those things, not trying to overemphasize any of those things, not trying to be something completely different.[4]

> It's just being yourself and doing your own thing, taking the risk of just putting your own stamp [on it] whether it's something done out of total

necessity that turns cool or just following your own gut and putting it out there to the world and taking the risk that no one will like it.[5]

An accurate reflection of what is. It's the moment when someone hears a story, sees a story, and they feel that shit.[6]

It's a buzzword now on social media. Everything is like, "Oh, that's being authentic." But obviously nothing's really authentic; everything in life is performative. Authenticity [can also mean] somebody trusts you or is something trustworthy. It is real and not a farce in some way.[7]

I think it's an imaginary construct. There's no authenticity. Nothing is authentic.[8]

When I taught introductory urban geography, I would start my lecture on cultural commodification by asking students to give me examples of things they would consider to be authentic. The answers are not much different from the quotes above. They talk about homemade food, classic artworks, and honest stories. Home-baked apple pie, a musician with an old guitar in a dive bar singing the blues, and grandma's stories strike us as genuine expressions of human talent, creativity, and care. They are not mass produced, which makes them feel both very intimate but also agnostic to our existence. An old pie recipe that existed before you were born could not have possibly been designed to appeal to your desires the way a frozen pie at the grocery store is taste-tested before showing up on the shelf. Authentic things just are—no pretensions, no gimmicks.

It is strange then, that food blogs will sometimes call a dish an "authentic" expression of a specific cuisine, even if it is made by a famous chef with no personal connection to the social world that produced the dish. There must be then, some element of authenticity that can be fabricated or intentionally produced, even if authenticity is all about originality. In short, authenticity may seem like a descriptor of how something was made, but what if it is actually describing how we feel?

Things get even more confusing when famous people and places get described as authentic. Donald Trump, quite possibly the most famous person to ever live, is routinely described as authentic.[9] How can someone who practically wrote (well, had ghostwritten for him) the book on being a celebrity businessman be described with the same word as a handmade Diné tapestry? Maybe nothing is authentic.

Trump is said to be authentic because he is, to put it more charitably than he deserves, "unfiltered" and expresses emotions like rage and joy in places and situations that are usually reserved for solemnity and poise.

He also flaunts his power and wealth while other politicians make attempts at approximating a "normal person" by eating a corn dog at the state fair. Even people who see Trump for what he is—a media-savvy demagogue—usually acknowledge that he is a more honest version of the Republican Party's long-standing value set. Authenticity isn't always pleasurable. But both Trump's supporters and his opponents acknowledge that the way he uses media confers a sense of authenticity.

Media, then, is a crucial component of our competing notions of authenticity. This checks out given all the tourism industry's advertisements for authentic experiences that let you see the "real" Hawaii, Los Angeles, or Thailand. These enormously popular destinations—along with famous people like Trump—appear to have some claim on authenticity, but how can this be? How can someone or someplace be intimate and famous or genuine and purposefully contrived all at the same time? This poses a paradox: how can Instagram posts with thousands of likes—for President Trump or Los Angeles—be authentic *because* of their media saturation? Doesn't that fly in the face of all that talk of apple pie and dive bars? One way to square this is to say that some people are just dupes who fall for marketing and see things as authentic when they're clearly not. But this explanation creates more problems than it solves. If there is a "real" and a fake authenticity, then we would have to have some objective measure of authenticity. But just the thought of creating such a metric seems perverse. Are you going to take out your authenticity detector and measure Aunt JoJo's pierogi recipe? Measuring something means you can easily compare it to something else, while the whole point of authenticity is uniqueness.

Another way to look at it is that there are multiple kinds of authenticity. Some people, places, and things are naturally authentic, while famous people and mass-produced objects are designed so well that they seamlessly fit into a culture and are thus perceived as authentic. Here we're treating authenticity like diamonds—something that can be produced through natural processes and be discovered—but also conceding that it can be manufactured so perfectly that the only way you can tell the difference is through authenticating something's origin. The problem here is we're still left with a natural/artificial dichotomy that can easily slip back into real/fake.

Perhaps, then, we should return to our initial supposition: authenticity isn't about a person's or a thing's origin; it is about how we feel. What if authenticity emerges out of a relationship between tourist and destination, audience and celebrity, or, generically, subject and object?

Rather than struggle to understand why some *thing, place,* or *person* is authentic, we might be better off understanding the contexts and relationships between things and people that create authentic experiences in the first place. Authenticity is a feeling, not a characteristic of an object. After all, the entire CapNY campaign is predicated on the idea that a place can be authentic but still need a "story" or cohering brand to convey this fact to the public. If authenticity is an experience, then advertising the things and places that will give you that experience is just shortening the discovery process.

We are going to spend this entire chapter understanding how and why authenticity is such an important force in our lives. In so doing it'll become clear why the authentic character of people, things, and experiences are tightly interwoven. This is a fairly fundamental investigation, so we'll have to zoom way out from the present-day Capital Region and instead look back in time and outward across multiple theories of what it means to be or experience the authentic. We'll begin with what it means to be an authentic person, but we will quickly find it is inseparable from being an authentic thing or experience.

PEG SEEKS HOLE

In season 3, episode 13 of the television show *The Handmaid's Tale* adapted from the Margaret Atwood novel of the same name, a little girl is about to escape Gilead and be put on a plane to Canada. Gilead has strict gender roles enforced through horrendous violence. Contrary to modern conventions, rebellious behavior is not answered with rehabilitation behind institutional walls. Instead, it is severely punished, often in public and on the body.[10] A woman cannot be anyone; she can be only her God-given role as human birthing stock or a domestic servant. The little girl knows this, and as she gets off the plane now safely in Canada, she asks, "Is this where I can be anyone?"

It is an admittedly ham-fisted declaration of what a liberal democratic society is like, but it does strike at the heart of the basic premise (and promise) of modern life. We look to create our own meaning in life and perfect ourselves. We are expected to rise and grind, find callings, and have passion projects. It is both a freedom and a burden to have so many choices. The late scholar Marshall Berman located the beginning of this entrepreneurial self in eighteenth-century France. It was here that Charles-Louis de Secondat, Baron de La Brède et de Montesquieu, referred to simply as Montesquieu, lambasted his fellow aristocrats in an epistolary novel titled *The Persian Letters* in 1721. Berman, who I lean on heavily in this chapter, and the incomparable bell hooks have done more to explain the modern condition than anyone else.

The Persian Letters follows a pair of Persian aristocrats: Usbek, a sultan, and Rica, his noble traveling companion. Together they tour France during the reign of Louis XIV and marvel at the strange emerging culture they find. To be clear, Montesquieu's Persia says much more about pre-Enlightenment France than the actual Safavid Empire of the time. Usbek and Rica are time-travelers of sorts, looking upon a country that is at the tail end of the era of Enlightenment and (unbeknownst to both the author and the main characters) primed for revolution. Usbek's harem has been left in the charge of loyal eunuchs, all of whom lament his absence. Their letters at the beginning of the story are full of love and longing. His role is not only to love them and rule them, but to give them purpose relative to his own. Without him, the gravity of the universe feels off.

Because everyone has a role to play, this fictional Persia, like Gilead, is a world where authenticity is not a problem. You either are who society expects you to be or you are severely punished. Marshall Berman explored this phenomenon in depth in his 1970 book *The Politics of Authenticity*, wherein he traces the emergence of the distinctly modern problem of choosing who to become amid peers' social expectations, rather than draconian laws. "In order to bring the problem of authenticity into clear focus," he writes,

> we should imagine a type of social experience in which authenticity is not a problem. In a closed, static society governed by fixed norms and traditions which are accepted by all its members, authenticity has no place in the vocabulary of human ideals. Here men are satisfied with the life options which their social system provides for them. . . . They experience themselves as pegs and aspire only to fill the hole that fits them best.[11]

Whereas Atwood's stories follow the subjugated woman, Montesquieu gives us the perspective of the supposed winner of pre-modern societies. Usbek seemingly has everything he could ever want and is confident in his status at the top of society. He is wealthy, powerful, and has a harem that he describes as among his "most precious . . . worldly possessions."[12] And yet all this pales in comparison to the vices that are still commonly associated with the Big City: casual sex, drugs, fast-paced life, and the ability to flee into the anonymity of the crowd. In his letters back home to his wives, he extolls the Parisians' freedom to make their own lives and enter relationships as equals. Usbek and Rica start to question how authentic the love of their wives and the obedience of their subjects truly are. How can, for example, a woman who is the property of a man ever truly show her love for him? Or as Rica puts it, "Such calm possession leaves us nothing to desire or fear."[13] This is the first hint of many that authenticity contains contradictions: to be truly recognized as genuine and authentic requires the possibility that such recognition can be freely revoked. It's only with the possibility of loss that life's gains are satisfying.

Usbek agrees, writing, "Everything smells of obedience and duty. Even the pleasures are sober, and the joys severe, and they are practically never relished except as manifestations of authority and subservience."[14]

These ideas are eventually put into practice by the eunuchs and wives who recognize themselves as subjugated individuals and demand and successfully fight for their freedom. Authenticity for Montesquieu, we learn in *The Politics of Authenticity*, is about stripping away contrivances and trappings of office and being who you want to be. But first you must learn to want to be anything. Berman is careful to show that anyone who thinks deeply about authenticity and the autonomy it brings will eventually arrive at the conclusion that these ideas are very disruptive. Montesquieu effectively revealed that self-awareness can lead directly to rebellion. If you know in your heart of hearts that you're more than a member of a harem, a worker in a factory, or a social media personality, you can start to question the institutions that keep those identities in place. You divorce your husband, unionize your workplace, or log off to show your oppressors that you are much more than your relationship to them.

From Montesquieu, Berman turns to Rousseau and then Hegel before concluding—and this is the book's big contribution to the humanities—that the works of Marx are essential to resolving the problem of authenticity that modern life presents to us. Authenticity is not just an individual problem, it has a class character as well. Rousseau considered the freedoms of self-determination and association as nothing more than new and more sadistic forms of domination and competition, which were, in Berman's words, "even more destructive because it promised men so much. The opportunity and the means for every man to be genuinely himself, extended with the left hand, were taken back by the right."[15] This domination comes not from an all-powerful king but from each other's judgment. Identity is as important as ever, but "in place of traditional identities as stagnant and rigid as stone, modernity had provided a form of identity as transient and insubstantial as the wind."[16] Rather than freeing us from anything, we are caught in a more insidious game of group action and individual consent: authenticity can be conferred only from long-standing social institutions that are constantly being reformed through authentic individuals' choice to be a part of them. Anything else is a contrivance. Hegel called this the "freedom of the void" because while we are free to be whoever we want, it comes at the cost of carving out deeply meaningful relationships situated within communities.

The logic here is actually simple: if people "are not given a real chance to be inauthentic, they could not really be authentic."[17] Of course the danger here is that too many people will choose to leave any given authentic community and never come back, thus destroying the community and its shared heritage. It is this danger of annihilation that is the most important paradox for authenticity: the very thing that ensures the authenticity of a community is its own constant threat of destruction.

As we learned in the first two chapters, Rust Belt cities are constantly fighting the outflow of residents to major metroplexes and the suburbs, and it is precisely this fight that makes the City Authentic regime of economic development so useful. The fact that it is in danger of disappearing gives it the authentic flair in the first place. Deciding where to live is a complex process dominated by work and family concerns, but when it comes to young and educated folks returning to the Rust Belt they were born in, they report to be motivated by a care for the people *and* an affinity for a place's character that they do not want to see go away. Jill Ann Harrison calls this the Rust Belt "boomerang effect."[18] It has become so powerful, according to Harrison, that Pittsburgh—the city whose loss of young people launched Richard Florida's career—"recently reversed the decades-long trend of out-migration among 18–[to] 24-year-olds, and in 2013—for the first time in many decades—its overall population grew."[19]

The Center for Economic Growth is also relying on this free choice of return as a means for growth. Mark Eagan sees the CapNY website as a "reservoir of information" about what is going on in the region, but "targeted social media placements" are what will drive traffic.

> The young person who is from Atlanta who's happy to live in New York or Boston is not going to hear from us. But maybe that person who originally was from here, somebody that maybe went to school here, maybe they're originally from Kingston or Springfield, Massachusetts, and they're living in one of those larger cities that might want to leave that city but their home-

town might seem too small, or their hometown might not seem like it has enough economic opportunity—we want to get on their radar, so they'll get something directly from us through a social media channel. That will then link them to our website to learn more, and then from there, if they want to engage or they want to connect with a young professional in our community, we'll do that and we're specifically targeting folks in their 20s and 30s.[20]

It is a bit too much to say that Mark Eagan and Katie Newcombe have harnessed the power of Rousseau's theory of authenticity, but his fingerprints are clearly all over the basic theory of change at CEG. Namely, that the prodigal sons, daughters, and nonbinary kids of the Capital Region can have one of the most authentic experiences possible: to be of a place and then freely choose to stay there, to both have roots and honestly enjoy where you live. We will return to the practical matter of social media marketing in chapter 5 because we must focus on the theoretical aspects of authenticity: namely, how do Enlightenment-era ideas of authenticity and identity play out in a modern capitalist consumer society?

What we see emerge from Berman's work is a definition of authenticity that requires a relationship to history and identity; it is not just a simple noun. Authenticity somehow implies both fragility and eternity— something that has lasted a long time but may be endangered by modern forces. The authenticity of a place and its people are deeply intertwined not only because people make up the culture of a place but because the very notion of authenticity is predicated on the choices we make as free individuals. A society without a concept of authenticity is a society with fixed and unchanging social roles; people are just pegs looking for holes.

In multicultural, cosmopolitan societies, it is inevitable that culture will not only change but will mix and evolve as it encounters more cultures from the margins. The mainstream media's conversation around this issue, largely described as cultural appropriation, has been disappointing. Google is more likely to serve you the opinions of people like David Frum (George W. Bush's speechwriter and author of the phrase "axis of evil") and Cathy Young (*Reason Magazine* and *Washington Post* columnist who frequently writes articles that are skeptical of the existence of rape culture and the need for affirmative consent laws) than anyone with training in cultural studies or a related field. Conservative and libertarian commenters like Frum and Young complain that "woke" scolds are picking fights with well-intentioned people looking to learn about and experience other cultures. Frum writes in the *Atlantic* that people who charge cultural appropriation want to freeze cultures in amber. They "must crush and deform much of the truth of cultural history—and in the process demean and infantilize the people they supposedly champion."[21] Young, in a 2015 *Washington Post* commentary, wrote that cultural appropriation has "become a common attack against any artist or artwork that incorporates ideas from another culture, no matter how thoughtfully or positively. A work can reinvent the material or even serve as a tribute, but no matter. If artists dabble outside their own cultural experiences, they've committed a creative sin."[22]

The title of Frum's *Atlantic* article is the core of these arguments: "Every Culture Appropriates." Which is, of course, true: culture is made just as much by sharing and remixing as it is by preserving and separating. But most people that raise questions and concerns about the role of nationality, ethnicity, and race in cultural commodification do not deny that cultural experimentation transcends boundaries. What Frum and Young miss (intentionally or otherwise) is the point that bell hooks asserts in her 1992 book *Black Looks: Race and Representation*. There she posits that the interest in Black people and the cultural artifacts they create are used in white-supremacist, capitalist patriarchy to satisfy the white person's desire to be transformed from alienated, bland suburbanite into worldly master of society. The problem with cultural appropriation is not that culture is remixed or even that there is a power differential at play. Rather, cultural appropriation is bad because it positions everyone as buffet-item choices for white consumption and gives very little back. "The overriding fear," in hooks's words, "is that cultural, ethnic, and racial differences will be continually commodified and offered up as new dishes to enhance the white palate—that the Other will be eaten, consumed, and forgotten."[23] The desire for Black culture by whites, according to hooks, has nothing to do with a love or care for Black people but is instead one of many efforts to relieve their anhedonia, their inability to feel pleasure.

Hooks's critique calls into question typical liberal solutions to cultural appropriation: appeals to patronize Black-owned businesses, checking for labels of various trade organizations that certify authentic sources of ingredients, and shopping local. These are admirable attempts to make the exchange more mutually beneficial but they are insufficient for two reasons. First, they don't do anything to end white people's magpie-like obsession with filling their lives with another's culture. But more importantly, they also risk diffusing the politically revolutionary aspects of cultures marginalized by white hegemony by reducing them to commodities and spectacle. Power structures are left intact but the people that take the power may be more diverse or bring new cultures into the power center. Take, for example, Beyoncé's *Lemonade*, which hooks says, "glamorizes a world of gendered cultural paradox and contradiction. It does not resolve."[24]

A hallmark of both hooks's and Marshall Berman's writing is dialectical thinking between the oppressor and the oppressed: oppressors are definitively the benefactors of the status quo, but they are also a kind of victim. They are Usbek, sitting around wondering if a single person loves them. People do not sort into oppressor and oppressed because of their personalities or dispositions. That is an idealist approach to the problem, not a materialist analysis. A materialist analysis requires that we look at the systemic inequalities that sort people with adherence to the prevailing hegemonic ideology and how the individuals within those groups go on to think about the world and either reinforce it or tear it down. The search for danger, grit, and the profane, hooks contends, is a natural consequence of white America's anhedonia brought about by a hyper-capitalist wasteland. Because nothing within the constant barrage of symbols and messages feels meaningful or historically grounded, alienated subjects seek out things that will feel intense or unfamiliar just to make sure they can still feel anything at all.

THE THREE FLAVORS OF AUTHENTICITY

In the last section I reviewed how the modern notion of being an authentic person arose from Enlightenment-era notions of how an individual can properly adjust to a capitalist society where you are supposed to *become* someone, rather than be a peg fitting into a preordained hole. Yet, as Rousseau and Hegel argued, the most authentic places and experiences are those under constant threat of elimination.

What we haven't addressed yet is the issue of validation: the recognition that you have achieved authenticity. You can't receive validation from just anyone. Your mom can tell you you're special; she is not the one to validate the authentic personality you have crafted. No, you need someone cooler than you to freely say you are cool. You come to desire this person and seek them out to be a potential lover, friend, or one of a number of parasocial media personalities that you hope will follow you back on Twitter one day. Everyone is selling themselves, seeking others' lives to buy, and to acknowledge this is both *very* authentic in the sense that you're not putting on airs, but it is also a terrible faux pas because it indicts everyone. *Maybe you are just looking for attention but I'm out here living a real authentic life!*

Now let's look at how people use their surroundings and experiences to both construct that identity and convey it to others because this change in peoples' lives is inextricable from society and its attendant cities. In the words of Marshall Berman, modern individuals'

> personalities, like their cities, were radically dynamic and expansive; if they lacked the means to express and develop themselves through activity in the world, their deepest impulses would be thwarted and their most vital capacities suppressed. Any adequate notion of freedom would have to include the individuals' power to experience, to change and to grow in pursuit of his greatest happiness: in other words, the freedom *to be himself*.[25]

The tourism studies scholar Ning Wang identifies three different flavors of authenticity.[26] Each kind poses a distinct question where "yes" is synonymous with the statement "This is authentic." First is objective authenticity. This is the kind of authenticity that an art historian or an archeologist may care about. It answers the question, Is the thing in front of me what it purports to be? The answer lies in documentation and expert observation. When Rick Harrison in *Pawn Stars* wants to authenticate an antique gun, he brings in an expert who looks at serial numbers, the patina of the metal, the details of manufacturing, and any accompanying documentation to confirm whether the gun on the counter is an *authentic* Brown Bess musket.[27]

Things get much more complicated from here on because while objective authenticity can be validated by referring to records and expertly debated concepts, the other two kinds of authenticity have no such fixed referent. The second kind is constructive authenticity. It answers the question, Have I witnessed what I expected? We experience constructive authenticity when expectations set by media and advertising are fulfilled. If you are told repeatedly that a quintessential and authentic Upstate New York experience is to go apple picking and then drink warm apple cider on the ride home, then there are dozens of apple farms ready to authenticate your trip. You might be told such things in an advertisement on the radio, or perhaps your church organizes an outing every year. Obviously, the latter is not as transactional as the former, which is where things get tricky. Where and how things get "constructed" as socially and culturally meaningful is very complicated and contingent on historical and even personal circumstance.

Note that since this definition of constructive authenticity relies on "a projection of tourists' own beliefs, expectations, preferences, stereotyped images, and consciousness onto toured objects, particularly onto toured Others,"[28] it leaves open many opportunities for the kind of "othering" that hooks talks about. It is easy to surmise how stereotypes, urban legends, and the contrivances of marketing can alter a culture in fundamental ways. It only takes a few cycles of setting and meeting expectations before the constructions just become part of culture.

Indeed, it is this perspective—that culture emerges out of contrivance and long-held beliefs—that represents the third version of authenticity, which Wang variously calls existential or postmodern authenticity. This kind of authenticity asks, Do you feel like your true self? The history of postmodernism is an interesting but ultimately distracting rabbit hole,[29] so I will only focus on Fredric Jameson's treatment of the term. For Jameson, postmodernism is marked by three characteristics: a breaking down of traditional categories or boundaries, a reverence for nostalgia, and pastiche.[30] Instead of new, boundless frontiers of culture, nature, and history, we are bound to remix and decontextualize what we already have. This manifests in lots of ways. In architecture we see buildings that look like nowhere in particular—airports that look like malls that have office spaces in them—but may also have a bit of nostalgic pastiche thrown in.

For example, in malls, the premium clothier Ruehl No. 925 would set up stores that looked like the first floor of a brownstone. The CEO of parent company Abercrombie & Fitch, Michael Jeffries "described potential customers as having graduated from college in Indiana and moved to New York City."[31] The company even came up with a fake origin story of the Ruehl family: a clan of Germans that immigrated to America in the 1800s and set up a leather goods shop at 925 Greenwich Street in the trendy eponymous village, where Jane Jacobs wrote *Death and Life of Great American Cities,* legends rioted at Stonewall, and someone from the Lark Street Business Improvement District got a great marketing idea. Everything about the stores seemed both jarring and desperate, which is probably why Abercrombie & Fitch shuttered them in 2010.

Had they "worked," they might have inspired some postmodern authenticity- something that you know is contrived or fake but nonetheless facilitates a rupture or break with everyday life. It is postmodern in the sense that context and history are reduced to a palette of possible design choices. But it can come off as authentic because it is clearly—deliberately—offering the option of consuming the essence of a place by extending its existence in time and space. In the case of Ruehl No. 925, this is almost literally true. Not only is the Ruehl family fake, so is the address—Greenwich Street ends in the 800s. Most tellingly, except for a small accessory shop on Bleeker Street, there were never any Ruehl stores in New York City.

Such a thing is also existential because it affirms the existence of yourself as you are and who you wish to become (e.g., a Hoosier turned New York City fashionista). Unlike objective or constructive authenticity, "existential experience involves personal or intersubjective feelings activated by the liminal process of tourist activities."[32] By *liminal*, Wang means that when we are on vacation, we aren't quite our everyday selves. When we take on the role of tourist, we are not just looking for interesting things, we are looking for a rupture from all the compromises we make in everyday life. When we shop, we are looking for things that fit not just our present selves, but the kind of person we want to become.

Communications scholar June Deery identified three "phases" of reality TV that map startlingly well onto Wang's three kinds of authenticity. First comes "edited reality in the observational mode."[33] These are almost documentaries but usually have some sensationalized or human-interest component to them. *Cops* is a good example of this kind of show. Then comes "contrived settings and preplanned activities."[34] This is where you get *Survivor, The Apprentice,* and *Big Brother.* Finally, in its most developed form, reality TV seeks to "reach out into the actual world to transform it."[35] Here we get makeover shows like *Queer Eye for the Straight Guy,* business rehabilitation series like *Bar Rescue,* and what I consider the apotheosis of the third phase: *Shark Tank,* where would-be entrepreneurs beg millionaires for money.

And like the existentially authentic tourist experience, the third phase of reality TV forces us to reckon with the difference between what is fake and what is fictional. Whereas the former might include deception, the latter can be a purposive dramatization or pastiche of several things that already feel authentic to the audience. When people go on *Shark Tank* to sell part of their business for equity, regardless of the deal they get (if they make one at all), their business is enrolled into two stories: First, there is whatever story the producers want to tell in that segment. But the second, much larger story is about the American dream and the ability to succeed through hard work. A good *Shark Tank* business lets the audience enjoy both fictions and may thereby be reasonably considered "authentic" by the viewer.

Authenticity collapses when something purported to be genuine is proved to be fake, expectations are not met, or we are not sufficiently convinced that what we are looking at or experiencing comports with our ongoing identity projects. In the previous chapter, we saw several institutions constructing a pastiche of authentic moments, people, and places, not unlike a third-phase reality TV show. Most notably, the CapNY project constructed authenticity as something that could be attained by getting a job at Goldman Sachs, buying a house for the monthly cost of renting a small studio in a bigger city, and consuming. This goes to show that, within reason, almost anything can be built up to invoke the feeling of authenticity if it's properly contextualized and fed into the discourse around the object or place in question.

Look at it this way: Early in our lives, we are encouraged to make expectations for ourselves and strive toward them. Often enough, those expectations go unmet, and while we can still find happiness, there is something within us that feels unfulfilled. Maybe you were supposed to be an undersea explorer and while that fascination and sense of adventure remains, your day job keeps you in an office. When you choose a vacation, you might select a place that offers scuba diving. This is appealing not only because the weather is warm and it is a good idea to check out the coral reefs before they're all gone, but also because this is the *real you* that life circumstances never let you become. The thing that you desire is not the reef itself but the idea of you experiencing the reef and all the media that you can create and share as evidence of your journey. You leave with swimmers' ear, tons of flattering photos to share, and a feeling of existential joy from an expectation achieved.

THE FREEDOM OF THE PARANOID

I opened this chapter talking about Corrigan's reluctant use of the hashtag #liveauthentic to get attention for her store. From there we chased authenticity's elusive definition from Enlightenment-era Paris to the set of *Shark Tank*. Obviously neither of these places are in the Capital Region and there was a reason for that: I want to impress upon you the fact that while the region may be small, the phenomena we are studying within it are at once globe-spanning and deeply intimate. And it is to that intimate space between our minds and our phone screen that this section now turns.

Under modernity, each person must be a piece in a jigsaw puzzle: completely unique but predictably so—a piece that is different from all those around it but still able to fit into a larger picture. We have more artifacts, both material and digital, than ever with which to enact our identities, yet we can never seem capable of staying unique for long.

These seemingly infinite combinations of symbols and things that we use to signal our identity, to our consternation, keep assembling into predictable patterns that are read by algorithms seeking to sell us more things that fit our delicately arranged identity. If I get into baking complicated French desserts and showing them off on Instagram, I will eventually get ads for stand mixers and artisanal flour. And if I get a significant following, the mixer and flour companies will give me these things with the expectation that I will show others that their products are compatible with (if not necessary components of) a French bakers' lifestyle.

Hopefully by now you notice that all these pressures and problems we typically associate with social media pre-date the technology by at least two hundred years. It's hard to tell if Berman is describing Montesquieu's Paris or twenty-first century influencers when he says, "Modern man's sense of himself was entirely relative, a function of his momentary success or failure" and "His body, his mind, his soul, all his faculties and capacities, appeared as nothing but competitive assets, to be invested prudently for a maximum return; he was forced constantly to develop and perfect himself, yet unable, even for a moment, to call himself his own."[36] In chapter 5 we will dive deep into the tools influencers use to gain attention, but for now let's look at how authenticity—in all its flavors and dispositions—plays in our digital era.

Since its beginning, the web has been a laboratory for identity formation.[37] With the relative comfort of physical distance, digital networks can let us experiment with how we want to be perceived, what we want to be called, and how we present ourselves. In years past it took moving to the city, as Lewis Wirth wrote in 1938, to find "a certain degree of emancipation or freedom from the personal and emotional controls of intimate groups" like family.[38] City life, Wirth argued, creates people who define themselves through voluntary associations with organizations like labor unions, religious movements, and sports teams. It is through this particular kind of urban social interaction that "the urbanite expresses and develops his personality, acquires status, and is able to carry on the round of activities that constitute his life-career."[39] Here, Wirth presages what the preeminent Marxist geographer Henri Lefebvre would conclude: to urbanize is to modernize.[40] Cities are synonymous with modernity not just because they usually contain the latest technologies or play host to the latest trends, but because they socialize us into modern people who seek status, validation, and uniqueness. Practically, they are also the only places that provide a decent assortment of options to try on. They also force us into cash economies because the scarcity of land makes it such that the necessities of life must be bought rather than made or grown on a homestead. Cities are, definitionally, social things.

It is usually at about this point in a book like this that the author is supposed to say something like "the internet did not create the phenomenon but it did accelerate it."[41] But that would be a misleading, partial truth because while the internet has undoubtably brought the variety and opportunities for experimentation that were once endemic only to cities, we will also see that digital technologies have been a homogenizing force as well. They interrupt, even as they intensify, the modernization and urbanization of the planet. This is, in essence, the problem that David Byrne warned us of in *True Stories*, and it is the sentiment expressed by those involved in what would become the CapNY campaign. If small cities like those in the Capital Region don't tell their own stories, they're liable to be flattened out to just another piece of the cultural hinterland of large metropolises.

If the city played home to Hegel's "freedom of the void," then digital networks host what I would call a "freedom of the paranoid." Whereas a void is an absence of immutable meaning, the paranoid references the existence of a haunting unknown something, a known unknown. Instead of a void, we have a nagging uncertainty at our core that must be resolved. Contra Richard Hofstader's well-known "paranoid style" of politics, I am not using our shared word as a pejorative. Being paranoid can be warranted: you may be preparing for an aggressor or uncertain of your place in a system that you can only partially see. According to Manuel Castells, a student of LeFebvre's and prominent urban theorist in his own right, our networked society has given rise to "new forms of social change" that take advantage of the "disjunction" between global and local.[42] We experience that disjunction as an uncomfortable desire to both preserve the things around us from a creeping global monoculture while at the same time be recognized as a valuable contribution to what will eventually become uniformity adopted.

In the Capital Region this looks like places, businesses, and people consolidating their definitions of what it means to live there, while also trying to convince outsiders that the region and its people can make a meaningful contribution to the global economy. Hegel's freedom of the void is filled with associations and membership to organizations that are voluntary, purposive, and foster solidarity among members. Subjects of the network society still come together like this, but they also take on what Castells calls legitimation, resistance, and project identities.

A legitimizing identity is directly related to a dominant force, usually the state. To identify as a "patriot," with all its connotations, helps to legitimate the power of the state by indicating that there are people willing to die for its continued existence. A resistance identity also related to power but is usually forged in reaction to an instance of unfair exclusion. Because the dominant force is necessary for the identity, Castells writes, its creation often involves "reversing the value judgement while reinforcing the boundary,"[43] much like what hooks says Beyoncé does in *Lemonade*.

Project identities, though, are truly fascinating. These are created when "social actors, on the basis of whatever cultural materials are available to them, build a new identity that redefines their position in society and, by so doing, seek the transformation of the overall structure."[44] It is a way of saying, "I exist, therefore society must change." Sometimes evolving out of resistance identities, the project identity exceeds the bounds of the existing order by saying that the boundary that separates the legitimate and resistance groups is itself inherently flawed. Castells uses the example of religious fundamentalists, who may evolve past the diagnoses of being the holdouts or chosen people of a fallen society and instead anoint themselves warriors of a transformative project to assert their morals as an aspiring new dominant force or hegemonic ideal.

For Castells and many theorists of identity since him, project identity is forged just like authenticity was for Rousseau: through constant threat of negation. Remember that for Rousseau there is no preexisting inner self; there are only games of choice and subsequent recognition by others. Being regarded as authentic is a function of others' evaluation of your performance. But if everything is in upheaval, then those others doing the evaluating have few points of reference. Because the network society is global in character, identity is constantly being contested and threatened from all sides. The freedom of the paranoid, just like the void, is scary because there are seemingly infinite options, no instruction guide, and the constant danger of choosing or arranging your information all wrong. And yet we do it anyway because we seek validation and belonging in a society where both are rare. "The dissolution of shared identities," Castells writes, "which is tantamount to the dissolution of society as a meaningful social system, may well be the state of affairs in our time."[45] Whereas in pre-modern times, you were just a peg looking for a hole and authenticity meant nothing, the postmodern condition tells us that authenticity is something you create rather than something you achieve. You are a drill boring holes to fit the pegs that life throws at you.

This is a deeply destabilizing prospect and given that the first edition of *The Rise of the Network Society* was printed in 1997 with a substantial rewrite in 2004, it feels safe to say that Castells's near-term predictions came true. The Catalonian independence movement, Brexit, and the rise of populist strongmen like Trump in the U.S., Duterte in the Philippines, and Bolsonaro in Brazil are all exercises in rearranging geopolitics by leveraging individuals' sense of belonging and freedom. And in each of these runs a thick, Facebook-blue line that is impossible to ignore. And for all he got right, Castells was writing in a time of relative optimism about what digital networks could accomplish. While no one could accurately describe him as a techno-utopian, even Castells's latest work does not sufficiently grapple with the material interests of the companies that control much of the internet—namely, Meta and Google, whose business models require sucking up as much information about as many people and things as possible. In *To Save Everything, Click Here*, Evgeny Morozov implores the reader to "inquire into how Facebook mediates the very conditions of authenticity, sometimes by erecting new barriers and constraints but, more often, by destroying them."[46] By this he means that Facebook is not only determining what kind of person you are, it is changing the basis by which authenticity gets measured. Here he quotes Facebook board member and one-time chief operating officer Sheryl Sandberg, who wrote in a 2011 *Economist* essay, "Profiles will no longer be outlines, but detailed self-portraits of who we really are, including the books we read, the music we listen to, the distances we run, the places we travel, the causes we support, the video of cats we laugh at, our likes and our links. And yes, this shift to authenticity will take getting used to and will elicit cries of lost privacy."[47]

Of note here is that Facebook, until a series of backlashes starting in 2015, was unshakeable in its mission to portray anyone that did not abide by its "real name policy" as untrustworthy and shifty.[48] To use the internet in precisely the way I and early internet pioneers originally described it—as a laboratory for self-experimentation or a playground to try on new identities—was absolutely wrong. Not only was it wrong, the Facebook party line went, it was immoral because platforms like Facebook are meant to be a tool of self-discovery, which was seen as different from self-experimentation. While the latter suggests infinite possibilities, the former assumes a static, preexisting self that must be found. As Morozov puts it, Facebook promises "to give us concrete, even numerical, proof that we have a deep and authentic identity waiting to be discovered, that we need to carry that identity with us when we log into Facebook, and that there will be something tangible and unique after, . . . we 'have taken stock of ourselves.'"⁴⁹

Somewhat ironically, in *The Authenticity Hoax* Andrew Potter calls this will to transparency the "experiment in authenticity." For a long time, we have valued candor because it reads to us as authentic. "We admire," Potter writes, "the apparent spontaneity of someone who tells us how they really feel."⁵⁰ But now, thanks to social media, we never feel like we have disclosed enough. We must be more transparent and divulge even more about ourselves. As the demands for transparency increase (this is part of the titular hoax that Potter is warning us about), our own ability to discern what is biased or fake becomes overly sensitive. We start to wring our hands about what kinds of echo chambers we have fallen into and decry polarization, unthinking obedience to authority, and groupthink. In reality, we have never been more obsessed with how we differentiate ourselves from the crowd or more curious about others' ways of thinking. The problem is that the goalposts have been moved too far away. The very moment we are most obsessed about inauthenticity, we are at our most honest about who we are.

Recall Caroline Corrigan's anecdote in the last chapter about seeing a billboard advertising Rensselaer County with a picture of a mountain that said, "The secret is out!" It was a bad ad not just because the message was confusing but because the presentation medium was impersonal. Maureen Sager seemed to recognize this when she told the *Albany Business Review* that the region needed was an identity "that feels real to us." The CapNY campaign sought to provide this by telling the stories of individual people in addition to describing the region itself because we are subject to the freedom of the paranoid: a frustratingly vague charge to build an identity that requires the validation of others who are just as uncertain about their identity projects as we are. A billboard can't help you with that, but a website with stories of people you're invited to identify with can. Even better if you can develop your resistant identity ("everything around me is fake and trivial") into a project identity ("I will move to Albany and make a new community worthy of my conformity").

But the campaign failed at this crucial point of transparency. The stories on the CapNY website are written by and about actual residents of the region—a rare distinction for an advertising project of this kind, which usually contains generic ad copy adjacent to stock photography. And Katie Newcombe even made a point to tell me that "many of the writers did not even know who was helping to fund the project." But the

ultimate takeaway is that this is a place that is eminently worthy of investment. To achieve a more believable identity would require more radical
transparency—a willingness to show something that seems as though it
should be hidden. This was well articulated by Newcombe herself when
she defined authenticity as "showing yourself warts and all."

The perceived effectiveness of the CapNY campaign hinges on
whether you think the stories on the website and on the social media
posts can subvert the expectations of advertising. The guys on the *Capital Region Business Podcast* didn't like the name but thought the campaign overall did convey a "gritty," authentic story about the area. Pat
Harris obviously disagreed, saying that what was described as gritty
was simply equal racial representation.

To truly read as "authentic" according to internet studies scholar Crystal Abidin, influencers have to "actively juxtapose this stripped-down version of themselves against the median and normative self-presentations
of glamour, to continually create and assign value to new markers—
faults and flaws, failures and fiascos—to affirm the veracity of their
truth-ness."[51] Through what she calls "porous authenticity," audiences
are "enticed into trying to evaluate and validate how genuine a persona is
by following the feedback loop across the front stage of social media and
the backstage of 'real life,' through inconspicuous and scattered holes or
gateways that were intentionally left as trails for the curious."[52]

A billboard with a mountain certainly leaves no opportunity to be
"porous." A website and social media presence does afford the opportunity to show some "faults and flaws, failures and fiascos," but the
CapNY project opts for a more existential approach, encouraging
would-be residents to imagine themselves living here and being the kind
of people depicted in the site. They are invited to make a rupture in their
present everyday life and, as the home page of the site and multiple people have told me, "come to a place where you can make a difference."[53]

Perhaps, though, the porosity comes across once you reach out
through the website to "get connected with someone living and working in the region."[54] By filling out a short form, potential residents are
paired with someone who is already living here. Katie Newcombe
explains how it works:

> A handful of people volunteered and said, "Hey, I'm happy to be part of this
> matchmaking. I'm happy to talk to someone." And then we work to make
> sure that there was sort of a cross section of people so that we represent all
> different types of lifestyles and backgrounds and all that kind of stuff, so, you
> know—maybe you're single, maybe have a family, you know—all that.[55]

The pool of volunteers came from the Young Professionals' Network (YPN), which falls under the Capital Region Chamber, an organization affiliated with CEG. YPN puts on regular events advertised through an active email newsletter. The panel discussion I described in the previous chapter was a YPN event, and I could imagine how porosity could establish itself during a one-on-one with someone from the network. But ultimately the point is that you can never be porous enough: our postmodern project identities are trained to be cynical, and perhaps that is why authenticity is still such a rare, valuable commodity.

CHAPTER 4

The Political Economy of Authenticity

In the eleventh-season episode of *Always Sunny in Philadelphia* titled "Dee Made a Smut Film," Frank Reynolds (Danny DeVito) puts on the persona of art collector Ongo Gablogian to lure a gallery director to the gang's pub as an elaborate ruse to get their friend Charlie's childlike drawings into a gallery to "prove that [art] is all bullshit." Frank pretends to be a "high society art type" when he goes to the gallery so that his invitation has the necessary credibility to get the director to show up. Frank assures his friend Mac, who assigned him the task, that "I've got this. I used to hang with an art crowd in the seventies. I know these people." Frank as Gablogian bursts into the gallery dressed in black, from turtleneck to loafers, and a fluffy white wig. After introducing himself to the director, he promises to invite her to the show. "But first," he says, "allow me to destroy your art gallery." Frank as Gablogian proceeds to pronounce everything he sees as "bullshit" and "derivative" before pointing to an air conditioning unit and saying, "That, I love! . . . I want it. It's everything. Look at us—we're just air conditioners after all."

Indeed, there is more to Frank's love of the gallery's air conditioner than meets the eye. Of course, his motivation is to con the art gallery's director into believing that he is the kind of person who can give her the attention, validation, and financial support that any art director needs to do her job. And as we saw in the last chapter, the concept of authenticity can be bent any which way so long as it aids self-actualization and a break from the ordinary. Whoever can convince enough people that their wares are the key to this process will have an opportunity to cash in. Or, as Sharon Zukin puts it, "Each form of commercial culture constructs a new form of authenticity that anchors the claim of new groups to live and work in that space. Consumers' tastes, backed by other resources, become a form of power."[1] If it's your air conditioner or a man-child's drawings, so be it.

But how can something as ordinary as an air conditioner be considered a radical break? Again, one way is to bullshit, as Frank does, and say something about how "we're just the air conditioners walkin' around on this planet, screwin' each other's brains out!" But another, perhaps more effective means of accomplishing this is to simply wait until the air conditioner signals a point in time worth remembering. "Ironically, the mass production of an earlier industrial era looks to our eyes like individuality," writes Zukin in her first book, *Loft Living*.[2] Here she isn't specifically talking about air conditioners but landscapes of abandoned industrial development, particularly the neighborhood of light manufacturing warehouses south of Houston Street in Manhattan famously dubbed SoHo. "Since the 1950s," she writes, "suburbia had so dominated popular images of the American home that it was almost impossible to imagine how anyone could conceive the desire to move downtown into a former sweatshop or printing plant."[3] But, of course, Americans (and now the world) have come around to the idea and, she argues, this is because of changes to both middle-class consumption patterns and the industrial lofts themselves.

In the sixties, there arose a growing concern among the white middle class for environmental protection and historical conservation. Rather than demolish the old, the new task was to preserve. The controversial demolition of New York's Penn Station in 1963 and the rise of Jane Jacobs's activism in Greenwich village to save Union Square from Robert Moses's bulldozers dovetailed into a romantic backlash against slum clearance and urban renewal. The City Efficient had gone too far in erasing the prior architectural achievements of the City Beautiful movement. To be absolutely clear—this sentiment, which ran from the San Francisco hippies to the New York literati, was concerned about cultural heritage first and housing affordability second, if at all. It is worth remembering that Jane Jacobs was more intellectually devoted to self-correcting markets and informal social control than to governmental power or redistribution. This is, in part, why her articles and interviews showed up in the pages of capital-friendly magazines like *Fortune* and *Reason*.

The finance capital directed at SoHo's lofts in the latter half of the twentieth century was not meant to retain them as cheap, open-ended DIY spaces in the center of the city. Rather, it was to preserve their aesthetic qualities while also emphasizing what lofts and suburban ranch-style houses had in common: airy, well-lit spaces with plenty of room to fill with consumer goods and art. They were also a safe way to rebel against the conformity of the suburbs and mass consumerism. The loft became a commodity to be bought and sold on the housing market and, like Gablogian's air conditioner, it had once been a piece of a mass-produced built environment. However, with the passage of time, each individual loft develops a history and charm that makes it unique and therefore builds value. Zukin puts it this way: "Living in a loft is an attempt to replace modernism's mass production of the individual with an individualization of mass production."[4]

The character of Gablogian as someone that you might meet in the seventies' art scene is instructive here, because by the 1980s the popular imagination seemed to be sick of such people. From neighbors Margo and Todd Chester in *National Lampoon's Christmas Vacation* (1989) to most notably the Deetz family in *Beetlejuice* (1984)—the yuppie artist was the derisive, pompous asshole that American families loved to watch get tortured by neighbors and ghosts alike. It was in this derision that American culture uncomfortably digested the idea that places were increasingly being preserved for their value as commodities, rather than their sentimental or historical value.

In early fall of 2020, when the pandemic was at a nadir between the second and third waves, friend Andy M. Gittlitz and I were sitting at a mostly empty bar in Troy when *Beetlejuice* came on. The bar, I explained, used to be the industry bar: the small, unassuming place where the bartender would let you smoke inside, the jukebox was three-quarters filled with the Rat Pack, and you could stay till the sun came up—but you could not, under any circumstances, curse. Bartenders like my wife would close up their bars at two and walk over to have a few of their own. It had become such an institution that every bartender had a Christmas stocking on the wall with their name on it. That bar had closed when the owner retired, and this new place did not retain any of that recent history. It had the same weathered wood and metal barstools of any other bar of its time. Having had a few, I said something like, "We are in the Deetzes' home right now."

One thing you forget about *Beetlejuice* is how it, as Gittlitz would write in his newsletter weeks later, is not a movie about the titular demon Betelgeuse, but about a class struggle over the identity and future of the Connecticut village of Winter River. Particularly relevant to the Hudson Valley today, the film begins with a situation I'd heard from several people on my trip—an annoying realtor stalking Adam and Barbara Maitland's (Alec Baldwin and Geena Davis) early 19th-century house, begging them to reconsider selling it to rich New Yorkers willing to buy based only on a picture.[5]

The Deetz family treat the Maitlands' old Connecticut home like an industrial loft: something with a unique past that gives its owner a sort of monopoly over the ability of others to interact with a potent symbol or story. In this case, the existence of ghosts does not diminish the value of the property but significantly increases it. As if Sharon Zukin herself were in the employ of director Tim Burton, the husband, Charles Deetz, is a real estate executive and wife Delia is an artist. Together they recognize they are at the precipice of a new frontier for capital accumulation. The first idea is a summer arts festival, but once the Maitlands are discovered, they realize a haunted theme park could be even more valuable. Who could compete with *that*?

The rest of this chapter is devoted to figuring out how the long-standing anxieties over authenticity are turned into profitable enterprises. That is, we have to investigate both why and how the history of a place create value for the FIRE industries. We already have the inner workings of authenticity under our belt. Now we can see it in action: how it transforms the landscape and ourselves.

I'm taking a Marxist approach, which means three things. First, while everything in the previous chapter was very heady and had a lot to do with how we *think*, the money that is made from authenticity has everything to do with *who* owns *what*. That is, ideas about what is or is not authentic are not enough to generate profit; there must be some fundamental material basis for this activity. We will find that geography, the natural and built environment, is ultimately the sources of wealth accumulation. Second, I take for granted that this is an antagonistic process with clear winners and losers. There is a relatively small group of capitalists that benefit from this activity and a much larger subset of workers whose labor creates this value but they do not reap the rewards of it. Finally, we are going to confront many contradictions in this chapter, meaning that when all goes according to plan, fundamental aspects of this system will undermine its success. Such contradictions are endemic to a Marxist analysis, and unpacking them will offer more insight into how it all works.

First on the docket, though, is answering the question, Why grow at all? Why do we keep building new stuff, especially if we valorize the old? Then the chapter will turn to the nuts and bolts of how to make money off authenticity—what in chapter 1, I called "authenticity peddling"—and then finally, we will explore the myriad contradictions that arise from the political economy of the City Authentic.

THE WILL TO GROW

People ask all the time, "Why are they building all this new stuff when what we already have is falling apart?" To answer this question, sociologist Harvey L. Molotch coined the term the "growth machine" in a 1976 paper and extensively expanded it in a book written with John R. Logan in 1987 called *Urban Fortunes: The Political Economy of Place.* The theory is very elegant: Elites agree that growth is good, so all effort must be put into assuring each parcel of the city has reached its "highest and best use" and extracting the profit that comes with it. Because the most powerful people in any given city agree that growth is good, planning, zoning, and government in general aid in the arrangement and staging of growth and not much else.

The growth machine, in this way, spans the political spectrum from bankers who want to invest in the new property to labor union leaders who support growth "because it will 'bring jobs' particularly to the building trades, whose spokespersons are especially vocal in their support for development."[6] Sure enough, one of the six people to spend all nine years on the Capital Region Economic Development Council (CREDC) was Jeff Stark, the president of the Greater Capital Region Building and Construction Trades Council. The growth machine even attracts the support of small business owners, who are more likely to gain competition from corporate national retailers than more customers, which is usually what they think of when new housing or highways are announced. "In this instance," write Logan and Molotch, capitalist "ideology seems to prevail over concrete interests and the given record."[7]

Logan and Molotch set their sights on what they call "structural speculators." These are leaders of firms that seek to benefit from future land-derived profits that they create through other market activity. They include not only real estate entrepreneurs and property developers but also local media and utility companies that can grow their markets only by increasing the number or wealth of paying customers in their geographically defined region. It would be accurate to describe the regional economic development councils (REDCs) as an attempt by New York State to capture and coordinate structural speculators. Rather than leave elites to duke it out across multiple jurisdictions, the REDCs do what Mark Castiglione described in chapter 2: bring power elites together in public meetings (rather than "backroom deals") to identify regional priorities.

The structural speculators at the helm of the growth machine are largely concerned with how well the city acts as a tradeable commodity (exchange value) and less interested in how it performs as a place to live (use value). This is understandably an unpopular position, so those in power work hard to "de-emphasize the connection between growth and exchange values and to reinforce the link between growth goals and better lives for the majority."[8] They focus on the jobs that new development will supposedly create or the amenities it will provide. These are often vastly overestimated or redound to the benefit of far fewer people than advertised.

Finally, and perhaps most crucially, the growth machine thrives on competition between city jurisdictions. This happens all across the world, but in New York and several other states, this dynamic is exacerbated by municipal governments' near-total authority over what gets built, or what is called "home rule." Rather than empowering city leaders, it actually sets them up for failure. Not only is each city caught in a version of the prisoners' dilemma—if I don't say yes to this crappy deal, they'll go to the next town over and we'll get less than nothing—it is outgunned at the negotiating table. City leaders and their staff (if they have any) lack the experience and know-how to go toe to toe with a legal team from whose legal department likely dwarfs most cities' entire budget. "In such a context" Logan and Molotch observe, "autonomy becomes a lead weight for the majority of cities, with only the most affluent towns able to create privilege from their formal independence."[9]

From this perspective then, the REDC system and the CapNY plan could do a lot of good. They de-emphasize inter-city competition in favor of a more coordinated strategy. The negotiating position and financial power brought to bear are bigger and better than going it alone. However, it appears as though the competition is stiffening across the country, with cities and towns doing whatever they can to compete in a fast-moving economy. *Urban Fortunes* may be more than thirty years old, but its observations are more important than ever. In fact, Logan and Molotch wrote in the preface to the 2007 edition of the book, "In almost all cases, we believe, the decades have seen an intensification of the trends we depicted, not a reversal."[10]

New technologies, collectively called "platform real estate,"[11] have given rise to what Jathan Sadowski calls "the internet of landlords."[12] Just as the owner of a building derives income from the tenants, so companies like Meta and Amazon accrue rents from their command of digital infrastructure by charging access to a collection of items, audiences, or services. From Amazon Web Services, which undergirds some of the most popular apps (Amazon-branded or otherwise), to Airbnb and Uber, which collect rent on the reallocation of physical space and cars, the internet of landlords is "materially essential for the new sources of rent, new infrastructures of rentier relations, and new mechanisms of extraction and enclosure."[13]

Platform real estate (PRE) offers landlords—of all stripes—"a new way of seeing," according to Joe Shaw.[14] Shaw's analysis of PRE shows that while much of the effort is being put into platforms that connect home buyers, sellers, owners, and renters with each other, there is also a burgeoning industry of financial technology that assists investment managers in identifying "market opportunities."[15] Whereas land development and real estate was mostly a regional industry, PRE makes it possible for a single firm to effectively manage a continent-spanning empire of real estate assets and rental properties.

With the advent of PRE, investment managers have much more information and many more trading tools to find just the right investment at just the right time, creating higher yields and potentially greater risk as more investors become more aggressive in their bidding and speculation. These new technologies could help smaller firms and even individuals locate "small off-market plots, up-and-coming neighbourhoods, home auctions, and proprietary algorithms to anticipate which houses will come to market,"[16] thus simultaneously increasing the concentration of market data in a few firms but also increasing the number of firms trading off that data. Crowd-investing platforms like Fundrise and Crowdstreet have already made it possible for anyone with disposable income to invest in real estate-backed assets.

What has yet to pass but whose elements are all already in place is the buying, selling, and speculating of land in real time in concert with the advertising of place and authentic living. Whereas, to date, real estate entrepreneurs have had to wrangle #liveauthentic and #upstatecurious and similar brands to market property, one can easily imagine PRE tools being utilized to align hashtags and other social media marketing directly to apartment listings or land prices.

In the three decades since Logan and Molotch's book, the growth machine has been "upgraded" in a two key ways. First is the realization by structural speculators that home rule, in some instances, must be overruled for growth to continue. This is a contentious issue that has caused a deeper rift in elites' growth consensus than any of the usual disagreements about how growth is to be achieved. At least three people I spoke to identified home rule as a major obstacle to regional growth but also knew that to say as much was verboten. It was taboo enough that separately each person told me that they did not want to be associated with the sentiment that home rule was a hindrance to growth and that things would be a lot easier if, say, smaller towns and villages were under the direction of county governments or some higher authority. To say as much is to burn significant bridges in the world of economic development. People are proud of their towns and cities and appreciate the control they have over their immediate surroundings. Some private-sector actors also appreciate the ability to play cities off each other for reduced taxes.

But for a new, emerging, upgraded growth machine, it is becoming increasingly important that elites get to choose the scale at which competition takes place. To attract talent and employers, elites want to work across and coordinate different jurisdictions and sell the biggest urban agglomeration possible.

The second key "upgrade" is the replacement of home rule with vertically integrated control systems. Like most large technical systems, the upgraded growth machine can work more efficiently through vertical integration of all the relevant components and standardization of inputs. Different democratic bodies and bureaucratic institutions with slightly different procedures, rules, and sanctions introduce complexity and uncertainty without necessarily contributing to the valuable uniqueness of any given plot of land. Even worse, municipalities can restrict access to their resources all together: Airbnb and Uber have been kicked out of several large markets, and that can happen again.

Social media, as we will study in detail in the next chapter, is increasingly used to target new employers and residents. It is too early to speculate on precisely how PRE and social media advertising will work together in this new, upgraded growth machine, but the outline is clear: direct appeals to potential renters and land buyers can be paired with detailed, proprietary knowledge of place to craft neighborhoods and developments with all the specificity and care of an algorithmically generated music playlist.

IT'S NOT A TROY-BILT UNLESS IT COMES FROM THE TROY REGION OF NEW YORK

This section is going to make ample use of David Harvey's 2002 essay "The Art of Rent," where he lays out the relationships between culture and capital. To make the most of it, we need to get some definitions out of the way. These are definitions pulled from the work of Marx as interpreted by Harvey.

Monopoly is commonly used to describe the sole ability of a firm to control access to, production of, or trading of goods, services, and let us add, experiences. For example, Apple holds an effective monopoly on what can run on the iPhone, and you can't call bubbly wine Champagne unless it comes from that region of France. But Marxists recognize that monopoly powers are much more diverse than that. One can have a monopoly over that piece of land and, because a piece of land is a unique commodity that is never exactly like any other, an owner can reap monopoly profits from those unique qualities. Hotels next to airports, a busker that shows up early to get a prime spot on the corner of two major streets—these are sorts of monopolies.

The other word we need to define is *rent*. More than just what you pay every month to a landlord, Marxists use *rent* to describe all incomes derived from the ownership of a piece of capital. Because Disney owns the rights to Marvel's cast of characters, everyone else must pay Disney a licensing fee to use them. That licensing fee is a kind of rent. Disney is the only owner of Marvel characters, and so it can charge what's called *monopoly rent*, which is how Marxists describe getting ripped off.

There are two kinds of monopoly rents, direct and indirect. Direct monopoly rent means a piece of land or a resource is traded, "as when vineyards or prime real estate sites are sold to multinational capitalists and financiers for speculative purposes."[17] A prime piece of Manhattan real estate or a chateau in Champagne, France, sells for obscene amounts of money because there is only a set amount of them and they are very desirable. Indirect monopoly rent "arises because social actors control some special quality resource, commodity or location which, in relation to a certain kind of activity, enables them to extract monopoly rents from those desiring to use it."[18] Champagne from the chateau can fetch a pretty penny (or euro) because it comes from valuable land. Less

FIGURE 5. A tote and throw pillow at a local hardware store. Photo: David Banks

indulgent and more common uses of indirect monopoly rent are found in airports, where you have to pay $20 for a cold sandwich because where else are you going to get it?

The value of direct monopoly rents works in degrees along a spectrum. If you sell a famous landmark, you'll probably get a hefty chunk of change. Sell a house that is next to a nice park, and you will also see an increase in the price of the property, which is derived from your direct monopoly rent of being one of the few houses next to the park. Lease a plum spot for a booth at the local farmers' market and you're likely to pay more than someone in a less trafficked spot.

Indirect monopoly rent is when you can buy and sell things based on their relationship to something that derives direct monopoly rents. We can imagine indirect monopoly rent working like a radio signal radiating outward from an antenna. A "Bitch, Please. I'm from Troy" bag (figure 5) will command the highest price tag when it is sold in Troy. The further it is from Troy, the less the bag is worth because its referent—the source of its value—is missing. What Troy? Troy, Michigan? Is this a reference to *The Aeneid*? Unlike direct monopoly rent, the buying, selling, and leasing may not change who owns the land itself;

you're trading on proximity or some other relationship. Every time you buy a souvenir on vacation, you're trading on indirect monopoly rent.

While it may be easier to get in on indirect monopoly rents—many more people can sell shirts about Schenectady than can buy land in Schenectady and you don't need to do the latter to do the former—that does not mean rent-accumulating properties are limitless. In fact, there is a peculiar dilution phenomenon that is endemic to indirect monopoly rent. Let's say you visit Lake George on vacation. There are plenty of car decals and T-shirts to take home that do the job of advertising the lake; however, according to Harvey, "The more easily marketable such items become, the less unique and special they appear. In some instances, the marketing itself tends to destroy the unique qualities (particularly if these depend on qualities such as wilderness, remoteness, the purity of some aesthetic experience, and the like)."[19]

Lake George has been a tourist destination for at least a century, so the indirect monopoly rent derived from souvenirs may be relatively low. This phenomenon gets more interesting when we think of what's going on with the "Bitch, Please. I'm from Troy" tote. The bag appears to be playing off a gritty, tough demeanor derived from being in a city that has seen it all. You might also interpret it in the opposite way as having very high standards. As in "Oh, do you think this place has nice cocktails? Bitch, please. I'm from Troy." But as the bag succeeds as a commodity, it begins to undermine the very basis of its value. As Troy becomes more obsessed with itself and goes from unique place to brand, the sheen wears off and the indirect monopoly rents will decline.

Then there is the issue of copycats, knockoffs, also-rans, and items that would stretch the definition of a geographic location. Authenticity peddlers must face all these challenges, but this last one is fairly common in direct monopoly rent scenarios where real estate is advertised to be in a hot neighborhood when, in fact, it is adjacent to it or even several blocks away. At the very beginning of this book, we saw the Fulton County Industrial Development Agency call itself the "new frontier of the Capital Region" in an effort to cash in on the monopoly rents associated with an adjacent well-performing land market.

There was a time when, if you wanted a really good rototiller, you would buy a Troy-Bilt, which was, you guessed it, built in Troy. But as globalization went apace, the company eventually sold its brand name to MTD Products, which has manufactured power tools under many other well-known brand names including Ryobi, Craftsman, and Cub Cadet. The point of buying a brand in this fashion is to trade on the indirect monopoly rent of the reputation of the previous manufacturer. If Troy wanted to protect its reputation as a manufacturer, it would have to create some sort of governing board and take legal action against MTD Products. If local elites wanted to market the region as a manufacturer of consumer goods rather than an innovation and culture destination, this might be advisable.

There is precedent for this in Europe, where brands and products like wine and cheese have deep ties to regions. Governments and industries establish very strict licensing boards to protect words and phrases that have accrued a reputation for quality. These protections increase or sustain both direct and indirect monopoly rents by throwing up barriers to dilution.

But, as the Comité Champagne—the body charged with protecting the word *champagne*—will tell you, this sort of monopoly rent protection is expensive. It spends approximately six million euros a year on legal expenses.[20] For a small city in the twenty-first century, the task is not so much to defend its name as to convince enough people that it has something unique to offer the world. If, as Marx wrote in *Grundrisse,* capitalism is capable of "the annihilation of space through time"[21] by using technology to speed up production and transportation, then the City Authentic seeks to preserve some monopoly rents through the construction of place through rhetoric.

Perhaps that is why I constantly heard from those I interviewed that economic development is about telling stories. As Katie Newcombe put it:

> The CapNY project is about being honest about who you are, so it's really telling our story. . . . It's about telling the stories of our industry clusters here. The most advanced chip was just announced from IBM, and that was made in our backyard—that's being honest. You know, I think it's easy to grab some flashy pictures, some stock images, and talk about a great place to live, work, and play, but unless you can drill down and talk about the why, then I don't think that you're being honest.[22]

Rather than see creative economies give way to innovation complexes as Zukin argues, we see the former instill the latter with meaning: an argument that says innovation would not have taken place if there had not been a talented group of people living, working, and playing in the region. Just as a label on a bottle of Champagne is meant to convince you that there is something unique to the terroir of the region that creates a fine Champagne, CapNY asks its audience to believe that the region is uniquely suited to bringing together creative people. And just like the unique microclimate of the hills east of Paris, this is something that cannot be moved or replicated.

THE THREE CONTRADICTIONS IN "THE ART OF RENT"

Dilution of authenticity through the commodification of a place's culture is just one of the many problems with making money through authenticity peddling. Harvey outlines three contradictions in "The Art of Rent" that will befall any agent looking to make money off arts and culture, so let's run through them.

The first contradiction concerns the balance one must strike between the special qualities of an authentic thing, place, or experience and the necessity of packing it into a recognizable consumable. One can have, essentially, the opposite problem of dilution and make something that is so unrecognizable that no one knows what to do with it, or it simply fails to fit into existing business models. Therefore, says Harvey, "while uniqueness and particularity are crucial to the definition of 'special qualities,' the requirement of tradability means that no item can be so unique or so special as to be entirely outside the monetary calculus."[23] Recall in chapter 2 I described a problem where a cash-poor entrepreneur wants to rehab an old building to make a restaurant. She is outmaneuvered when it comes to finding financing because, in part, the bank sees an old building as a risky investment when compared to the near plug-and-play adaptability of relatively new construction in the suburbs. Unique, funky buildings are cool, but their special qualities cannot get in the way of commodification. Striking the right balance between bespoke authenticity and market compatibility is what I call "predictably unique." Something is different enough that it can transport us, offering an existential experience or fulfilling a previously constructed expectation, but it is not so alien that it gets rejected outright as too intimidating or simply a bad fit for the prevailing market conditions.

The second contradiction is the trend toward monopoly. "Competition, as Marx long ago observed," writes Harvey, "always tends towards monopoly (or oligopoly) simply because the survival of the fittest in the war of all against all eliminates the weaker firms."[24] For authenticity peddling, this often takes the form of corporatization and gentrification. It is the deconstruction of CBGBs that I discussed in chapter 2. It is Caroline Corrigan questioning whether organic discovery has been replaced by Instagram. Places that could foster experimentation or less-than-marketable fare could do so because rent is cheap and the clientele is loyal. As more money comes to the area, rents and property taxes go up, and developers begin to speculate on land, which can drive up the price to the point where only they and other well-resourced firms can buy the land, often leasing it for relatively high rates to make back the money spent acquiring it. We have already seen, from an analysis of commercial service industry locations, that chain stores in the region exclusively lease their spots, indicating that this is indeed at play in the region.

The third contradiction may prove to have some of the longest-lasting ramifications. This one requires some setup. Harvey writes,

> Urban entrepreneurialism has become important both nationally and internationally in recent decades. By this I mean that pattern of behavior within urban governance that mixes together state powers (local, metropolitan, regional, national or supranational) and a wide array of organizational forms in civil society (chambers of commerce, unions, churches, educational and research institutions, community groups, NGOs, etc.) and private interests (corporate and individual) to form coalitions to promote or manage urban/regional development of some sort or other.[25]

Clearly the Capital Region fits this description very well, especially given the institutional makeup and actions of the regional economic development council. Its job is to sufficiently convince enough people that it has a monopoly on something and effectively market that something to as many people as possible. We see this kind of rhetoric in the CREDC's reports. For example, the Saratoga Performing Arts Center (SPAC) will rehabilitate a long-vacant building in its effort to become "a unique international cultural tourism destination."[26] In its 2015 report, the CREDC brags that "the Capital Region goes global," which, in addition to providing markets for its manufactured goods, will also "promote arts and cultural assets to international travelers to the North Country (from Canada) and New York City."[27]

We have seen that the region has become more diverse in the past decade and international migration has increased to the metro area. We further investigated how urban branding efforts like renewing city flags and CapNY can trigger culture-war debates about nationalism versus cosmopolitanism. Harvey notes that this is common and leads us to the third and final contradiction: "The most avid globalizers will support local developments that have the potential to yield monopoly rents even if the effect of such support is to produce a local political climate antagonistic to globalization!"[28]

I witnessed this contradiction firsthand as an organizer in Troy. Back in 2017, I and a few other concerned citizens organized an effort to make Troy a sanctuary city. This means that city officials, including the police department, would not proactively collaborate with Immigration and Customs Enforcement (ICE) in the deportation of immigrants. We were harassed, some even assaulted,[29] as we demanded the city recognize the rights of the undocumented. After nearly two years of fighting, the city council passed a resolution, only to be vetoed the next day by the Democratic mayor.[30]

A short while after the veto, in July 2019 a developer was giving a public presentation to build a very prominent building in the center of the city. The positioning of the building near the Hudson River and several important utility lines in addition to its prime location meant that the construction costs would be very high and therefore the office space in the building would have to attract a very deep-pocketed tenant. During the Q and A, I brought up Richard Florida's three *T*'s of creative-class development—technology, talent, and tolerance—and asked whether the mayor or the developer was concerned that a recent vetoing of the sanctuary city resolution would hurt the chances of getting a tenant. Some in the audience groaned; some people I knew in city government sent me texts calling me an "asshole" (this was half joking); and the developer became visibly angry. The developer dismissed the idea that political issues were pertinent to development at all and had no patience for those sorts of questions. He said this while wearing an enormous American flag lapel pin.

This stands in stark contrast to Schenectady, whose Republican mayor in 2002 went to great lengths to persuade Guyanese immigrants in New York City to move a few hours north. The *New York Times* reported that Mayor Albert Jurczynski would act as "their guide on a weekly bus tour that brings dozens of Guyanese immigrants [to Schenectady] every Saturday for a three-hour tour of the city. He takes them to Schenectady's own Central Park for ice cream cones. He takes them to his in-laws' house for homemade wine. He promises to build them a cricket stadium one day, to personally review all their résumés, officiate at their weddings and learn to love their spicy soups."[31]

This got the mayor into hot water with existing ethnic communities in Schenectady, who said they'd never received such treatment and balked at his comments that implied the Guyanese were uniquely hardworking and clean compared to Black and Latino people. In both cases, we see a resentment on the part of at least some portion of the people who have lived in their cities during the lean times and understandably resent the incentives given to new residents. This also echoes Collective Effort's Pat Harris's comments in chapter 2 about investing in the people who had been in Troy for a long time, rather than seeking out well-heeled managerial types. As we see, this frustration with bringing in new residents and making attachments to a "globalized" economy runs the gamut from very well-founded disappointment to outright xenophobia.

It is through these three contradictions that we see some of the darkest aspects of the City Authentic. It is overstating things to call retro bars inherently fascist—they're not—but there is a clear, material linkage between the rent-seeking behavior of authenticity peddlers and fomenting turf battles over definitions of place and time. Crucially, the particular nature of these battles encourages support for the predictably unique, which by its very definition, severely limits the ability to ask tough questions or challenge existing power hierarchies. In this way, authenticity peddling can, at best, engender a liberal cosmopolitan ethos that may convince a Republican mayor to try spicy soups. It may offer limited opportunities for ethnic minorities to open businesses, so long as they cater to a majorly white audience seeking opportunities for self-actualization. At its worst, authenticity peddling appropriates marginalized cultures while fomenting a xenophobic backlash against people who may or may not financially benefit from interest in their culture at all.

AUTHENTICITY PEDDLING AND ITS DISCONTENTS

In a very general way, we should recognize that for every eighties yuppie and early aughts hipster seeking some predictably unique item from an authenticity peddler, there are at least an equal number of people who see this as an existential threat to their way of life. It may not be a coincidence then, that the rise of New York City art types in the style of Gablogian were followed by the Reagan revolution or that a cultural landscape dominated by Brooklyn was followed by the presidency of a certain developer from Queens. But just because the cosmopolitan liberal cultural trend generally comes before the reactionary political achievement does *not* mean the former causes the latter. In fact, there is much stronger evidence to suggest both are popular cultural reactions to the three contradictions of rent.

For the liberal cosmopolitan looking to live a conspicuously authentic urban life, there are material and psychic difficulties. The trappings of authenticity are expensive—big cities charge indirect monopoly rents on those experiences and items that confer urban authenticity. You can get more mass-produced ones (Ruehl No. 925 comes to mind here), but the first and second contradictions do their work making it feel less authentic and not necessarily less expensive. In a cruel irony though, the job that might get you enough money to live in a place that feels authentic is likely going to be a bullshit job that is devoid of meaning altogether.[32] In which case, you may feel as though your evenings are only canceling out your day job.

For the conservative, their project is to preserve an authentic life that either once existed or that they believe is threatened but not quite gone. The artifice and cosmopolitanism that is creeping into their life is dangerous and must be repelled through an assertion of nationalist values and a focus on family life. The same corporate forces that sterilize downtowns for cosmopolitans are also reducing job opportunities in more rural areas as employers chase the clustering effects of growing cities.

CEG's CapNY campaign aims to resolve this tension by using its regional approach to offer both rural seclusion and urban cosmopolitanism. The website lets its visitors know that "whether you long to live at the foothill of a majestic mountain, with your grocer being a nearby farm or prefer pounding urban pavement with cafes and entertainment all around, New York's Capital Region has a hometown for you."[33] This promise that there is a "hometown" for every kind of person suggests a very intimate kind of power. Zukin again:

> Our tastes as consumers—tastes for lattes and organic food, as well as for green spaces, boutiques, and farmers' markets—now define the city, as they also define us. These tastes are reflected in the media's language and images, from lifestyle magazines to local wikis and food blogs; this discourse, which has become more participatory through the Internet, forms our social imaginary of the "authentic city," including the kinds of spaces and social groups that belong there. Filtered through the actions of developers and city officials, our rhetoric of authenticity becomes their rhetoric of growth.[34]

Let's put it all together. As with drugs, we develop a tolerance to the wares of authenticity peddlers and trends move on, but we are not the same afterward. Our resistance identities (to use Castells's language) begin to feel hollow because they've been transmuted into just another shirt to put on, another cuisine to sample. With each failed effort at substantive societal change, the desire of the predictably unique compounds. Capitalists build cities designed for bourgeois identity performance and commerce only to invest in them so heavily that all that can afford to exist are carefully managed environments: postmodern corporate mishmashes of symbols and architectural referents that have no discernible connection to a past, only a technologically mediated amalgam of intellectually property. The modern identity-seeking subject described by Berman is disappointed, and the postmodern project identities of Castells begin to take hold. This necessitates a massive influx of creativity and pastiche, but the authenticity peddling in this environment is a poison pill. Project identities become shot through with nationalism and empty cosmopolitanism, leaving people better poised as subjects to be marketed to than full subjects aided in their self-actualization. Don't like the direction your city is headed? Be like Shepard Fairey or Banksy and make what Sarah Banet-Weiser calls a "counterbrand": a loyal opposition to the corporate branding that instigates "a kind of ambivalence within the branded city."[35] The late cultural theorist Mark Fisher gave a name to this dynamic: precorporation.[36]

Where is all this headed? I have written[37] that the emerging market for leasing a subscription to a network of housing—what I term the "subscriber city"[38]—calls to mind Marx's writing that capitalism requires workers freely to sell their labor to whomever is buying and make it such that their labor is the only thing they can sell. The former has been well established for a long time: individuals' rights under liberal democracies ensure that most people—save prisoners and some migrant farmers—are no longer slaves, indentured to land or a particular person. Removing individuals' ability to be self-sufficient has been more challenging. The ownership of land and the ability to grow food or make goods is still possible, though getting rarer all the time.[39] Many people are pushed off their land, but many more are pulled into the conveniences of renting as gainful employment becomes more temporary: selling a home and seeking out a new one is an expensive, difficult process. Getting more people to rent can speed up labor markets' ability to respond to the whims of capital.

Because the City Authentic encourages us to think of place in predictably unique genres, rentable shelter can be organized and rented like digital media. Each offering is unique, but they also have enough in common that an algorithm can suggest things you might like. The branding of regions at the right scale and price range is one way to make places comparable. Another is to make them actually look and behave predictively unique. We see this forming online as entrepreneurs like Caroline Corrigan use hashtags not just to promote the store but to decide how it should look so it will be recognizable as something Brooklynites might want to go to.

There is, of course, more than just brand exercises pushing us in this direction. Following the Great Recession, private equity groups and venture capital–backed enterprises went on a buying spree, snapping up thousands of homes and office buildings and adding them to their portfolios of available rentals. These firms have begun buying homes in bulk using another recent invention called an iBuyer. An iBuyer streamlines the home-buying-and-selling market by bringing in title searches, inspections, and other services in-house and automates some aspects of the process to cut costs.[40] Together these companies simultaneously centralize land ownership, drive up housing prices to a point that only institutional investors can afford, and package housing into readily marketable forms that match the scale of the purchasing.

We see hints of that with Redburn Development which, as I described in chapter 2, builds websites that advertise its renovated historic buildings within a context of citywide enticements including discounted dog-walking services and bundled parking permits in city garages. The site's URL is liveindowntownalbany.com and Redburn's name is hardly seen. Recall, also, Redburn's other properties like the River Street Lofts with links to the *New York Daily News* written from the perspective of and for an outsider considering a visit or move. It may only be a matter of time before smaller developers like Redburn make the turn to (or are absorbed by) larger firms that are already fully embracing platform real estate technology.

PART THREE

Governing the City Authentic

CHAPTER 5

Policies and Tactics

When Hank Hill discovers on a family hike that his beloved rock formation Teakettle of the Mount has been vandalized, he tries to get the
town of Arlen's city manager to clean it, but he refuses. "Should I spend
the town's limited funds on fire engines and police cars or on helping
you recapture your childhood?" Undeterred and ever the intrepid journalist, his wife, Peggy, dives into the *Arlen Bystander*'s archives to write
a history of the Teakettle to drum up support for its restoration. She
finds photos of many famous men posing in front of the rock and a few
unknown women. After digging a bit deeper, Peggy finds that the women
were town founders and Arlen used to be called Harlen, which was a
contraction of the original name Harlottown. She breaks the news to
Hank, who is scandalized that "our beloved Arlen began life as the
most notorious brothel in Texas."

She publishes the story anyway ("I am a journalist and I will not kill
a story because it's unpleasant!"), and the city manager calls Peggy and
Hank back into his office. To their surprise, he loves the story and wants
to make a whole festival celebrating the history. The manager explains
his "equation": "Scandal plus time equals tourist dollars. Look at
Salem, Massachusetts. Almost everyone thinks burning witches is bad
now, but Salem is using their unique past to bring in tourist dollars. I've
been there, Hank. They have a sewer system par excellence."[1]

This episode of *King of the Hill* ends with a perfect example of the
third contradiction of "The Art of Rent": the townspeople reject the

tawdry branding of their suburb and create a petition to return to their PG rating.

"Harlottown" came out in 2005, just a few years after Richard Florida's *The Rise of the Creative Class*, and cities were plumbing the depths of their histories for a predictably unique story to tell tourists and potential new residents. It was a story line many Americans could recognize as plausible, if not characteristically exaggerated for animated television. Perhaps one of the more instructive parts of the episode is the reaction of the Hills' status-climber neighbor Kahn Souphanousinphone, who was originally against the rebranding before realizing that the upper crust of Arlen society saw *Harlottown* as "sophisticated" and immediately changed his tune: "Oh, very progressive. I'm in!"

Part 2 was all about how authenticity works—so you can guess how competing notions of authenticity play out in this episode. Peggy's article constructs a story and a theme that events can refer to for authentic flair. History is displayed in such a way that it sets attainable expectations for an authentic experience. A town based around sex work can prove to be existentially authentic as you break from everyday life to experience something scintillating but sophisticated. Kahn's about-face proves the effectiveness of the city manager's equation, not to mention the social pressures of class distinction.

This chapter is dedicated to putting that theory into practice and understanding the behind-the-scenes policies, tactics, and tools of the trade that make the City Authentic "work." The constituent parts of the City Authentic are not endemic to only the Capital Region, the American Rust Belt, or even the United States, but they come together particularly well here, under the aegis of the Economic Development Councils (EDCs), to grow the region's economy and built environment. Because the EDCs have been so instrumental in focusing the City Authentic's main components—social media branding promoting predictably unique experiences and utilizing creative-class theories of development—they are a useful starting point for our investigation into how the City Authentic works.

ECONOMIC DEVELOPMENT COUNCILS

The EDCs, according to then Governor Cuomo's office, were the "cornerstone of his economic development agenda," yet they do not directly disperse funds. Instead, they serve an "advisory" function to the various state agencies that review and select competitive applications through a "consolidated funding application," or CFA.[2] Each region's EDC hosts its own competition among CFA applicants for subsidies, grants, and low- to no-cost loans, and each region competes for additional funds to be directed to them from the state. This is touted as a way for smaller municipalities like the ones in the Capital Region to compete for the same amount of funds as New York City's boroughs. Brooklyn and Troy never directly compete for the same pot of money; instead, they compete for separate pots of money against their more immediate geographic neighbors. Each EDC creates a portfolio of proposals submitted through the CFA and turns them over to Empire State Development, which then ranks the portfolios, granting extra money to those that look particularly good.

The CFA is where non-EDC actors are enrolled in the councils' goals. Each aspiring CFA grantee makes up its own application based on which funding source they are applying to. For example, if a user wants to apply for a grant meant to disburse funds within the Erie Canal heritage zone, it selects that grant on the website. The site will add a collection of questions to the applicant's personalized CFA, such as "Explain in detail the recreational or historical contribution of the project and how this will affect the vitality of the surrounding area or community." Another asks how the proposal supports "a specific bicentennial milestone or event; cultural, heritage or educational programming; or an infrastructure project that includes recognition of the legacy of canal history and the vision for the next 100 years."

More common questions only have to be asked once, and the answers are then distributed to the appropriate funding body. For example, multiple grants ask applicants to write their own two-sentence press release blurb. Instead of answering that question for each grant, they only do it once. The rules and decisions about who wins and loses do not appear to be all that different from reality TV or a game show: once a winner is announced, there are press conferences, interviews, and photos of the winners holding their oversized checks. To date, a total of $6.9 billion has been allocated to cities in ten rounds of funding through the Regional Economic Development Councils.[3] These nested competitions within and between regional EDCs are punctuated by special themed competitions, as in 2015, when Governor Cuomo announced an Upstate Revitalization Initiative with a $500 million grand prize.[4]

Like most neoliberal policy programs, this process appears to be very efficient: only the best applicants win a custom-tailored package of incentives, loans, and grants. In practice, however, it produces a lot of waste in the form of time and money spent on failed applications. I know this because, for a summer, I was one of these expensive consultants and despite a very well researched and well argued proposal, my client did not get the money it applied for. I was subcontracting under a consultant company that charged a sizable fee for doing the requisite research and applying for the grant. There is a whole cottage industry for this work, largely built on informal knowledge of how the program "really works" and personal relationships with people who know which strategic plans, development projects, and opportunity zones are ripe for more state assistance.

These thirst games, as I explained in chapter 2, are organized around reports and plans published by the EDCs. Firms within the Capital Region EDC's jurisdiction compete to interpret their projects within the language and goals of these reports and repeat them back to the EDC in their CFA applications. One of the first of these documents from the CREDC is the 2011 *Capital Region Economic Development Council Strategic Plan*, which lays out a "Capital Region economic ecosystem" made up of "the Region's distinctive strengths in technological innovation; business; public and private schools; an educated workforce; a bountiful and productive natural environment; and a diverse population and cultural opportunities."[5]

To develop this ecosystem, the CREDC lays out seven goals, three of which are central to the City Authentic: First is "bring cities to life" by "return[ing] them to centers of influence that are alive with business, residential, and cultural programs that will revitalize them as active neighborhoods." Second is "spotlight our strengths," which aims to "create and celebrate our distinct and comprehensive Regional identity by reaching out to other geographies to feature these assets and make the Capital Region the first destination in New York." Finally, there is "celebrate and optimize surroundings" that will "attract visitors, new residents, and businesses by sustaining and optimizing our rural assets and working landscapes that provide a backdrop for the Region."[6]

The Capital Region's submission for the 2015 Upstate Revitalization initiative, titled *Capital 20.20: Advancing the Region through Focused Investment*, marked a significant shift from the original 2011 plan and moved away from the ecosystem model in favor of "five mutually reinforcing strategies."[7] Though one could be forgiven for not understanding the difference between "five mutually reinforcing strategies" and an "economic ecosystem" or between "bring cities to life" and "metro," the change in jargon between 2011 and 2015 also marked a significant shake-up on the council.

The first two years of the Capital Region's EDC were lackluster, with the second year coming in dead last in amount of funding for its projects.[8] It was after this poor showing, on October 3, 2012, that the cochair and president of the SEFCU credit union, Michael J. Castellana, resigned via email, taking the rest of the council by surprise.[9] His fellow cochair and president of Rensselaer Polytechnic Institute, Dr. Shirley Ann Jackson, resigned not long after. Before the 2013 progress report was published, nine of the twenty-one councilmembers had left, six of whom were halfway through their two-year term. By 2014 the CREDC seemed to have stabilized. Thirteen of the council members who had been serving in 2014 were still serving by the 2019 report.

Overall, tenure on the committee is a mixed bag. The average and median time spent as a council representative (not including ex-officio members, some of whom are elected leaders serving longer terms) is four years. In total, forty-four people have served on the CREDC, ranging from one year for three members (two of whom served between 2011 and 2013) to all nine years for six members, including the cochair from 2013 to 2016 and CEO of Albany Medical Center, James J. Barba. Some offices (besides the ex-officio elected officials), like the president of the University at Albany (my employer), have been represented every year even though four people had held that position over that time. The six members who have been on the committee for all nine years when a progress report was published come from a wide range of organizations, including Albany's economic development nonprofit agency, the Center for Economic Growth (CEG); a paper products company; and the local building trades council.

Then there are people like Andrew Meader, who has managed to stay on the council even though he has changed jobs multiple times. When he started on the CREDC in 2014, he was the corporate alliances director for a Six Flags theme park in Queensbury, New York. The 2017 progress report lists him as partner at 46 Peaks Studios, which, as far as I can tell, produced a single movie in 2020 called *Spy Intervention*, a romantic comedy that has 33 percent on Rotten Tomatoes. The address listed in the New York Department of State corporation database is a few doors down from fellow longtime CREDC member Omar Usmani's Aeon Nexus Corporation. By 2019 Meader was the film commissioner at the Adirondack Film Commission, whose goal is to "attract and support filming projects in the greater Glens Falls area."[10] He seems to have succeeded in getting the HBO series *Succession* to film on location at his previous employer's park. But it also seems he left that job fairly soon, because in January 2020 the *Glen Falls Post-Star* ran an article titled "Washington County Tourism Social Media Numbers Come under Scrutiny," which describes a tense County Board of Supervisors meeting wherein Meader had to explain why the $152,544 the county had paid him had not translated into significant increases in social media interactions and attention to the area's farms, fairs, and events.[11] As of 2021 he was no longer listed as a member of the CREDC, but it is unclear when between 2019 and 2021 he left.

The EDCs are unique to New York, but the myriad organizations that interface with them are very common: industrial development authorities, community loan funds, business improvement districts, and chambers of commerce are eligible to apply for assistance from the EDCs and may act as staff for the EDC. Mark Eagan of the Center for Economic Growth told me that his organization and the CREDC "are directly aligned. There's not a dedicated staff to a Regional Economic Development Council, so the staff is really sort of part and parcel development staff and part staff by CEG."[12]

CEG has received nearly $200,000 from Empire State Development through two CFA grants administered through the CREDC, including a $125,000 grant for "completion of an Economic Analysis and submission of an application for a Regional Center under the Dept. of Homeland Security's EB-5 Immigrant Investor Program" in 2012[13] and a $65,000 grant two years later to write a "Strategic Plan that will (1) define what constitutes the creative economy in the Capital Region, (2) create a data base of the creative economy participants, (3) extrapolate the creative economy's current economic impact and potential future economic impact, and (4) generate a plan that recommends how to maximize the potential economic impact of this sector."[14]

As confusing and seemingly nepotistic as this might seem, the process of a governor-appointed council telling a state bureaucracy to pay its not-quite staff thousands of dollars for research and planning is much closer to state-capitalist economic planning than corruption. Katie Newcombe, also of CEG, describes the system as a "symbiotic relationship between state economic development, local economic development, and regional economic development." She gives an example:

> There may be somebody looking at the region: they want to locate here, they want to invest, they want to grow jobs, all that stuff. And we have to help make the business case, so we put together that pitch. It's a lot of data and analysis: What's your labor shed? How many degrees are you graduating each year in a certain area? You know, livability-type stats. Workforce devel-

opment, research and development, whatever it is. So we're able to do that and then at the end of the day, they may go to a local economic development agency for that PILOT [Payment in Lieu of Taxes] agreement.[15]

A PILOT agreement is a popular way to reduce the initial costs of new construction by suspending property tax collection and replacing it with an agreed-upon reduced payment schedule that eventually rises to the full property tax rate. PILOT agreements are made by a county's or city's Industrial Development Agency (IDA). There are over a hundred IDAs in New York State alone.[16] It is common for an IDA to cut deals that reduce property tax rolls by millions of dollars each year, which are defended as short-term losses for longer-term gains in jobs, housing, and, eventually, taxes.

The EDC system was so closely tied to the governorship of Andrew Cuomo that it seemed unclear at first if it would survive his August 2021 resignation. Not only were the EDCs described as the centerpiece of "his" economic strategy, but it seemed clear that his strongman, kiss-the-ring style of governing and need for constant validation were essential to the program. Out of the 744 news articles and press releases on the EDC website, 540 contain his name.[17] Regardless of the longevity of the EDC system itself, Cuomo had merely (though effectively) wrangled a system much larger and older than he or his governorship.

COMMUNITY CONTROL SYSTEMS

In the nineteenth century, the American federal government made a handful of direct attempts—mostly canal and road building—to manage domestic economic development. Since World War II, however, economic development has been greatly expanded but almost never in a nationally directed way. Through the establishment of the Small Business Administration in 1953 and the Economic Development Administration in 1965, the federal government set local governments against each other to compete to be the spatial fixes[18] for postwar spoils. By 1988 the influential policy expert Peter K. Eisenger declared American capitalism was a "mixed economy" because the state "has fashioned a far more intimate form of involvement in the private market than anything to which Americans have been accustomed."[19] Widespread was not the same as organized though, because even by the 1990s, community development scholars described these institutions as "ad hoc and poorly coordinated."[20] Industrial Development Authorities, Business

Improvement Districts, and other local development organizations are still an overlooked but increasingly crucial part of American capitalism. Textbooks on the subject reassure readers that these institutions are a part of a "community development system that began to solidify by 2001."[21]

I don't want to give the impression that these organizations are uniformly bad. There are some nonprofit housing organizations, community-based development organizations, and land trusts that do a lot of good work, and I'll highlight some in the book's conclusion. But generally, the move from government provision of housing, food, and jobs programs to this network of semiprivate organizations introduced perverse incentives into life-sustaining institutions. The result has been a wealth transfer of public money to boards of directors staffed largely by local elites that are more likely to be responsive to real estate interests than those of the poor. This community development system is more accurately described as a community *control* system because while development (or growth) certainly happens, the main function is really control over land, resources, and labor.

Community control systems do the necessary planning and research to keep market economies afloat. Without the work done in community control systems, it would be even harder to plan within capitalist firms. They would have no counterparts to negotiate land use terms with, nor would they have the necessary information about workforce development or natural resources. This section is not meant to be exhaustive about everything community control systems do, nor does it significantly cover other kinds of organizations that could be accurately described as part of the community control system, like chambers of commerce, housing authorities, or local development corporations. Rather, it covers how a select few of them interact to maintain the updated growth machine and the City Authentic.

The atomized, competitive nature of American economic development was forged amid the City Efficient: downtowns were bulldozed in urban renewal programs that sought to increase car infrastructure and build according to the modernist architectural ethos of form follows function. Crucially, the slum clearance campaigns that were central to the urban renewal programs included substantial grants to local development agencies that were willing to turn over downtown land to private developers. City governments, through their development agencies, would use eminent domain to assemble land plots that were substantially larger than the row houses they were set to demolish. It is in this context that the thirst games as we know them first took shape, not necessarily as competitions for who can look the most authentic but for who can give away enough land and resources to the best developer they can find.[22]

At about the same time, the great builder Robert Moses pioneered the use of public-benefit corporations to generate revenue and fund major public works outside general tax money.[23] New York State's early and frequent use of public authorities, quasi-private-public corporations formed by the state legislature for economic development, is unique.[24] There are state authorities for highways, bridges, parking lots, ports, and land banks. In 1969 the New York State legislature let counties and municipalities create public benefit corporations whose chief purpose would be to promote and develop regional economies. Those corporations generally took the form of Industrial Development Agencies, or IDAs.

As of 2022 there were 108 active IDAs listed on the New York State Authorities Budget Office website.[25] The Capital Region's IDAs as of 2021 had $5.3 billion in outstanding debt.[26] IDAs use their quasi-government status to provide bonds, cheap financing, and other financial instruments to private companies to establish a presence in their county or municipality. Each IDA has a board with a small staff. Board members are appointed by county and city governments and can stay on for a long time. Joseph Fava, the chairman for the City of Schenectady Industrial Development Agency, for example, has held the position for seventeen years.[27]

While there are rules against intentionally poaching another New York State IDA's project, there is stiff competition. As Rocky Ferraro told us in chapter 2, "The metrics in terms of financial support for that organization or for the executive director to continue is primarily what have you done for this community, this county." That usually takes the form of increased economic activity in proportion to the grants, loans, and tax money that was foregone in PILOTs and other enticements. Their role in the City Authentic is to keep the upgraded growth machine moving by lobbying for business-friendly policies and enticing new companies to set up shop. Albany has been at the forefront of IDA-based financing since at least the eighties, when a local law firm was one of the first to specialize in arranging and promoting bonds offered through IDAs.[28]

The ad from the Fulton County IDA shown in chapter 1 is somewhat anomalous. The public presence of IDAs is usually quite minimal, with sparse websites containing almost exclusively legally required documents and lackluster social media accounts—if they exist at all. IDAs do, however, regularly publish press releases citing their own numbers on job retention and economic stimulus.

It behooves IDAs to remain in the background given that their main task is deeply unpopular: to utilize their tax-free status to reduce the amount of money going into city coffers from developers and employers. There's also the fact that IDAs are likely very corrupt. The New York State Comptroller's office in a 2006 report called IDAs' financial reporting "inconsistent and inaccurate."[29] In 2015 New York's IDAs were moderately reformed to include a uniform application process and policies to suspend or end PILOT agreements,[30] but that does not seem to have done enough. In late 2019 the New York State Senate published a report outlining widespread waste and possible corruption in public authorities in general; in particular it stated that the "extent to which IDAs have been providing questionable benefits brings into question whose interests are being served by the system."[31] Given this, it makes sense that IDAs rarely participate in overt publicity campaigns and instead opt to play the thirst games quietly. Even when everything is above board legally, their consolidation of power looks unseemly. For example, when Cathy Gatta, the director of marketing and communications for the restaurant group Mazzone Hospitality was named chair of the Scotia Business Improvement District, the *Albany Business Review* made sure to note that "she also is a Schenectady County Legislator, serves on the Schenectady County IDA and the Capital Resource Corp. and works with the marketing committees of both the Schenectady Chamber and the Downtown Schenectady Improvement Corp."[32]

The Center for Economic Growth (CEG), which I have mentioned several times in this book, is not an IDA; it is a nonprofit organization tasked with regional economic development in the eight Capital Region counties.[33] In addition to assisting the CREDC with research and administrative duties, CEG does many of the same things as an IDA, including courting developers and employers, finding loan and grant programs, and building incentive packages for those that do decide to do business in the Capital Region. It also runs workforce development programs, conducts research on the region's economic indicators, offers pitch coaching to entrepreneurs, and maintains a stable of angel and institutional investors.

It is useful to think of CEG as a clearinghouse for the necessary precursors to growth-machine politics. In addition to its work promoting the region to outsiders, it does a lot of research that the community control system needs. Counties, cities, corporations, universities, newspapers, and banks all invest in CEG because pooling and coordinating their resources—at least partially—is better than going it alone. CEG offers the major players in the community control system information on how to develop relationships, gain the attention of relevant market actors, and find grants and loans that few others are in a position to provide. As Mark Eagan puts it, "Albany can't survive or thrive on its own—none of our communities are able to do that." During the first year of the COVID-19 pandemic, it also administered a $150,000 Small Business Stabilization Fund to minority- and women-owned businesses.[34]

Unlike an IDA, CEG has been very visible in the media. It has been the institutional home of the CapNY campaign since it merged with the Upstate Alliance for the Creative Economy in early 2019.[35] It is also affiliated with the Capital Region Chamber, which runs the Young Professionals Network (YPN), which hosts talks, panel discussions, and mixers for creative-class types. More importantly for our purposes, anyone that reaches out through the CapNY website by filling out a short form is paired with someone from YPN to talk about the region and answer questions. When I asked Katie Newcombe and Mark Eagan about YPN, they were quick to point out that there's no fee to become a part of the network and anyone can volunteer to respond to questions posed through the site. The people who answer questions, according to Newcombe, are volunteers from the YPN network who "represent all different types of lifestyles and background—maybe you're single, maybe have a family, you know—all that."

Eagan tells me, "When it was originally created, it was meant for people that were forty and under, and I think that sort of sweet spot is probably twenty-five to thirty-five. You'll find the person that's forty, but most are probably in their mid-twenties to mid-thirties." When I went to a YPN event in the summer of 2021, the room was full of well-dressed young people—more women than men and while white people were probably overrepresented, it was not a monochromatic crowd—who seemed legitimately excited about what the panel had to say about the future growth of the region. When Jeff Buell, the panel's moderator and a principal for Redburn Development, asked the room who was born there, only a smattering of hands went up.

Equally, if not more important than getting people to come to the region is organizing them once they get here. IDAs exist ostensibly to attract new business to an area (though there are more than enough stories of developers looking for PILOT agreements *after* they decide to build somewhere), but once they get there, it is up to a Business Improvement District, or BID, to maintain those favorable conditions. BIDs act as private governments within public ones. Within the defined boundaries of the BID, companies and landlords voluntarily enter a defined tax pool that is collected by the city but is managed for and by the sole use of the businesses within the BID jurisdiction. This money can go toward hiring private security, trash pickup, beautification projects, and other services. BIDs also take percentages from the events they throw.[36] In the Capital Region, BIDs have an annual operating budget between just under a hundred thousand to over a million dollars. They can also get startup funds from their local IDA, like Troy did when business owners started forming a BID in 2008.[37] The small staff of BIDs generally come from and eventually leave for the communications and real estate businesses.

BIDs were first invented in Toronto in 1970.[38] In the Capital Region, BIDs came relatively late (the largest, the Downtown Albany BID, was established only in 1996 and Troy didn't have one until 2011) but have since become essential community control systems. During the COVID-19 pandemic, they responded by publicizing lists of businesses to support, which is a good indicator of how BIDs respond to problems in general: with publicity. They went into overtime publishing press releases and using social media to draw attention to stores and encouraged residents to "shop local." The Downtown Albany BID also offered matching funds for outdoor heaters so that restaurants could keep serving customers well into the fall.[39]

In normal times they host events like the Troy's Chowderfest, Schenectady's weekly farmers' market, and Albany's lunchtime concert series; lobby for infrastructure improvements they cannot pay for themselves;[40] and run flashy websites and social media profiles highlighting their constituent businesses. Around 2012, BIDs in the region started realizing the importance of social media and began hiring dedicated staff to post every day to multiple platforms. They share that expertise too, hosting workshops for business owners to build their own profiles.[41]

Being the image-conscious institutions that they are, BIDs are likely to oppose things like a methadone clinic that was meant to go in downtown Troy, stating, "Of the various challenges we face in achieving our goals, perhaps the most daunting is that of public perception."[42] And when Downtown Albany's BID director Pamela Tobin was found to have dodged paying 736 parking tickets over seven years, she resigned.[43] Elizabeth Young, then head of the Troy BID, told the *Albany Business Review* in 2013 that the buzz around events was the best antidote to the rough reputations of Rust Belt downtowns: "It's a tough thing to quantify. But when you mention Troy now to someone random on the street, they might say, 'Oh, yeah, I went to that barbecue festival last year. I hear there's that new wine bar.' And maybe they don't spout out some crime statistic from the '80s that has long since changed."[44]

Those changes also come from altering the streetscape. In 2001, the Lark Street BID in Albany was involved in a $6.5 million renovation of its eponymous street's infrastructure, including restoration of cobblestone intersections and the installation of reproduction historic light fixtures. They also received money from the New York State Council on the Arts to work with the Historic Albany Foundation to install historic markers and develop audio walking tours.[45] This was also the first year they had a website.

More recently, the alterations of the streetscape and online advertisement have merged. For example, in 2014 the Downtown Albany BID worked with a local artist to install large red, ornate picture frames all around the city and asked visitors "to take pictures of themselves and others in the frames, and share the images on social media with the hashtag #captureALB."[46] When thirty five-foot-tall fiberglass statues of Uncle Sam were installed all around downtown Troy, the BID encouraged passersby to pose with their favorite, take a picture, and post it to social media with the tag #unclesamproject.[47]

Engagement with these two projects varied widely. On Instagram the #capturealbany hashtag has 238 associated images, while #unclesamproject only has 22. A few things contribute to this difference beyond Albany being twice as big as Troy. One is that the Uncle Sam project was in 2012, two years before the Capture Albany campaign, so Troy might have been a bit ahead of its time. More importantly though, the #captureALB campaign's red frames gave people something to work with in composing their photos, rather than simply posing with a statue. The most popular Uncle Sam statue was outside a popular bar and his stovepipe hat was painted to look like a pint of beer, which gave tipsy patrons something to pose with. Probably the most important thing about #captureALB is the way it invites porous authenticity. #CaptureALB contains inside jokes, deprecating photos of discarded liquor bottles in a gutter, and even a few wedding photos. #CaptureALB is also on the frame itself, reminding viewers to use the hashtag, whereas no one would know about the hashtag #unclesamproject unless they'd already seen it on the Troy BID's social media accounts.

And BID social media accounts, while active and regularly updated, do not have high engagement numbers. On August 5, 2021, I took a sample of the follower counts on two Albany BID pages (Lark Street BID and Downtown Albany BID), Troy BID, and Upper Union Street BID in Schenectady. Downtown Albany had by far the most followers, with 13,303, followed by Lark Street, with 4,224; Upper Union Street, with 3,886; and Troy, with 2365. Upper Union Street, however, was the only one with decent engagement numbers, usually about two dozen reactions and a scattering of comments on posts about new businesses opening, new deals, and shares of news coverage about BID member businesses. Downtown Albany's BID would get significant interaction only when it would wish business owners a happy birthday and tag the owner in the post. Given that many of these owners are well-known and active on social media themselves, this was an effective way to boost engagement. Troy and Lark Street BIDs posted very frequently, but the posts were effectively ads for their constituent businesses and not much else.

These community control systems are some of the main organizing institutions of the City Authentic. It is in these semi-democratic councils and boards that elites come together to organize reputations, money, and the built environment. Their social media campaigns can sometimes be lackluster. Most of BIDs' authenticity peddling comes from the way they use experiences, events, and urban infrastructure to produce constructive and existential authenticity. They then use media to advertise these efforts, but with modest success.

THE BRANDED LANDSCAPE

In the *Journal of Marketing Management*, scholars Julie Napoli, Sonia Dickinson-Delaporte, and Michael Beverland put together a study of "brand authenticity" that builds on previous work, which they say demonstrates that "consuming authenticity helps consumers experience a perceived connection with the past and perceived evidence that they have escaped phoniness, shallowness, and [the] artificiality of modern-day life."[48] They introduce their study by observing:

> An organisation's marketing and brand strategies are often directed towards establishing a strong brand presence in the marketplace and attaining a

desired position in the minds of consumers. In the postmodern era, consumers are more inclined to seek out authentic objects or brands that help them express their authentic selves . . . and supplement, if not drive, their personal identity projects. This presents a unique opportunity for firms to position their brands, either explicitly or implicitly, as authentic.[49]

Postmodern is the operative word here. In a modern era, brands would not necessarily be a source of meaning or identity. Who you are or what you make of the world would more likely come from state propaganda, religion, or your family. In these older institutions, you would not only be expected to find purpose but also a grand narrative to chart the progress of society. Brand advertising of the modern era, not yet burdened with task of telling you who you are supposed to be, focused mainly on quality, price, and feature sets. To be sure, 1950s car commercials flattered viewers by describing them as smart and lured them to dealerships with the promise of neighbors' adoration as they pull out of the driveway. But the bulk of advertising used what communication scholars call the "direct route of persuasion," where the narrator tells the audience, "Buy a Ford truck and get the best towing capacity for the lowest price." Or some such.

The *indirect* route takes a detour through ideology, emotional commitments, and one's sense of self. This detour is necessary because, as Napoli and colleagues say, "the 'cynical' postmodern consumer . . . often associates brands with deception, trickery and exaggeration."[50] Only a chump believes what a salesman tells them. Instead, the advertiser must carve out a need or identify some hole in the world and make a reasonable argument that its product fills the void. The more ephemeral and abstract the thing is, the more postmodern the advertising can be because, ultimately, the goal of postmodern advertising is to elicit an emotion and attach the object to that emotion as quickly as possible. Insurance, fragrances, banking, and services like Airbnb are best sold by eliciting an emotion because their products barely exist.

Naomi Klein's first book, *No Logo*, tracked the rise of mega brands like Nike and Apple that realized that it was more profitable to protect and leverage branding than focus on the quality of the product itself. Her book became a touchstone for the so-called antiglobalization movements that fought against corporate domination of the public sphere and human rights. Napoli and colleagues have their own way of acknowledging this when they note that in the 1990s and early 2000s, "aggressive growth strategies dilute[d] perceived authenticity." Their antidote is a four-tier strategic approach to authenticity, with each tier geared toward brands at different stages of their development. Newer "novice" brands need to use a "germination strategy" that establishes the company's sincerity and emotional connection to consumers. "Apprentice" brands are prescribed a "cultivation strategy" that requires they show their commitment to both their heritage and present work. "Professional" brands must consolidate and control those external factors that may be a threat to their authentic reputation. This might mean downplaying their Chinese manufacturing operations or making sure their products are sold in the right stores under the best conditions.

These first three tiers are entirely in the control of the firm, but at the highest echelons of brand authenticity—what Napoli and colleagues call "master brands"—authenticity is no longer controllable by the firm. "The iconic status of the brand," they write, "resides in the minds of consumers and it is not something that can readily be shaped by a firm."[51] All it can do now is *preserve* this iconic status in a defensive posture. That means maintaining not just the build quality of the product but the reputation of the symbols, stories, and contexts that represent the brand. All a company can do at this point is screw up the good thing they have going.

In a society such as ours where our everyday lives are increasingly ordered by the logic of brands, it is essential that we understand their political dimensions. Such is the thesis of Sarah Banet-Weiser's *Authentic*™, which shows that some of the best-known and most effectively leveraged brands eschew the traditional buying of ads on billboards and opt instead to manage "organic" engagement. This strategy can take the form of underwriting the costs of the kind of artistic production that you want your brand associated with, as when the shoe brand Converse sponsored an "underground recording studio" in Brooklyn—whatever that is.[52]

Reading Banet-Weiser's book, one gets the sense that the BIDs in the Capital Region are outgunned by their big city counterparts. Not just because big, global cities, to use Napoli and colleagues' typology, have achieved master-brand status but because they have all the tools and talent to keep that status. The best brand managers are "*curators* of content" that are constantly hosting, producing, and managing cool stuff "instead of relying on industry-produced statistics or imagined audiences."[53] The result is a seamless web of brands and culture that is difficult to separate into clearly authentic and contrived categories.

Authentic™ came out in 2012, yet the tactics it details feel years ahead of whatever those Uncle Sam statues or #CaptureALB could accomplish.

The Capital Region seems to deploy some of the master brand techniques, but I have seen more professional branding tools: consolidating control over what it means to live in the Capital Region and redistribute it across various media channels. CEG's CapNY campaign in conjunction with the Young Professionals Network is slightly more sophisticated than what the BIDs have done. Its CapNY campaign reaches further with more precise and targeted advertising. In addition to the CapNY site, which it sees as a destination for curious people, social media advertising is meant to be the initial touch point, the lure that brings you in. In June 2021, CEG started taking out ads on LinkedIn, Instagram, and Facebook targeting twenty-five- to thirty-five-year-olds in Boston and New York. Specifically, it wants people who have had some prior but temporary relationship with the region. "We're looking if somebody has some familiarity—they've been on vacation here, they visited a friend here, they went to school or lived in proximity." Katie Newcombe tells me that while CEG is relying on a previous personal connection to enhance the ad's message, the ad doesn't let on that that is who it is targeting. Rather, its message is how "we have far more breweries, ciders, distilleries, and wineries compared to where they are, so [we're focused on] lifestyle."

This campaign is informed by the needs and recommendations of recruitment departments at the region's large employers who, according to Newcombe, tell her that the site will be "a valuable tool, so that when they are talking to people about moving here, they have a way to show what it's like. That it's not, you know, just Albany or Saratoga Springs—that it's something much larger, because oftentimes it's the recruiter that's doing the sales pitch."[54]

Mark Eagan chimes in: "We realized that a lot of younger professionals want to have more of an urban environment. They want to be able to walk to a restaurant or a bar or do whatever they want." That desire for the authentic urban experience, however, comes at a cost. Eagan continues, "All of a sudden if they moved to the Capital Region but they were still working in New York—you know, doing it remote—if they're getting called back, it is our hope they might say, 'You know what. I'm not going to move back because 80 percent of my income was going to my rent, and when I live in the Capital Region, it's 50 percent instead so that means that . . . I do want to go out with friends. If I want to save for a home, I can do so, versus New York or Boston, I can't.'"[55] (Recall from chapter 2 that while this is true for now, it is getting less true. Indeed, that is one of the core contradictions of the growth machine.)

This close relationship between CEG and individual firms' recruiters shows that the audience for CapNY and similar campaigns isn't just the potential new resident; it is the executives at companies that are already there. It is a very fine needle to thread, which makes authenticity both crucial and intensely difficult to convey. On the one hand, an ad campaign that works at the cutting edge of brand management would likely need to be porous in the Abidinian sense, offering both a polished presentation with hints behind the curtain of something messy and relatable.[56] That might be a bit too much for an image-conscious company that would rather CEG show only the best parts of the region.

Indeed, this is an old playbook. In 2004 two consulting companies, Impresa, Inc. and Coletta & Company, produced a study for Portland, Oregon titled *The Young and the Restless: How Portland Competes for Talent*. They suggested many of the same tactics that CEG is using now: keep in touch with former residents; use symbols and stories in local media to define a narrative of the place; and—most importantly— "deliver an appealing reality" because "substance is what counts. Young people are very savvy in assessing cities. They use the internet to get information and check facts. They are tied into their own extensive networks of people with first-hand knowledge of how things really are."[57] The next year the same two companies released a report in Tampa titled *The Young and the Restless: How Tampa Competes for Talent*. Jamie Peck, writing soon after the Impresa and Coletta reports, explained why these recommendations for "manipulating street-level façades, while gently lubricating the gentrification processes" spread so quickly: these "ideas may have traveled so far, not because they are revolutionary, but because they are so modest."[58] Reports like these tell civic leaders that they can do wonders simply by being cool.

The Impresa and Coletta reports are right though: young people do, in fact, use the internet to check facts and are savvy consumers of culture, which is why the technology used to sell place is constantly evolving. The most sophisticated form of advertising I came across in my research was in Ulster County, just to the south of the Capital Region. Toward the end of chapter 2, I introduced Megan Brenn-White, a real estate entrepreneur whose Instagram account @upstatecurious is at the center of her business. She and her husband moved from Brooklyn to a small town in Ulster County in 2016. I sent her a message over Instagram asking for an interview, and she responded with the timeliness and charm of someone who has done a lot of business over the platform. We set up a Zoom call, and she told me how @upstatecurious got started:

"We were buying a place with the intention of it being a weekend place or splitting our time and then ended up being able to move here full time right away, so we actually never had it as a weekend place." The account began as an outlet for

> processing my feelings about living here and thinking about it. And sharing it is, like, was just so natural to do. I actually didn't start this with any strategy. I just started it because I was so excited about being here and I was like, "Instagram seems like a cool thing." . . . It was such a different life than what I had lived in Brooklyn, you know, and I loved living here so much. It just felt really kind of exciting to share it somehow and to be like, "Oh, look at this tree I'm seeing" or "I'm figuring out how to deal with, like, bears."[59]

However, she is quick to mention, "I moved to Brooklyn around I guess 1997 or '98, and if Instagram had existed then, I would have done the same thing."

Brenn-White wasn't even a real estate agent when she moved north. She had done digital-content marketing for higher education programs since 1997. She didn't work just with universities but "with regions, countries, and cities to really help them refine why an international student would want to go there." It was only after she moved upstate and fell in love with it that she made a significant and incredibly successful career change. She now has a sixteen-person team that is "going to do $100 million in business this year, and we do not have a website." What they do have is her Instagram presence, which has "driven the growth of our business 100 percent," and an iPhone app by the same name.

The Upstate Curious app launched in the midst of the pandemic, on March 2, 2021, as a tool to help people in the region find friends, meet up safely, and share information. The app became an instant success, with 1,500 downloads in a week.[60] It was especially popular with those who'd left the city for greener pastures. It grew so quickly that fellow Brooklyn transplant Marcy Langworthy was brought on part-time as the community manager. Her full-time job though, was similar work for a place called Inness, which offers "lodging, dining, swimming, tennis, membership, golf and outdoor activities for creative individuals and families" in Accord, New York, and private cabins start at $522 a night.[61] The app requires that you make a profile (which signs you up for a newsletter, of course), and then you are greeted with a timeline similar to Facebook. It's active too, with people looking for general contractor recommendations, help identifying weird bugs, and tips for where to park on the cheap for the Albany International Airport. There are advertisements for a drag show in Hudson and a hairdresser that claims to be "bringing SoHo to Olive, NY!"—a town of less than five thousand in Ulster County.

I tell her about *Scare Me* and what its star and creator Josh Ruben had to say about Ulster County becoming an "alt-Hamptons" and putting writers looking to #escapebrooklyn in his movie. Brenn-White agrees that "probably 90 percent" of her business comes from Brooklyn, but she connects it to a larger global phenomenon by describing a project from her previous job:

> One of our clients was the Glasgow School of Art, and they had just opened a big branch in the Scottish Highlands for exactly that reason—a lot of artists don't necessarily want to be in the middle of London anymore because they see it as associated with finance and attorneys and not creativity. I think it's interesting. I for sure have met so many more people here . . . I mean, if you do specific kinds of art, you need more space and you can't get a huge loft in Bushwick anymore for like $1,000 a month.[62]

Just like the SoHo lofts of the sixties and Bushwick at the turn of the century, it appears that upstate New York has once again become a place to do creative work on the cheap. This isn't unprecedented; Brenn-White points out:

> It's been like this since the nineteenth century! For as long as there's been colonialism in this country, there has been a connection between this area and New York City, whether it was like bluestone and cement [two building materials that were brought south to build the city]. It's been tourism; it's been gentlemen artists coming up building places. This has been a big tourist area for a long time. And that to me is weird. People have like really short memories. If you look back, yes, prices have gone up and things have changed and gotten busier since like the '90s, early 2000s. But then, I talked to people who grew up here before IBM left, and they're like, "Kingston was thriving. I grew up here, and there were like tons of restaurants, and my friends' parents had like good jobs, and we were able to do things,, and then it went really south for a long time."[63]

Of course, what is different now is the ability to lash together a region through continual mediated communication. And the question we have been following in this entire book is how that new communication technology has impacted this much older relationship between environment, self, and political economy. Put another way: if a freshly minted real estate company can use Instagram to sell $100 million worth of real estate to Brooklynites in search of nature, then something worth investigating must have changed in how people choose where to live and what to do once they get there.

What we know so far from chapters 2 and 4 is that the City Authentic has a significant impact on land and housing prices that far outpaces actual demand for housing or increases in population. The value that brand management instills in the land is the possibility of existential fulfillment of a particular kind of life made up of authentic human connections and experiences. This requires a cultivation of an aesthetic and a story that signals to audiences that a particular place is linked to those promised existential experiences.

Brenn-White tells me that "most real estate agent Instagrams are like, 'Just sold!' 'Just listed!' 'Just sold!' 'Just listed!' or, like, 'Here's Barb's five tips.'" These are goofy but effective, she tells me. And so I stop her and say that only a third of her Instagram posts are listings. "If you count the stories, actually it would be way less than a third, I would say, because, like, I do a lot of stories that are all about, like, events and things that are happening." It reminded me a lot of Escape Brooklyn, the company that Corrigan courted to show off the Fort Orange General Store, and I said as much. Brenn-White said she'd advertised with them too, but as her business grew, its audiences became too similar for her to get any new clients. I asked if she saw a distinctive collection of media dominating the region. She told me that after studying what other businesses attracted similar audiences,

> I realized it was And North, Escape Brooklyn obviously. But then it was also certain hotels, restaurants, and shops that had a direct overlap, so it was [restaurants like] Scribners, you know, like Clove & Creek in Kingston. And I guess that maybe to your point, those shops and hotels and restaurants kind of do belong to the media universe now because of Instagram. So, even though they're not like Escape Brooklyn, they're not like And North and they're not publishing articles, the same people are looking at them for information and to like get a sense of the place and to get a sense of the people behind that.[64]

This merging of media presence is at the heart of the upgraded growth machine and the indirect monopoly rents that it relies on. More important than any one account is how they come together as a genre or aesthetic of authentic Upstate living. And while the properties Brenn-White sells and advertises certainly have a rural character, the fact that she shares a "media universe" with other accounts that are distinctly urban confirms what Lefebvre and Castells have said about urbanization in the past: that it is a social and economic relationship as much as a description of the built environment. Or as Brenn-White told the *Times Union* when the Upstate Curious app launched: "You can't explore rural areas the way you do urban areas where you say, 'I'm going to get to know this place' and plunk yourself downtown and walk around.'"[65] The app, in a way, creates that urbanity. Without it, there is little evidence that traditional media would be able to sustain the amount of specialty and luxury businesses in Ulster County or the Capital Region to its north. At least that is the sentiment of the business owners and economic development professionals that I spoke to.

Social media is many things to many people, but to economic development coordinators, real estate agents, and hospitality business owners, it is a crucial tool for extracting both direct and indirect monopoly rents from a region. Through the image-dense affordances of platforms like Instagram, regions can be packaged into discernible locations that one can go experience. While those involved in creating these experiences talk often and openly about the importance of transparency and showing the good with the bad, there's little evidence of the porous authenticity that Crystal Abidin says is so crucial for maintaining credibility in the influencer market.[66] Instead, there is a lot of constructive authenticity at work: building up expectations of what Upstate New York is like and meeting those expectations with luxurious, curated experiences that may also achieve existentially authentic moments. But by and large what we see is a careful crafting of a place's aesthetic and culture that can be easily recognized and sold for both direct and indirect monopoly profits.

MEMES OF PLACE

"How does, like, a hydroflask and Timbs come to represent East Greenbush?" Elroy McDaniels is being patient with me as I ask him to walk me through how "starter pack" memes work. His @upstatenymemes Instagram account had a rash of them for a few months and I'm trying to understand his process.

> Somebody had requested, "Make a Guilderland meme." But I do not live in Guilderland, so I asked, "What would you want to see?" And they listed off, I think it was, "people drive BMWs; we have like the biggest Walmart; everyone goes to Crossgates [mall]; and we're bad at sports." So, I was like, "Huh? Why don't put it all into one and make a starter pack."[67]

The conceit is that a collage of items under the headline "X Starter Pack" contains all the necessary items for becoming or fitting into X. People in East Greenbush wear Timberland boots, and Guilderland does, in fact, have the world's largest Walmart. Therefore, they go in their respective towns' starter packs. They are easy to make collaboratively because all you need is a list of things and phrases to make the meme.

But what I'm trying to understand is how these mass-produced, name-brand consumables can be useful in describing very specific places that no one outside an hour's drive has likely ever heard of. "Technically these things can represent anywhere, right?" I ask. "Because they are available all over the place."

He responds: "Exactly. And I think that's also like one of the reasons people got, you know, a little tired of the starter packs. A lot of the towns ended up having the same things, you know? Give or take one or two. It's just what people happen to enjoy consuming and buying there."

"And does that, say, maybe in a roundabout way, describe the income level, the demographics of the region, or something like that?"

"In a way, yeah. Like, I remember again my Guilderland one—I think I put like a BMW in there. I think that kind of goes along with, you know, Guilderland has this reputation as a more affluent area."

When he says this, I can't help but share one of my favorites, which was one for Bethlehem, a posh suburb just south of Albany, which included the phrase "My dad is a lobbyist."

Most of the towns that got starter packs are best described as suburbs, and so it makes sense that McDaniels's audience, which he describes as containing lots of high school and college students, would resort to these fine distinctions in consumption patterns between otherwise indistinguishable places. BMWs, pregnancy tests, and SoundCloud rappers—all requested items for various starter packs—are proxies for race, class, and any number of other social markers. This is the people of a region talking to each other in the language of mass-market consumer capitalism, not a region selling itself in the market of branded places.

With its pop culture references, mainstream brand references, and deprecation, @upstatenymemes is just as important a part of the City Authentic branding regime as those stylized photos of log cabins and brownstones. It is not the only meme account making fun of small differences between neighborhoods. In fact, McDaniels started the account because when some friends from Long Island were talking about a similar kind of account, he realized none existed for the Capital Region. These sorts of memes—let's call them memes of place—are common and provide a glimpse into the paradoxes of authenticity. Although these memes are for anyone who grew up in the region, their content is dominated by mass-market brands and symbols. But as you zoom out and try to sell the same places to outsiders—as Upstate Curious or Escape Brooklyn tries to do—the global brands are eschewed for very specific kinds of content that read as uncommodified experiences or sumptuous objects. Whereas authenticity peddling relies on the predictably unique, memes of place use very common symbols in unpredictable ways.

The kinds of eye-rolling jokes found in @upstatenymemes are for insiders; they would elicit defensive pride if an outsider said them. This is where the warts are on full display, so in that way, it is *very* authentic. There are more posts about convenience-store chains and annoying car dealership commercials than there are sun-dappled photos of latte foam art. Given all the self-deprecating memes he makes, I ask if he thinks people should move to the Capital Region and if he likes living here. His response is immediate and echoes some of the economic developers' ad copy: "I think people should move here. I've enjoyed growing up here and what I think is so great about like Upstate New York, especially the Capital Region is, like, it's got something for everyone." Yet McDaniels's advice to those building advertising campaigns for the region is different from what they've been doing:

> Humor always helps. I've noticed people don't want to feel like they're being, you know, advertised to. They don't want to feel like they're just seeing, you know, "Come visit Albany." I don't know—I feel like it almost has to be humorous, and human in some way—how specifically I'm not necessarily sure. But people don't like ads. They don't want to feel like they're being, you know, preyed on almost. So if they can find a way to make it feel less like that—and, you know, as you say, like, more authentic. I would say that would be the way to go.[68]

Given the content, it makes sense that when McDaniels runs an ad on his account—there have been several—they take the form of a trending meme and the advertiser is usually a real estate agent looking for homes to sell, not encouraging outsiders to buy a house in the Capital Region (figure 6). The ads are straightforward and easy to spot, wrapped in a small joke.

FIGURE 6. A paid post on @upstatenymemes from a local real estate agent.

The Upstate Curious app I discussed in the last section, while not funny, definitely does not feel like advertising. In fact, there are advertisements in the app itself, which has a way of making you forget that you're using an app made to encourage the buying and selling of property in and around Ulster County. It is almost as if, to paraphrase the French scholar Jean Baudrillard, the ads in the app exist to make you think the rest of the content is authentic.[69] The economic development professionals we've heard from in this book would likely agree with McDaniels that no one really wants to be advertised to, but instead of being funny, the definitely-not-advertisements have been exceedingly earnest. They also keep chain-stores out of their posts, while @upstatenymemes is full of name brand consumer goods and chain stores. Instead of listing rankings about how the school districts perform, there are memes about which school kids drink White Claw versus Natural Light. And when the ads come, there's no question you're being advertised to, but they come with a wink and a nod, as if to acknowledge that ads suck but hey, we all gotta get paid.

TO THE INFLUENTIAL GO THE SPOILS

I want to take a step back now and survey the field of influencers and reality TV for two reasons. First, we will find many parallels to what has already been covered about authenticity and branding the city. Remember that my contention here is not necessarily that city elites are consciously importing the tactics of influencers and reality TV stars. Rather, all three are responding to the same pressures of the political economy of attention and authenticity.

The second reason, and why I've put this discussion toward the end of this book, is that cities' relatively late adoption of these tactics means we intuit the near future of the City Authentic by looking at the present state of the influencer industry, with the important caveat that real estate never quite behaves like any other commodity. Each part is connected—physically and culturally—to all others. No one can make more land (sure, you can dredge up the sea and make some islands or extend the shore, but it's not enough to make a serious dent in land prices), and as we saw in chapter 4, the growth machine is really only capable of expanding itself by creating new investment opportunities.

An influencer is a person with a significant number of followers on a major social media platform who monetizes both your and their attention. Influencers monetize yours through advertisements and charging for access to ever-deeper parts of themselves. They also charge to gain access to their attention through apps like Cameo, OnlyFans, and PearPop, which let influencers charge for anything from collaborative videos to personalized birthday greetings. These parasocial relationships are neither wholly transactional nor intimate, but they definitely trade on intimacy as a product.

Within this world of emotionally evocative symbols and identities, authenticity can exceed the terrestrial bounds of the city and enter reflexive, even fantastical heights. Because "everything is for sale" on social media, writes media scholar Zoe Hurley, it is assumed that "everything and everyone participating in the social media landscape is doing so for commercial gain. Projecting a fantasy or giving a perform-ance of 'authentic' life is the important thing as authenticity itself becomes commodified."[70] Contrivances and staging are expected—that is, we expect fiction and are on the lookout for fakes—but a peek at the "backstage" through displays of disorganization or intimacy can give an influencer a boost of authenticity. That is the porous authenticity Crystal Abidin described in chapter 3. This subversion buttresses the credibility of influencers when they later recommend a real estate agent or a new lip gloss. Rather than contradict one another, expertly curated photoshopped selfies sit next to candid moments to create a picture of a fully formed person that also happens to be famous.

One of the first people to realize the power of the influencer industry and take it seriously was Taylor Lorenz, who started reporting on influ-encers back in 2009.[71] Lorenz's career has always tracked closely with the mainstream acceptance of her beat: the way influencers and content creators shape the world and how they get treated in return. She went from freelancing in web-only niche publications to her current position as a staff business reporter for the *New York Times* in twelve years. I talked with Lorenz over the phone in late August of 2021 about the state of influencers in the real estate industry. She was laser-sharp and had an example for nearly everything I asked her.

The mainstreaming of influencers, she tells me, means that they are "just another line item in a lot of people's marketing budget the way TV ads or print ads or classifieds once were." When Lorenz says this, a little red flag pops up in my mind. My experience in researching the internet has led me to be suspicious whenever someone says a new technology is just a different version of something older.

I ask her if the change in marketing methods and technology also changes the subject that is being marketed.

"Cropping up all over cities are places to stage and shoot content for social media. So I would say that's definitely a change." She also points me to the story of photographer and influencer James Jackson, who was paid by the D.C.-area developer Ditto Residential to stay in a condo it had just listed for the weekend to take pictures and generally be cool in a posh one-bedroom that costs half a million dollars. In a write-up of the event in the *Washingtonian*, Jackson tells reporter Marisa Kashino, "94 percent of my followers are in the DC area, so I'm a really good person [for a client like Ditto]. . . . Someone who lives in the area can walk through the door and give Ditto money, whereas someone who lives in Peoria will just go 'Oh that's a cool picture.'"[72]

Lorenz also clues me in on New York City actress and magazine editor Tavi Gevinson, who advertised the apartment complex she lives in to her five hundred thousand followers. A representative for Two Trees, the building developer, told *The Cut* that "we are partnering with a few creative influencers who are great fits for our residential buildings. . . . In a rental market crowded with perfectly staged model apartments, we wanted to show what it's really like to live in a Two Trees building." The selling doesn't stop at the screen though; she'll also host parties in her *own apartment* as part of the deal with the developer. "We think it's an exciting addition to our marketing efforts and a terrific amenity for tenants."[73]

We start talking about the pandemic and how Upstate developers are bragging about buildings full of ex-Brooklynites. "You know when the pandemic hit, a lot of people obviously were looking to figure out their next move," she tells me. "And I think a lot of them turn to influencers and people in their social network to see where they were going and see what people they aspire to be like or people in their social circle were doing." We'd already talked about Washington, D.C., and New York City, but now Taylor Lorenz is talking about Miami:

> The mayor was acting like an influencer, responding to people on Twitter. He generated this big audience by, like, promoting the city and basically leveraging influencer marketing tactics. He got key people in the tech world to come out with their family and get those people to influence their peers and then, again, it's down to aspiration: what you see is a lot of these big tech leaders moving to Miami, which generates a lot of hype and conversation. Then it trickles down and suddenly they had a lot of random tech workers in the Bay Area move to Miami. Obviously, some thought [it] was about the zero income tax, but there are a lot of places that they could move with zero income tax, and the reason that they wanted to move to Miami was because of this hype that was generated through big, influential people in the tech space and the way the mayor was leveraging Twitter.

I want to start moving the conversation to my neck of the woods, so I share my hypothesis about how smaller cities position themselves as boutique thrift-store finds to the more mainstream name brands of big cities. Lorenz is quick to confirm my hypothesis: "That's a hundred percent what it is. It's back to the aspirational stuff: people see influencers they aspire to online, cool creative people like [food writer and chef] Alison Roman or whatever moves to somewhere upstate, and then suddenly she's posting about her lifestyle. There are scenes from her life and her apartment. Then that becomes an aspirational lifestyle. They see that an aspirational lifestyle can happen there." That "somewhere upstate" was Hudson in Columbia County. By my count, Roman gave three different interviews where the first or second answer mentioned that she was staying with friends in Hudson, hiding from both COVID and a recent firestorm around comments she made about fellow influencer Chrissy Teigen. More importantly though, Roman started investing in the region, reportedly buying one restaurant and acting as guest chef at two others, all within a day's drive of Hudson.[74] "If you've been in the city for a couple of years," Lorenz explains, "and then you see someone manifesting this lifestyle on social media in maybe an unconventional place, it becomes very easy to picture yourself there."

When she says this, I immediately think of the writer Alana Massey, who, as her website puts it, "is a writer working, decorating, and tending to her collection of petty grievances in the High Woods of upstate New York."[75] Lorenz remembers when Massey announced to the Brooklyn literary scene that she was moving to a big house in the Catskills: "I was at a party in Brooklyn, and there were so many people talking about it being like, 'Should we all move upstate?' It's funny how one loud person on the internet can sway so many people, but it is a thing and I guess that's how gentrification happens, and obviously, these real estate developers have an interest in courting those people too. They're making a very easy pathway for people to be like, 'Oh, okay. Small-town America is really nice."

But what are people doing *now* to sell land? As late as 2016 or so, cities were still doing what Albany and Troy had done: making specific hashtags and creating opportunities to use them with events and public art. But hashtags, Lorenz explains, have become

> a very outdated discovery mechanism. They're from a different time on the Internet. Nobody really use them much anymore. I mean a little, maybe, if it's a very hyper-specific hashtag, but a lot of people were doing these big hashtags [like #liveauthentic] to get distribution, but the thing is now, we have all these algorithms for distribution—we have TikTok—which will serve you content that's related to what you're interest in, and hashtags can play a part in it, but the algorithm is the primary mode of discovery.

Getting noticed in an algorithmically ordered world is hard and essentially comes down to going through all the different social media platforms and, as Lorenz puts it, "leveraging all of these platforms to the fullest and developing an influencer marketing strategy on each." You have to either understand how a platform works or find someone who does. Some cities—Lorenz mentions Baltimore—have outsourced this to influencers who they fly in and give an all-expenses-paid trip to cover everything they want to highlight in the city. Then the influencers just do their thing: create really engaging content that reaches millions.

To the influential goes the spoils, and so professionals tasked with promoting and selling land can't farm out attention-getting tactics. That's why, as Lorenz says, "real estate agents themselves have become influencers. I'm also thinking about the cast of *Selling Sunset* [a reality TV show about real estate agents in Los Angeles]. Those women are influencers and were influencers, which is what got them on the show. Having an audience—obviously real estate agents want a huge audience to sell to—means you have to project a certain lifestyle about their listings and market themselves, but also I think it's also important to project just lifestyle sort of content."

And there we have it. In a few short sentences, we go from sellers of real estate to social media, to mass media, to cultivation and performance of the self, and finally to using the audience that is attracted to your performance to sell real estate. It's everything we've explored in this book thus far, in a nutshell: the City Authentic in action, albeit with more sun and Botox than what you'll find in Upstate New York.

Sticking with reality TV for a moment and speaking in more general terms, it is exceptionally good at "creating impressions, selling lifestyles, and iconicizing the hollow and the flawed," writes communications scholar June Deery. This is how, in her words, "reality TV also answers a nostalgic desire for the authentic."[76] Rather than provide *the* or even *a* truth, reality TV provides opportunities to seek out the truth among partially scripted scenes and characters. Audiences know they are getting an adulterated product: something in between artifice and genuine humanity caught on camera, and part of the joy is guessing which is which.

This guessing game can bring us anxiety too. "While it draws on the real," Deery writes, "one can argue that RTV is contributing to its scarcity, turning more of raw experience into a commodified media product and overlaying lived experience with yet more TV grammar."[77] Is it an overlay? Or as Jean Baudrillard famously argued, life has become increasingly dominated by representations of things—simulacra, if you want to be fancy about it—rather than the things themselves. We have entered a hyperreal era where simulacra come before, and therefore define, that which we call real. To put it in the language of authenticity: the media that is essential to constructive authenticity has now come to influence the character and selection of subjects that might be chosen for authenticity peddling in the first place.

Consider again the difference between @upstatenymemes and Upstate Curious: they each have wildly diverging descriptions of the region and yet both are true simultaneously. The latter, however, sits more nicely in the pantheon of marketable places, whereas the former reminds us that the Capital Region is just like everywhere else. The only way both can be true is if we take for granted the fake Ecclesiastes quote[78] that acts as epigraph to Baudrillard's *Simulacra and Simulation*: "The simulacrum is never what hides the truth—it is truth that hides the fact that there is none. The simulacrum is true."

A DAY IN THE LIFE OF THE CITY AUTHENTIC

In this chapter I have tried to show how the City Authentic actually works. Lifestyle branding and financial speculation have come together to make a heady brew of seeming existential fulfillment and return on investment amid declining rates of profit and increasing alienation. I still don't feel, however, that I've fully described where it's all going because all the pieces aren't quite there yet. I think a short vignette of speculative fiction might do more to explain how this all ties together. So, if you'll indulge me by way of conclusion, let's look at a very possible near-future scenario:

Rosa must sleep. The dim screen on her watch suggests a breathing exercise and a discount for melatonin. She takes neither. There will be no sleep until she decides: live in Chico, California, or Athens, Georgia. Otherwise, she is off to the nearest labor campus. The Waterford, New York, data center is up and running—another job well done—but now she had to move to the next job. Her last payment came in at noon today. She watched it blink into her bank account and divide like a cell into payments for her rented apartment, the meal subscription plan, the ice-fishing classes she was really getting into, and the porn that she had been meaning to cancel. What had been a healthy paycheck is now a dozen different prepaid subscription packages.

She always made sure to watch the payments clear in real time. This sour ritual helped Rosa remember where her efforts went and what she got in return. This time a little note popped up after the cells did all their dividing: "There are no scheduled credits for your account. If a new credit is not scheduled in three days, your subscriptions will be automatically removed for your convenience. Now that's savings!"

Her gig dashboard is open, with Chico and Athens sitting under big, bold text that reads "CURRENT OFFERS." Like a midnight refrigerator grazer, she searches the Chico listings for new morsels, but it's the same bad choices that were there two hours ago: too-small apartments next to busy highways and free mountain biking lessons.

Instead of looking at Athens again, she closes the dashboard entirely and starts scrolling through the images and videos her friends are watching and sharing. A young girl is rolling her eyes at her mom just off camera. The caption floating above her head reads, "Millennial Mom telling me to keep a bank balance instead of subbing to work clothes." Rosa remembers having the same fight with her mother. "No one keeps a bank balance, Mom. That's for old rich people!" She gives it a heart and flicks her finger up on the screen to beckon a new video from the ether.

The next is an old man skateboarding down a tree-lined road. "This is Chico, baby!" he yells into his camera before dousing himself with milk. She'll have to figure out what the milk thing is later. Flick. A house crumbles underneath the massive, webbed foot of a bright yellow duck. The duck's bill opens, and the loud, resonant sound of a truck horn comes out, causing the leaves in the trees to shiver. Bright purple bubbly text scrolls up from the bottom of the screen: "Athens Music Cabal Has It All." Flick.

An unfamiliar lock screen fills her phone. A voice with the slightest hint of simulated humanity states flatly, "This really just happened to me. Can't believe I was recording it." A message notification pops up on the screen: "DAD: She'll always be with us, honey. I know it's hard. I miss your mother too, but you can't just skip out on work like that." The message soon gets pushed down as an avalanche of unsubscription notifications piles up. First it's music, followed by meal deliveries, then an eviction notice, all within seconds of each other. For just a moment the screen goes blank and in white text, it reads, "Screen recording ended." Flick!

Rosa opens the preview for Athens again. The housing rental companies are cheaper; there are lots of ads for festivals (including the Athens Music Cabal); and the job ad is identical to the one in Chico. She opens both offers so she can compare. Under "vibes," Chico is described as "outdoorsy, crusty, hip, resilient, TexMex, ReIndustrial." Athens is "South, foodie, Indie, FolkTrip, Post-National." The last two places Rosa had lived in were described as Post-National. and she couldn't tell what they held in common except a predilection among long-term residents to call soccer *fútbol*.

Rosa had never lived in a place tagged "ReIndustrial." She taps and is greeted with a board of images, some clothing labels, and a cocktail list. There's a write-up in her favorite magazine that she had never noticed about the ReIndustrial trend and how it had been started by a failed unionization drive that made some very cool merch to raise money for the strike fund. It all seems enticing, so she opens up a private tab and does a search for other places labeled ReIndustrial. She finds a few cities that she was hoping would come up in the offer list but didn't, including Green Bay, Houston, and Charleston. She goes back to the offer listing and sees that it has now changed for the first time, ever so slightly. The pay has gone up half a percent and there's a new apartment listing that includes discounts at the clinic on the ground floor.

A sigh that feels as though it came from her shoulders as much as from her mouth fills the space between her face and the screen. Rosa takes a long hard look at the fishing poles propped up in the corner of the room. She notices that renting a mountain bike costs about as much as the poles, and she could probably halve her workout subscription too. After a quick search to figure out what the milk thing was all about—nothing worth factoring into the decision—she accepts the offer.

CHAPTER 6

What Is to Be Done?

There is a question I've had for most of my life that I deeply want answered. Few have proffered a satisfying answer. The answer could tie together everything we have explored together into a nice little bow. It would resolve and synthesize issues of political economy, culture, meaning, and place. The answer to this question could provide us all with a path toward a more egalitarian civilization while also maintaining the fun, creative entrepreneurship that so many people cite as the most important thing state provision cannot provide. With this answer I would sleep better at night.

The question is this: how do restaurants work in *Star Trek*? For those who don't know: the Earth-based, interplanetary United Federation of Planets is a communist utopia where there is no money and all basic needs are met, thanks largely to abundant free energy that, with a technology called replicators, can be converted to almost any kind of matter. There are, however, periodic complaints from characters that replicated food just isn't the same as that which is grown and prepared. Captain Benjamin Sisko swears that nothing that comes out of a machine is as good as his father's jambalaya.

You don't have to like *Star Trek* to appreciate the thought experiment it implies. If a civilization has the technology and material abundance to never exchange money for cooked food ever again, how would restaurants function? We don't go to restaurants *just* to satiate biological needs; we fulfill social needs (humans' or any space-faring civilization's) as well. Eateries and bars are places of culture, community, and creativity. Therefore, it seems logical that the focus would go from pushing product to creating a place that both host and guest find pleasing to be in. Daily concerns would move from profitability to something else: prestige, furthering the arts of cooking and hospitality, or preserving tradition.

But without money, how does a proprietor apportion access to the limited number of tabletops and handmade food? If you wanted some of that famous twenty-fourth century jambalaya and teleported on down to Sisko's Creole Kitchen, how easy would it be to get a table? Maybe there's a daily lottery for who gets in? First come, first served? Perhaps we are thinking too narrowly, and if the camera panned back from Sisko's restaurant, we would see thousands of other equally good restaurants that serve the same purpose. And absent a profit motive and capitalist land markets, we would likely not run up against issues like gentrification, cultural appropriation, or cartoonish facsimiles of cultures and cuisines. We would stop eating the other and finally nourish ourselves. Truly a utopia worth striving for.

My point here is this: once we eliminate all the thirst games and wage slavery, how will cultural institutions function? One answer can be found at Saint-Sixtus Abbey in Westvleteren, Flanders. It is here that, some say, the best beer in the world is brewed. The monks sell their world-renowned beer in only one way: through a reservation system on their website that allows customers to pick up the beer in person from the abbey, sometimes months after making the initial reservation. They go to great lengths to make sure it is not resold in stores at a markup. The three different kinds of beer are meant to be sold only at the "correct" price set by the monks. They give preference to new customers over returning ones and limit purchases to only three crates. Why do this? Because, as their website says, "We brew to live. We do not live to brew." Their interests simply lie elsewhere—in charity work and prayer—and the money from the beer is meant to support that and nothing else.[1]

Clearly, some people do live to brew. They enjoy the process and the product. So not everyone would live and work like these monks, but what Saint-Sixtus Abbey and Sisko's Creole Kitchen demonstrate is that we must exercise a good bit of imagination when it comes to not only what goes on inside cultural institutions, but also what we do with the rest of our lives. By now (unless you're the kind of person that reads the conclusion of a book first), it should be clear that the City Authentic is deeply intertwined in not just local economics but our identities and worldview and the culture that shapes all of these. We seek out authentic experiences because we want a break from modern drudgery and to experience something untouched by marketing and the profit motive. But because fulfillment of this desire is so valuable, our search for authenticity is "precorporated," a word coined by the cultural theorist Mark Fisher to describe the "pre-emptive formatting and shaping" of community and human desire into yet another subgenre or aesthetic to buy.[2] It stands to reason, then, that to truly break free from the City Authentic, we have to not only rethink cultural planning and its attendant industries, but we need to rethink modernity itself.

This final chapter will accomplish two things. First, we're going to look at alternatives to the upgraded growth machine. Instead of an ever-growing capitalist economy that demands more bodies and buildings be thrown into its insatiable maw, the immediately following section will trace out some promising leads for more stable, reasonable local economies. This will involve a study of state-financed worker cooperatives and unions' once-powerful ability to build housing for its members.

Although the bulk of this final chapter is grounded in the material changes necessary for creating life-sustaining twenty-first-century cities, this book will close on a more cerebral note. We cannot substantially change our cities without changing ourselves too. And this transformation goes in both directions: if we substantially change how cities work, we will also become a different kind of people and vice versa. That's why I have chosen to end on a humanist note: confronting not just what kinds of cities we want to build but what sorts of humans they will nurture.

WHO RULES?

If there is one thing that capitalists and Marxists agree on, it is that American cities' home rule laws must go. The problem is not that cities lack power to say what happens within their borders, rather it is the *structure of power* across the whole landscape that is all wrong. Similarly, IDAs and chambers of commerce are strongly incentivized to compete in the thirst games, resulting in a race to the bottom for public revenue, environmental protections, and labor standards. The result, as we have seen, is that corporations make out like bandits and everyone else gets less than they would have if they'd worked together. The home rule question—how can power over economic development be reorganized to serve people over capital?—must be addressed.

New York's capitalists answered the home rule question with economic development councils, where power players are strongly incentivized to hammer out regional priorities among themselves and dole out state money in concert with their own plans for private investment. As far as organizational design goes, this is a very effective system, which has done a very good job at juicing the growth machine: increasing land prices and rents and staving off the worst of population loss to Sunbelt cities. It also recognizes the reality that leaders of private firms are responsible for the well-being of thousands if not millions more people than those directly under their employ. As my interlocutors pointed out, getting them all in one, publicly announced meeting could be understood as a form of harm reduction: these people make deals anyway, so why not induce them to do it out in the open in a more organized and civically minded way?

A Marxist may respond like this: no one elected these people, and not only do we not share priorities, much of their profit-seeking interests are in *direct opposition* to most of the population. The state helping capitalists organize how they'll extract value from workers and rape the land is not progress. This is just an exercise in greasing the skids that will deliver us to further immiseration. An upgraded growth machine is a machine better at growing, not at nurturing or anything else having to do with human flourishing and social reproduction.

This leads to a few important questions: How do we preserve the regional scale of the Economic Development Councils (EDCs) while democratizing who gets to serve on them? What can be done to ensure whoever is on these councils thinks about human welfare before profit? What new power configuration replaces home rule, and how do we ensure that it fosters cooperation among common people and their representatives, rather than competition that serves a wealthy few? I remain convinced that the best and fullest answers to these questions get worked out in situ, through struggle and political victory. There are, however, some easy mistakes to avoid that I want to list here.

While it seems that the quickest, most effective route to democracy would be the direct election of Economic Development Council members, this would be catastrophic. Popular election of EDC members would inevitably result in some of the most corrupt, bought-and-paid-for elections in human history. There is simply too much at stake and the scale would be small enough that too few journalists would be able to cover them and keep everyone honest. Even if there were more robust monitoring and plenty of transparency laws, we know from chapter 4 that elected officials are already an integral part of, not a check on, the growth machine.

Another dead end would be to increase the proportion of higher-education and nonprofit sector leaders to serve on EDCs. Not only are both industries just as entrenched in the growth machine as any other, but it may even be necessary to—all else being equal—*reduce* the amount of participation of university and nonprofit leaders. Case in point: as of 2021, every EDC had a university or community college leader as one of the cochairs and there has been no appreciable difference in their behavior. Moreover, while working on this book, I was an untenured faculty member of the University at Albany, SUNY, which made it somewhat awkward, if not difficult, to be critical of the CREDC given that it was cochaired by the president of that institution. In the interest of transparency, I messaged the president's office about this book project, requesting an interview. It was the only interview request in my research that was turned down. With the protections of tenure eroding, it would be a mistake to let the bosses of universities have more responsibility that cannot be studied critically by their employees. The same goes for news organizations, nonprofits, and nongovernmental organizations with missions that include writing reports and investigating inequality. In their current form, none of these institutions can increase democratic control.

Universities, along with local media and trade unions, have roles to play in the growth machine too and are incentivized to grow the city based on exchange value just as much as for-profit companies, if not more since their road to increased revenue and profitability is hemmed in by the geographic footprint of the region. None of these institutions, which may appear at least adjacent to common people's interests, are properly situated to defend them. It may be the case then that the EDCs are not the first site of reform here. We need to look at the institutions just below the development councils.

WHOEVER OWNS

The Cleveland Foundation is the oldest community foundation in the country. Founded in 1914, it is a charity organization that raises money for social projects. There are over seven hundred such foundations across the country—most of which are much younger—serving their respective communities; together, they manage an estimated $30 billion.[3] In 2007 the Cleveland Foundation embarked on a unique economic development strategy called the Greater University Circle Initiative. The foundation and municipal governments worked to convince the area's hospitals and universities to act as guaranteed customers for new worker co-ops, financed with the same kinds of financing usually reserved for big developers and corporate employers. Evergreen Cooperatives, the umbrella corporation that was eventually created to house the commercial laundry, greenhouse, and solar installation companies created from this initiative, have received national attention.

Worker-owned co-ops are great in that they offer pay and benefits competitive with private companies as well as the opportunity to build equity in the company through shares that accrue over time. The Evergreen model is different in that "rather than concentrate on workforce training for employment opportunities that are largely unavailable to low-skill and low-income workers, the Evergreen Initiative first creates the jobs, and then recruits and trains local residents to take them."[4] These are not just local people, but people in neighborhoods and with backgrounds that are regularly left out of the job market. As of September 2016, all three cooperatives employed a total of 119 people, 83 percent of whom are Cleveland residents, 84 percent are minorities, and 39 percent are formerly incarcerated people.[5]

There are mistakes worth learning from as well. "The Evergreen model," writes Stacey Sutton, associate professor of Urban Planning and Policy at the University of Illinois, Chicago, "is a cautionary tale for . . . cities that prioritize large-scale, institutional-led cooperatives that fail to integrate community groups and transition ownership early on." The universities and hospitals lined up to be the first big customers for these companies had a hard time ending contracts with previous suppliers, restricting necessary cash flows at critical moments. With everything else in place, it understandably discouraged the worker-owners, who Sutton predicts "will likely become disenchanted by the slow pace of establishing economic democracy and blame the cooperative model when what hindered Evergreen was overreliance on anchor institutions for market opportunities."[6] She also points out that only 26 percent of the workers at these cooperatives have actually become worker-owners. The rest are all just regular employees because they either have not worked there long enough or have not met some other qualification for owner status.

Still though, another benefit of the Evergreen Cooperative model is that it is already seemingly "compatible" with the REDC system. Rochester imported it in 2015 as part of its Market Driven Community Cooperatives Corporation incubator program. In 2018 it rebranded to the catchier OWN Rochester (OWN stands for Owner Worker Network) and now has two firms: an LED lighting installation company and a floor care and custodial business. OWN Rochester was built off $300,000 in philanthropic donations and $350,000 of city money.[7] But even with the regional priority-setting power of the REDC, securing the patronage of area institutions was even more difficult than it was in Cleveland. In an interview, OWN Rochester CEO Katie Washington described the early days of the co-ops as a "rude awakening. We went into it thinking we had all these anchor institutions represented on our board [of directors, so] we'll have no problem getting work, and as it turned out, we had great difficulty getting the business going."[8] The success of the worker cooperatives did not outrank board directors' desire to cut costs at their day jobs.

Another avenue might be more successful. Both Evergreen and OWN Rochester began as "incubators" building co-ops from the ground up, but Washington says that the "silver tsunami" of retiring business owners has a lot of potential:

> We realized very quickly that the best strategy for us is to go into conversions. . . . That is our current strategy now and that is where we plan on going in the future. . . . We have actually been very fortunate in that we have a revolving loan fund that we received from a partnership that we have with the City of Rochester and our local Rochester Economic Development Corporation that allows us to have funds to apply towards the purchases of businesses.[9]

Evergreen Cooperatives has also launched a fund for employee ownership that finances the conversion of small businesses into employee-owned cooperatives. During the pandemic, it advertised "an exit strategy for business owners." The fund stated it was "looking to buy good companies that were performing well in their industry, pre-pandemic, even though their performance has since taken a hit by the crisis. And here's the crucial point: If you have taken a hit from the pandemic, we will value your company by looking only at your pre-coronavirus performance. That means no pandemic penalty."[10] Since that post, it has announced the conversion of an insulation business and a coffee shop.

This conversion strategy syncs nicely with Sutton's recommendation that rather than relying on the largesse of political leaders and powerful institutions (as was necessary in Cleveland and Rochester), cities build "enabling environments" where worker co-ops are supported from the ground up, rather than being pieced together by consultants and political leaders. Revolving loan funds and other forms of "patient capital"[11] that help employees buy companies from their present owners are both relatively low risk and equitable for all involved. They are especially appropriate at a time where younger people are saddled with debt or otherwise cannot get access to the kinds of credit that previous generations received to build their businesses.

Workplace democracy, at least one of whose forms is the worker cooperative, can provide both a constituency and pool of qualified candidates for REDC board seats and appointments to other community control systems. A democratic economy, if it is going to avoid the worst aspects of the thirst games, must mature at these lower levels and build upward. Otherwise, we are just building new spectacular nepotism contests that catapult people to the top of a patronage network. This slow buildup is essential not only because it can ensure more face-to-face, holistic relationships among workers, but it also socializes people into a more democratic society where they are better trained to make decisions that impact others. A mature enabling environment for worker cooperatives would not only secure funding for conversions, but it would also normalize the idea of worker ownership and start to assert authority over community control systems, thus tipping more resources to their advantage. Media, real estate, and elected and appointed boards would start to behave in ways that redound to the benefit of worker owners, not capitalists.

WHICH SIDE ARE YOU ON?

The Albany area enjoys the highest union density in the country at 34.6 percent[12] (compared to a national average of 10.8 percent), thanks largely to a handful of dominant employers: state offices, universities, and hospitals. Unions have long been a powerful force for economic stability and workplace democracy, and they can continue to serve that function today. Unionizing larger firms can be a nice complement to the worker ownership models in small businesses. Not only do worker ownership and unionization democratize the workplace and raise the standard of living, but unions build a significant backbench of leaders that have an intimate understanding of the issues and needs of the region.

Unionizing big employers can be a huge boon to economic development if it means increasing the baseline pay of a major employer in a region. For example, Albany Medical Center (AMC), which has been well-represented on the CREDC fought a protracted three-year battle with its nurses after they voted to unionize with New York State Nurses Association (NYSNA) in 2018. As a member of the Troy Area Labor Council, I walked the picket in solidarity and helped swell their ranks during a day-long strike in the winter of 2021. In that time, I heard some disturbing things. The nurses claimed that AMC took advantage of their regional monopoly as the only level-1 trauma center in the region to pay low wages. Nurses need experience in trauma centers for professional development, so it was very common for nurses to take the pay cut to work at AMC while they got the experience they needed, only to leave for better wages elsewhere. This meant perennial under-staffing and high turnover. Michael Fitzsimmons, a registered nurse at the cardiac ICU and member of the negotiations committee put all this in context in an interview with the labor magazine *Strikewave*:

> Our nurses definitely understand Albany Med and the importance it plays. 10,000 employees, 2,000 nurses, $1.2 billion operation—that precedes its mergers with Hudson [Columbia Memorial Hospital], Glens Falls [Hospital in Glens Falls], and Saratoga Hospital [in Saratoga Springs] and all the clin-ics opening up everywhere. Ahead of the strike, Albany Med management bought a full page ad in the newspaper [stating there would be no interrup-tions in service during the strike] and a lot of the nurses saw that. They understand this is not only important for ourselves but that it's also part of a bigger picture. They pick up on it at the picket lines with the solidarity we get from local labor. We're in this big fight and it's hard, but we have to hang in there because of who we are up against. We're fighting for our commu-nity, for our patients. We feel that deeply.[13]

The nurses eventually prevailed, but what this underscores is that CREDC members cannot, by virtue of the institutional positions they hold, simultaneously care for the region and the interests of their capi-talist enterprises. James Barba, as cochair of the CREDC from 2012 to 2017, was tasked with raising the profile of the region and attracting high-paid professionals from bigger cities. However, in his role as CEO of Albany Medical Center (he retired in 2020), he was suppressing wages, short-staffing his facilities, and violating human trafficking laws even during a pandemic.[14] The same goes for state-run organizations like my own University at Albany. Even though the university's presi-dents have served on the CREDC for most of the years of its existence, hiring for full-time faculty actually went *down* after the 2008 recession budget cuts as reliance on tuition instead of direct state aid doubled.[15] This means that while successive university presidents worked on the CREDC to attract a highly educated labor pool that would fill jobs in

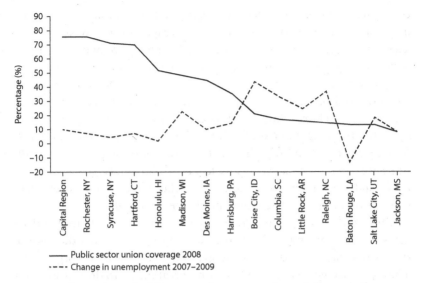

FIGURE 7. Comparison of public sector union concentration and changes in the unemployment rate in selected cities. Sources: U.S. Census; Barry T. Hirsch and David A. Macpherson (2019), unionstats.gsu.edu.

advanced manufacturing, healthcare, and creative industries, they made attaining that training more expensive and hired fewer people in their own institution both to do these jobs and to train others. The only people in the appropriate position to care for and defend the economic health of a region are those looking out for the interests of thousands of workers, not a handful of board members or investors.

Recall that Shelby Schneider attributed the Capital Region's resiliency through the 2008 recession to high public-sector employment. While that did likely help, figure 7 shows that being a capital city with high public-sector employment does not ensure economic resilience. I took all the cities that CEG studied in its *Capital Region Indicators: Benchmarking Progress in New York's Capital Region* report (see "A Solid Return on Investment" in chapter 2) and arranged them in order of most to least union coverage in the public sector as of 2008, according to Hirsch and Macpherson's Union Membership and Coverage Database,[16] and then compared that to the change in overall unemployment from 2007 and 2009. While there are many other factors to consider, including the size of government in these respective states both in absolute terms and in relation to the private sector, the health of the unions in these states, and the historical contingencies of each regional economy, one can see a general relationship to union coverage and unemployment, especially once union coverage dips below 50 percent. The only outlier here is Baton Rouge, which had a public-sector labor force of only 67,486 compared to 407,863 for Albany, a very small sample size used to calculate coverage, and a statewide increase in construction and business repatriation.[17] Much of this is likely thanks to the rebuilding effort following Hurricane Katrina, which opened up an opportunity for spatial fixes for capital and all the attendant business-friendly policies that go with it. All this makes sense given that recessions are often used as excuses by leaders to introduce austerity measures, and so union protections, not the largesse of government expenditure, is a better determinant of recession resiliency.

Outside the workplace, area labor federations are venues for delegates of different unions in the region to meet and discuss the state of their workplace, coordinate strategy, and share ideas for organizing. These can also be, in addition to co-ops, great places to draw leaders for IDAs, EDCs, and other community control system organizations.

Still though, nothing about unions or worker cooperatives guarantees progressive or anti-capitalist politics; they only open the door for them. It is essential that any coordinated effort to influence the community control system keep this in mind and develop a long-term plan for power that seeds the vast network of elected and appointed positions in unions, cooperative boards, and beyond. Recall also that the president of the Greater Capital Region Building Trades Council has served on the CREDC since its inception and yet unions were only mentioned once, in the first CREDC progress report, and never again. Many cities have rules that require their IDAs to have union representation, but the requirements are followed to the letter, rather than the spirit, of the law. In Troy, for example, the union seat on the IDA is filled by a city employee who just happens to be a member of Civil Service Employees Association (CSEA).

I am not suggesting a palace coup, where today's unions take over community control systems and operate them under the same rubrics and goals as bosses presently do. What we need are more unions, and those unions must be ideologically grounded in the belief that workers should democratically control a peaceful, human-centered economy.

What about housing? One of the perennial problems of cities—regardless of their economic, social, or political order—is how to move people from their housing to sites of productive labor. Commutes in American cities today are long, arduous, and dangerous journeys on crumbling roads in expensive cars. Mass transit is poorly funded and rarely faster or more convenient than the worst car drive. In the Soviet Union, following the reconstruction from World War II, the government prioritized building and operating factories and was therefore able to establish sites of work faster than housing. This meant the parts of the government responsible for housing would take years, sometimes decades, to replace slap-dash dorms with more permanent housing.[18]

What frustrates most efforts to link affordable housing to jobs is that convenient transportation is highly desirable and therefore raises prices on the land around it, effectively displacing the very people the transportation was meant to help. Therefore, keeping housing prices insulated from land markets is critical for disrupting the worst aspects of the City Authentic and its attendant gentrification. The only question is how to do it. As with worker cooperatives, government can be both a provider of patient capital and an instigator of grassroots organizing. Community land trusts have been an effective means of urban development, especially in Rust Belt regions that have a lot of vacant buildings and brownfield sites that traditional development financing is incapable of profitably using. Community land trusts are organizations that own land and lease access to the building rights on top of it, effectively preventing excessive land price increases and retaining control over how shelter is allocated. Housing co-ops, where residents own shares in a company that owns both the building and the land it sits on, are also very effective at stabilizing prices while also providing some equity to individuals.

Labor unions have a significant role to play here as both potential financing partners and incubators for leadership. Co-op City in the Bronx was built for and financed by unions and state loans secured through the Mitchell-Lama program, in partnership with Robert Moses's constellation of authorities, which would eventually provide the legal grounds for the community control systems that were the subject of chapter 5. This kind of cooperation between state financing and union organizing must be reinvigorated because even today the fruits of that work provide the most racially integrated, affordable housing in the country. Nothing else has even come close, in the American context, to housing so many people in a sustainably affordable way.

THE ART OF WORK IN THE AGE OF
DIGITAL REPRODUCTION

What is it all for? What is the animating idea that could move people to put aside the comfort of cynicism and organize their workplace, run for office, and start a co-op? Much of this is already happening. Young progressives, many inspired by Bernie Sanders's campaigns for the presidency, are running for and attaining public office. There are robust unionization efforts in Starbucks cafes and Amazon warehouses, the likes of which have not been seen in a lifetime. What, though, could unify these trends into a broad social movement recognized as such? Put another way: even though the American left has mainly organized around resistance and counterculture, what would be something worth conforming to? How do we build the hegemonic ideas that hold together a burgeoning new order? The City Authentic, as I have described it in this book, is the latest form of capitalist urban development and so it will take nothing less than a new society to defeat it.

I introduced the City Authentic as a set of policies, practices, and ideas that leverage our modern desires for meaning and belonging to drive economic development. Meme accounts running ads for real estate agents, well-connected councils bankrolling algorithmically targeted media blitzes, and entire apps designed to establish hip, urban archipelagos within a rural county are all proof enough that the City Authentic is an economic force to be reckoned with. But what do we do about the psychic toll of all this? The paradox I introduced in chapter 1 and followed throughout the book—that the search for meaning in cities' amenities and landscapes begets a cynical, postmodern tapestry of symbols, brands, and algorithmically selected aesthetic motifs that are anything but unique or meaningful—is not something that automatically goes away with a change in the material base of labor. We can still yearn for meaning amid plenty; indeed, the yearning becomes ever greater and more prescient as other, more basic needs are met. Therefore, we have to assess the political dimensions of the City Authentic beyond their ability to spatially fix surplus capital, define monopoly rent opportunities, and maintain the upgraded growth machine.

Walter Benjamin's famous 1936 essay "The Work of Art in the Age of Mechanical Reproduction" posits that the context and uniqueness of a piece of handmade art, what he calls its "aura," is lost when something is near-infinitely reproducible. A painting or a sculpture can be copied or forged—which does nothing to the aura of the original—but a photograph has no original, only a negative to develop and therefore has no original aura. If you know this essay, this is most likely the part you remember. The less repeated portion is the political upshot of this phenomenon. Because reproduced images allow for mass consumption of the same piece of media, it follows that the producers of media make things that the masses can appreciate. But because movies and even photographs have no aura to contemplate, they must be arresting regardless of context and so they are attention-grabbing rather than thought-provoking.

It is from this shift—from unique artworks in a specific context worthy of contemplation to mass-produced art meant to be understood in any condition—that politics, according to Benjamin, replaces the traditional ritualistic function of art. Because Benjamin is writing in Europe in the 1930s, he gives us only two opposing political formations to consider: communism seeks to politicize art while fascism aestheticizes politics. In so doing, the latter,

> attempts to organize the newly created proletarian masses without affecting the property structure which the masses strive to eliminate. Fascism sees its salvation in giving these masses not their right, but instead a chance to express themselves. The masses have a right to change property relations; Fascism seeks to give them an expression while preserving property. The logical result of Fascism is the introduction of aesthetics into political life.[19]

It can be added that contemporary liberals attempt, with varying degrees of success, to *replace* politics with art. Clearly, I am a fan of using fiction in conjunction with theory and history to spin a compelling narrative about future political projects. What is truly dangerous though—and most important to the City Authentic—is the magical thinking that public art and other forms of creative expression are useful starting points for, if not sufficient resolution to, the issues of inequality in cities. Art as a replacement, rather than an entry point, for politics gets it precisely backward. The political program of Mulgan and Worpole (to say nothing of the constructivist art and architecture movement of early Soviet society that Benjamin was likely thinking of) saw politicizing art as a means toward political organizing. Cities and corporations have done a good job of appropriating the image and culture of marginalized groups and using this further exploitation through commodification of ethnic cultures as proof of substantial political change when none has taken place.

We have seen how city leaders, eager to be the elected equivalent of the weekend dad, green-lit the infrastructure and attendant institutions of creative-class leisure and art. These projects were easy to implement because they had no politically powerful opponent—no one else with clout had urban redevelopment ideas. The safe, vapid art of this era did more to signal that a place was ready to be gentrified than to express any specific idea. Art-as-politics has been devastating for both politics and art.

How easy, though, is it to slip from a liberal's relationship to art to a fascist's? Can one replace politics with art only to eventually find oneself aestheticizing politics as Benjamin described? David Harvey argues that the turn toward arts- and culture-fueled economic development can induce progressivism but can also "easily veer into local, regional or nationalist identity politics of the neofascist sort of which there are already far too many troubling signs throughout much of Europe as well as elsewhere."[20]

Still though, Harvey has hope that "by seeking to trade on values of authenticity, locality, history, culture, collective memories and tradition [capitalists] open a space for political thought and action within which socialist alternatives can be both devised and pursued." He concludes by listing a few promising examples of culture and art that do "not trade on monopoly rents in particular or cave in to multinational capitalism in general,"[21] such as Red Bologna of the sixties and seventies or turn-of-the-twenty-first-century Porto Alegre, where the Brazilian Workers' Party has been developing its own socialist cultural program.

Sharon Zukin is also guardedly optimistic that authenticity can be used to "reshape the rights of ownership." Declaring a neighborhood "is authentic suggests that the group that makes the claim knows what to do with, how best to represent, its 'authentic' character."[22] Citing Benjamin and the religious contemplation inherent to the origins of art's aura, Zukin suggests that communities take control over what is deemed "authentic" and reserve it for communities' attachment to place rather than mere aesthetics and experiences.

To further complicate things, a study in Norway about perceived authenticity of political candidates found that "populist right-wing politicians were overrepresented among those politicians mentioned by voters as being themselves." But that may have more to do with populism than political orientation because "populism is characterized by anti-elitism, spontaneity, and outspokenness, which are also strategies to construct authenticity, and in a mediated environment which favors the authentic, populist politicians might get a strategic advantage."[23]

I am not as optimistic about art and authenticity's political ambivalence. More specifically, I believe that the best course of action is to dispense with authenticity talk altogether. Authenticity is a poison pill at the end of a long rat race. Nothing short of dispensing with the inherently capitalist notion of authenticity will give us relief. Both the intellectual history of authenticity and the recent scholarship on how authenticity behaves in media and tourism settings are indicative of an irredeemable system of striving and false hope. Rather than continue the modernist project of building an authentic self through the deft navigation of expectations, performance, and urban settings, I would contend that we need something genuinely new that leaves the capitalist centuries behind.

A postauthentic order—and by extension the postauthentic city—would have to reimagine nearly everything about identity formation, consumption, and culture. Such a society should seem alien, but exciting—a world of new possibilities that foretell a civilization based in compassion, care, and cooperation, where ambition is moderate, tempered by the needs of the moment, not the ego. What is authenticity? It is nothing at all.

CODA: A POSTAUTHENTIC ORDER

Rosa wakes up in a bed made of down and something else that was installed last year that she doesn't understand. There's a pamphlet somewhere around here that explains why it is better but she can't find it. No matter though, her mothers' linen sheets can make anything feel like a cradle. She pads down to the living room with her favorite mug, a toothbrush, and a few ideas for how she'll spend the day.

The living room is busy. Three hundred people are spending the morning sitting at tables of all different sizes, organized under several terraces that host a never-ending farmers' market selling everything from apples to dresses. The corn this year is particularly good and has been selling out fast. The grocers look halfway to sold out as hungry customers take the corn and turn around to the cooking booths, where they hand their recently purchased ears to someone who will make it into elote, fritters, or breakfast tostadas. A band must have set up just outside the building because over the din of breakfast is the muffled sound of live music. Hopefully, there is some left for lunch because Rosa doesn't want it for breakfast: she doesn't want kernels in her teeth when meeting her new coworkers. She descends a staircase while making mental notes of how long the line is at the pancake station and how much her agriculture credits are trading for. Not much today, so breakfast will be more expensive than usual.

She finds an unused private bathroom at the base of the stairs and freshens up. Back in the living room, she gets her pancakes, fills her mug with coffee, and sits down at an empty table for three but is soon joined by friends Jacob and Alaya. "That must have cost you an arm and a leg," the latter says pointing to Rosa's plate.

"Don't get me started. Dale has been riding our ass at the orchard, but our credits still suck against services. Glad I'm cutting my time there in half and switching to phone repair. I need something other than agricredits in my wallet."

"A fresh start doesn't hurt either!" Jacob adds.

"Sure. Still nervous though."

"That sounds like you but you'll do fine," Jacob reassures her while distracted by a gaggle of children screaming and playing with a dog two tables over. He's lived in three different cities, making him the best travelled person at the table despite also being the youngest. It's a distinction that has earned him skepticism from most people, which may be why he'd never climbed higher than house delegate. Jacob's flitting eyes reminded Rosa of a drunk conversation they'd had two nights prior. It was cold and he wouldn't stop looking at the fire they'd built. "I don't like power and when it shows up at my doorstep, I find a new door. In the back. I go through the back door, where power can't find me."

The memory scatters and, desperate to not think of herself, Rosa turns to Alaya. "Speaking of doing fine, congrats on the vote yesterday."

"Thanks! I really appreciate you sending those letters." Alaya said in that sincere voice that helped her earn a spot at the regional planning council. "No one thinks an artist is going to have a knack for numbers, and your recommendation really did the trick."

The three friends commiserate about the strains of the twenty-hour workweek, make plans to get drunk around a fire again soon, while the weather is still crisp, and wish each other luck at their new endeavors. Jacob, characteristically, is the first to clear his tray and catch the train to work. Alaya soon turns somber, and Rosa knows few things earn this kind of response from her friend. "No one wants to say it, but at least two hundred people are going to have to move, maybe more." Rosa's eyes get wide. She knew the housing was crowded but not that crowded. "Construction crews are too busy. We have a request out but they're not gonna get to building another complex here for a year, at best. As soon as I got on the council, they handed me their first incentive offer that they're gonna circulate next week. It's okay but I don't think it's going to be enough to get that many people to pick up and go. The moving cost vouchers are generous, but no one wants to move this close to the holidays at any price. The New Year season is gonna be tight. Visitors are gonna have hard time finding rooms."

"Maybe I'll go." The short sentence floated between the women before falling like a stone on the table. Alaya's eyes move as if to follow the words to the floor before her hands come up to catch her head. "Don't be like that. I'm already starting a new job. It'd be easier for me than most!" Alaya counters that before she asks anyone to leave, she will give up her room—and her new seat on the council—to someone else.

The two fight, each accusing the other of being generous to a fault. It is a sad, beautiful argument that will ultimately end in stalemate, but they do not know that yet. Their table becomes the loudest one in the room. Louder than the children with their dog. Louder than the sizzle of ripping-hot grills full of elote or the bands' muted rhythms coming from just outside. It is a fight of recognition, each wanting to be seen as something more than themselves. They have been offered a chance at something so much bigger than a new city, a new life, or a new job. They will both, in due time, get their chance to give willingly to a society that they love and that loves them back all the more.

Notes

CHAPTER 1

1. "Move Your Business | The Capital Region's New Frontier," Fulton County Industrial Development Agency, https://capitalregionsnewfrontier.com /move-your-business/.

2. Dave Lawler, "A World of Boomtowns," *Axios*, August 16, 2018, https:// www.axios.com/2018/08/16/population-of-world-cities-growing-urbanization.

3. See David A. Banks, "The Edifice Complex," *Real Life*, October 18, 2016, https://reallifemag.com/the-edifice-complex/.

4. Lark Street Business Improvement District (BID), Albany, NY (website), accessed January 22, 2021, https://larkstreetbid.org/.

5. "All About Historic Lark Street in Albany, NY," Hotspots, Albany.com., accessed January 22, 2021, https://www.albany.com/hotspot/lark-street/.

6. Paul Nelson, "As GE Continues to Fade, Schenectady Moves On," News, *Times Union* (NY Capital Region), October 19, 2018, https://www.timesunion .com/news/article/As-GE-continues-to-fade-Schenectady-aims-to-move-13293279 .php.

7. Paul Nelson, "Rivers Casino & Resort Opens in Schenectady," Local News, *Times Union* (NY Capital Region), February 8, 2017, https://www .timesunion.com/local/article/Hundreds-line-up-for-opening-of-Schenectady-casino-10917265.php. State aid listed in Capital Region Economic Development Council, "Capital Region Creates: 2018 Progress Report" (Albany, NY: Capital Region Economic Development Council, 2018), 38.

8. Schenectady Metroplex Development Authority, "New Center City Celebrates Five Years of Success in Downtown Schenectady—Schenectady Metroplex Development Authority," January 15, 2016, http://www.schenectadymetroplex .com/news/new-center-city-celebrates-five-years-of-success-in-downtown-schenectady/.

9. Unlike "Albany's Greenwich Village," I have heard people who at least appear to be made of flesh earnestly say "The New Brooklyn."

10. I'm serious about the hot dogs. The last Troy mayoral race ended with a question to the candidates about which hot dog vendor they preferred: Hot Dog Charlie's or Famous Lunch. The winning candidate said both.

11. "Move Your Business," Fulton County Industrial Development Agency, accessed January 14, 2021, https://capitalregionsnewfrontier.com/move-your-business/.

12. Others we could add are the City Humane, the City Functional, the Garden City Movement, and the Radiant City. I won't be covering these as they are variously smaller in their impact and less coherent in their outlook than the two we'll be looking at.

13. Peter Hall, *Cities of Tomorrow: An Intellectual History of Urban Planning and Design in the Twentieth Century*, 4th ed. (Oxford, UK; Malden, MA: Blackwell Publishers, 2014), 205–6.

14. Joan Cook, "Harland Bartholomew, 100, Dean of City Planners," Obituaries, *New York Times*, December 7, 1989, https://www.nytimes.com/1989/12/07/obituaries/harland-bartholomew-100-dean-of-city-planners.html.

15. See Daniel Serda, "Planning, Community, and Renewal: Harland Bartholomew Associates and the 1951 Armourdale Redevelopment Plan" (master's thesis, Massachusetts Institute of Technology, 1996).

16. Peter Hall's *Cities of Tomorrow* is widely regarded as the definitive history of urban planning, but a much more approachable book that covers the highlights is Wade Graham, *Dream Cities: Seven Urban Ideas That Shape the World* (New York: Harper, an imprint of HarperCollins Publishers, 2016).

17. David Harvey, *The Limits to Capital* (London: Verso, 2018), 426.

18. Kurt Andersen, "You Say You Want a Devolution?" *Vanity Fair*, January 2012, https://www.vanityfair.com/style/2012/01/prisoners-of-style-201201.

19. My favorite book on this topic, which doesn't quite fit here but is worth checking out is Wolfgang Schivelbusch, *The Railway Journey: The Industrialization of Time and Space in the 19th Century* (Berkeley: University of California Press, 1986).

20. Graham, *Dream Cities,* 59.

21. Lewis Mumford, "The City," in *Civilization in the United States: An Enquiry by Thirty Americans*, ed. H. E. Stearns (New York: J. Cape, 1922).

22. Nick Srnicek in *Platform Capitalism* (Cambridge, UK: Polity Press, 2017) writes: "The problem for capitalist firms that continues to the present day is that old business models were not particularly well designed to extract and use data. . . . A different business model was necessary if capitalist firms were to take full advantage of dwindling recording costs. . . . Often arising out of internal needs to handle data, platforms became an efficient way to monopolize, extract, analyze, and use the increasingly large amounts of data that were being recorded" (42–43).

23. Steven Pinker, "Is the World Getting Better or Worse? A Look at the Numbers, " TED Talk, May 21, 2018, https://youtu.be/yCm9NgobbEQ.

24. From Thomas Piketty's *Capital in the 21st Century* (Cambridge, MA: Belknap Press, 2014): "The only continent not in equilibrium is Africa, where a

substantial share of capital is owned by foreigners. According to the balance of payments data compiled since 1970 by the United Nations and other international organizations such as the World Bank and International Monetary Fund, the income of Africans is roughly 5 percent less than the continent's output (and as high as 10 percent lower in some individual countries)" (68).

25. Richard Florida rose to prominence in 2002 with the publication of *The Rise of the Creative Class*, which centered the needs and desires of upper-middle class creative professionals in economic development strategies. His 2017 book *The New Urban Crisis* detailed the extent to which his 15-year-old prescriptions had contributed to vast inequalities within and between American cities.

26. Raquel Rolnik, *Urban Warfare: Housing under the Empire of Finance*, trans. Felipe Hirschhorn (London: Verso, 2019), 4.

27. Harvey, *The Limits to Capital*, 427.

28. Harvey, 434.

29. To get the full effect of modernization, see Silvia Federici, "Women, Land-Struggles and Globalization: An International Perspective," *Journal of Asian and African Studies* 39, no. 1–2 (January 1, 2004).

30. See Rolnik, *Urban Warfare*, especially ch. 3.

31. See Neil Smith, "Toward a Theory of Gentrification A Back to the City Movement by Capital, Not People," Journal of the American Planning Association 45, no. 4 (October 1, 1979): 538–48, https://doi.org/10.1080 /01944367908977002.

32. Naomi Klein, *The Shock Doctrine: The Rise of Disaster Capitalism* (New York: Picador, 2008), 4.

33. See Neil Smith, *Uneven Development: Nature, Capital, and the Production of Space* (Oxford, UK: Blackwell, 1991), 148.

34. Realty Wired, "Most vacant zip codes in the United States in 2016, by ratio of vacant single-family homes with deceased owner to single-family homes in area," Statista, October 28, 2016, chart, accessed July 14, 2021.

35. Richard L. Florida, *The New Urban Crisis: How Our Cities Are Increasing Inequality, Deepening Segregation, and Failing the Middle Class—and What We Can Do about It* (New York: Basic Books, 2017).

36. U.S. Census Bureau, "Unemployment Rate for Civilian Population in Labor Force 16 Years and Over, 2019," table A17005, *American Community Survey 2019 (5-Year Estimates)*, https://www.socialexplorer.com/data/ACS2019_ 5yr/metadata?ds=SE&table=A17005.

37. U.S. Census Bureau, "Physical Housing Characteristics For Occupied Housing Units," table S2504, *American Community Survey 5-Year Estimates 2016–2020*.

38. Harvey, *The Limits to Capital*, 420.

39. The book's strange title is a play on the working-class novelist Alan Sillitoe's *Saturday Night and Sunday Morning*, which Mulgan and Worpole use to bring attention to the "long-standing tension between political seriousness and 'self-indulgent pleasure.'" To their intended audience of fairly well-educated leftists, the association with Sillitoe was meant to signal an allegiance to the everyman whose interests and attitudes were rarely seen on the BBC.

40. Geoff Mulgan and Ken Worpole, *Saturday Night or Sunday Morning? From Arts to Industry, New Forms of Cultural Policy*, Comedia Series 44 (London: Comedia Publishing Group, 1986), 74.

41. Quoted in Leif Weatherby, "Politics Is Downstream from Culture, Part 1: Right Turn to Narrative," *Hedgehog Review*, February 22, 2017, https://hedgehogreview.com/blog/infernal-machine/posts/politics-is-downstream-from-culture-part-1-right-turn-to-narrative.

42. See also Munira Mirza, *The Politics of Culture: The Case for Universalism* (London: Palgrave Macmillan UK, 2012).

43. Mulgan and Worpole, *Saturday Night or Sunday Morning?*, 109.

44. Mulgan and Worpole, 110.

45. Mulgan and Worpole, 43.

46. As quoted in Mulgan and Worpole, 38. I don't know what to do with this information, but it is also worth noting that this is extremely close to an apocryphal Henry Ford quote popularized by Steve Jobs: "If I'd ask customers what they wanted, they would've told me a faster horse." Jobs goes on to clarify that "people don't know what they want until you show it to them. That's why I never rely on market research. Our task is to read things that are not yet on the page." Perhaps this is just the garden variety paternalism of the rich and powerful, but it seems more important than that.

47. Raymond Williams, *Keywords: A Vocabulary of Culture and Society*, rev. ed. (New York: Oxford University Press, 1985), 90, quoted in Deborah Stevenson, *Cities of Culture: A Global Perspective* (New York: Routledge, Taylor & Francis Group, 2017), 152.

48. Stevenson, 57.

49. This definition is based heavily on Donald Macleod, "Cultural Commodification and Tourism: A Very Special Relationship," *Tourism Culture & Communication* 6, no. 2 (June 1, 2006): 71–84.

50. Stevenson, *Cities of Culture*.

51. Stevenson, 59.

52. Stevenson, 59.

53. Geoff Mulgan, "Ideas into Action," Ideas, *Geoff Mulgan*, accessed July 13, 2021, https://www.geoffmulgan.com/ideas.

54. Charles Landry, *The Creative City: A Toolkit for Urban Innovators*. (London: Earthscan Publications, 2000), 50.

55. See Jamie Peck, "Struggling with the Creative Class," *International Journal of Urban and Regional Research* 29, no. 4 (December 1, 2005): 740–70.

56. Peck, "Struggling with the Creative Class," 742.

57. Stevenson, *Cities of Culture*, 123.

58. Roger Luckhurst, "Cultural Governance, New Labour, and the British SF Boom," *Science Fiction Studies* 30, no. 3 (2003): 417–35, 420.

59. Quote from Luckhurst, "Cultural Governance," 422.

60. Geoff Mulgan, "Impact Investment, Arts and Culture: A Field—at Last—Comes of Age," *Geoff Mulgan* (blog), January 20, 2021, https://www.geoffmulgan.com/post/impact-investment-arts-and-culture-a-field-at-last-comes-of-age.

61. Sharon Zukin, *Naked City: The Death and Life of Authentic Urban Places* (Oxford: Oxford University Press, 2011), 2–3.

62. Zukin, *Naked City*, 3.

63. Sarah Banet-Weiser, *Authentic™: The Politics of Ambivalence in a Brand Culture* (New York: NYU Press, 2012), 110. See also Oli Mould's *Against Creativity* (London; Brooklyn: Verso, 2018).

64. Richard Florida, "The Creativity Bubble, " interview by Erin Schell, *Jacobin*, October 3, 2014, https://jacobinmag.com/2014/10/the-creativity-bubble.

65. Schumpeter was, at least, very wrong about Nazi Germany, telling the *Boston Globe* in 1933 that Germany under Hitler "looks much worse than she actually is; in a few months the Nazi Government will settle down to a more rational, conservative routine—and then Germany will become a power not only to respect but also, possibly, to fear." Quoted in Irwin Collier, "Harvard: Schumpeter Opines on Germany's Future under Hitler, 1933," *Economics in the Rear-View Mirror* (blog), July 15, 2021, http://www.irwincollier.com /harvard-schumpeter-opines-on-germanys-future-under-hitler-1933/. After the war, he opposed charging Nazis with war crimes because he "did not believe the Nazis had killed 6 million Jews, and his thinking that only 2 million had died seemed to make some kind of difference to him." From Robert Loring Allen, *Opening Doors: Life and Work of Joseph Schumpeter*, vol. 2 (New Brunswick: Transaction Publishers, 1994): 166. Quoted in Laurence S. Moss, "Robert Loring Allen's Biography of Joseph A. Schumpeter," ed. Robert Loring Allen, *The American Journal of Economics and Sociology* 52, no. 1 (1993): 112.

66. Florida, "The Creativity Bubble."

67. Bob Sullivan, "Millennials Spend Huge Amounts on Rent, Using Up 45% of Income Made by Age 30." *USA TODAY*, May 18, 2018, https://www .usatoday.com/story/money/personalfinance/real-estate/2018/05/18/millennials-spend-large-percentage-income-rent/609061002/.

68. U.S. Census Bureau, *Longitudinal Employer-Household Dynamics*, data, 2002–2017, https://lehd.ces.census.gov/data/.

69. Pam Allen, "Sandy Flooding Keeps Troy Wine Bar Dry for Now," *Albany (NY) Business Review*, October 31, 2012, https://www.bizjournals.com/albany /blog/2012/10/flooding-from-sandy-keeps-troy-wine.html.

70. Pam Allen, "Coffee, Cheese or Vino? Troy Wine Bar Will Have It All (Slideshow)," *Albany (NY) Business Review*, October 30, 2012, https:// www.bizjournals.com/albany/blog/2012/10/coffee-cheese-or-vino-troy-wine-bar .html.

71. Kenneth C. Crowe, "Troy Suspends Economic Development Coordinator," *Times Union* (NY Capital Region), April 6, 2012, https://www.timesunion.com /local/article/Troy-suspends-economic-development-coordinator-3462882.php.

72. Andrew Beam, "Troy Economic Development Coordinator Vic Christopher Resigns," *Record* (Troy, NY), https://www.troyrecord.com/news/troy-economic-development-coordinator-vic-christopher-resigns/article_fod65a13 -9dfo-5bba-ad14-d9c1999a5c07.html.

73. Vic Christopher, "We decided that Bradley's Tavern is perfect just the way it is," Twitter, December 6, 2016, https://twitter.com/vicchristopher /status/806218543750643716.

74. Graham, *Dream Cities*, 59.

75. Jimmy Vielkind, "Hello from The Bradley, a bar around the corner from @SenGillibrand's 2020 headquarters in Troy," Twitter, January 15, 2019, https://twitter.com/JimmyVielkind/status/1085404021446377472.

76. Vic Christopher, "The Bradley is and remains authentic for one main reason," Twitter, January 17, 2019, https://twitter.com/vicchristopher/status/1086040910213902336.

77. Vielkind, "Hello from The Bradley"; and Jimmy Vielkind, "State Street: Gillibrand Brings Her Campaign Home," *Wall Street Journal*, eastern ed., January 22, 2019.

78. Chris Churchill, "Is Troy the New Brooklyn?," *Times Union* (NY Capital Region), July 21, 2014, https://www.timesunion.com/upstate/article/Is-Troy-the-new-Brooklyn-5625682.php.

79. Simone Kitchens, "Can These Towns Become More Like Hudson Without Becoming Hudson?," *Intelligencer*, September 20, 2018, http://nymag.com/intelligencer/2018/09/newburgh-catskill-troy-new-york-real-estate.html.

80. For Mayor Madden's speech, see Troy City Hall, "Mayor Madden Delivers 2020 State of the City Address," City of Troy, NY, February 5, 2020, https://www.troyny.gov/mayor-madden-delivers-2020-state-of-the-city-address/. One year's worth of private investment attracted by Madden, $125 million, divided among Troy's population in 2018 would mean $10,204 of private investment per resident. New York City posted a record $56 billion in construction spending in 2018, according to the *New York Daily News*. Divided among the population of New York City, that would be "only" $5,330 per resident. Michael Gartland, "NYC Construction Expected to Keep Rising in 2019, New Report Shows," *New York Daily News*, sec. New York, October 24, 2019, https://www.nydailynews.com/new-york/ny-construction-building-congress-jobs-20191023-tmrvaqg2m5cy3ms2gkttv5vrii-story.html.

CHAPTER 2

1. "David Byrne on 'True Stories,' His Tabloid-Inspired Vision of Eighties America," interview by Kory Grow, *Rolling Stone*, November 26, 2018, https://www.rollingstone.com/movies/movie-features/david-byrne-true-stories-interview-754919/.

2. See Sharon Zukin, *Naked City: The Death and Life of Authentic Urban Places* (Oxford: Oxford University Press, 2011), 114.

3. Shara Sprecher, "CBGB to Reopen as Restaurant in Newark Airport," *Rolling Stone* (blog), December 21, 2015, https://www.rollingstone.com/music/music-news/cbgb-to-reopen-as-restaurant-in-newark-airport-59529/.

4. In case you don't know, Shea Stadium was demolished and replaced by Citi Field in 2009.

5. Richard L. Florida, *The New Urban Crisis: How Our Cities Are Increasing Inequality, Deepening Segregation, and Failing the Middle Class—and What We Can Do About It* (New York: Basic Books, 2017), 186.

6. David A. Banks, "Where the Streets Have No Numbers," *Real Life*, October 23, 2017, https://reallifemag.com/the-edifice-complex/.

7. Zukin, *Naked City*, 121.

8. Samuel Stein, *Capital City: Gentrification and the Real Estate State*, Jacobin series (London; Brooklyn, NY: Verso, 2019), 53.

9. Stein, *Capital City*, 53.

10. U.S. Census Bureau, *American Community Survey 2019 (5-Year Estimates)*, https://www.socialexplorer.com/data/ACS2019_5yr.

11. Sharon Zukin, *The Innovation Complex: Cities, Tech, and the New Economy* (New York: Oxford University Press, 2020), 7.

12. Zukin, *The Innovation Complex*, 200.

13. Florida, *The New Urban Crisis*, 21.

14. Florida, 21.

15. Florida, 33.

16. Zukin, *The Innovation Complex*, 15.

17. Capital Region Regional Economic Development Council (CRREDC), *Capital Region Creates: 2019 Progress Report* (Troy, NY: CRREDC, 2019), https://regionalcouncils.ny.gov/sites/default/files/2019-10/2019CapitalRegionProgressReport.pdf, 7.

18. Zukin, *The Innovation Complex*, 214.

19. Riordan Frost, "Who Is Moving and Why? Seven Questions about Residential Mobility," *Housing Perspectives*, Joint Center for Housing Studies of Harvard University, May 4, 2020, https://www.jchs.harvard.edu/blog/who-is-moving-and-why-seven-questions-about-residential-mobility.

20. Frost, "Who Is Moving and Why?"

21. Frost, "Who Is Moving and Why?"

22. Fulong Wu, *Planning for Growth: Urban and Regional Planning in China*, RTPI Library series (New York: Routledge, 2015).

23. Weizhen Tan, "Evergrande Stays Silent on Its $83 Million Dollar Bond Interest Payment, Leaving Investors in Limbo." CNBC, September 24, 2021, https://www.cnbc.com/2021/09/24/evergrande-debt-crisis-83-million-interest-payment-on-dollar-bond-.html.

24. Regional Economic Development Councils, "About REDC," n.d., accessed June 16, 2020, https://regionalcouncils.ny.gov/about.

25. Regional Economic Development Councils, "REDC FAQs," n.d., accessed June 16, 2020, https://regionalcouncils.ny.gov/redc-faqs.

26. Jesse McKinley, "Development Money, in Cuomo Era, Is Disbursed With Dazzle," sec. New York, *New York Times*, December 11, 2015, https://www.nytimes.com/2015/12/11/nyregion/development-money-in-cuomo-era-is-disbursed-with-dazzle.html.

27. Urban Dictionary, s.v. "Thirst," accessed July 19, 2021, https://www.urbandictionary.com/define.php?term=Thirst.

28. CREDC, *Capital Region Economic Development Council Strategic Plan*, November 14, 2011, https://regionalcouncils.ny.gov/sites/default/files/2017-12/CREDCStrategicPlan2011_online_version.pdf, 19.

29. "Mainly Greene: Cultural Tourism Corridor," Consolidated Funding Application, Regional Economic Development Councils, accessed June 15, 2021, https://regionalcouncils.ny.gov/cfa/project/38216.

30. "Hudson River Greenway Water Trail Marketing Materials," Consolidated Funding Application, Regional Economic Development Councils, accessed June 15, 2021, https://regionalcouncils.ny.gov/cfa/project/37262.

31. CREDC, *Capital Region Economic Development Council 2015 Progress Report: The Tech Valley in Focus* (Albany, NY: CREDC, September 21, 2015), 3.

32. CREDC, *Capital Region Creates: Capital Region Economic Development Council 2017 Progress Report* (Albany, NY: CREDC, 2017), https://regionalcouncils.ny.gov/sites/default/files/2017-12/2017ProgressReportCapital Region.pdf, 8.

33. CRREDC, *Capital Region Creates: 2019 Progress Report.*

34. Mark Castiglione (executive director, Capital District Regional Planning Commission) in discussion with author, June 8, 2021.

35. Rocco Ferraro (former executive director, Capital District Regional Planning Commission) in discussion with author, January 14, 2021.

36. Shelby Schneider (president Saratoga County Prosperity Partnership) in discussion with author, June 3, 2021.

37. Katie Arcieri, "Virginia's Amazon HQ2 Win Wasn't Just Based on Traditional Incentives," *Washington Business Journal*, November 14, 2018, https://www.bizjournals.com/washington/news/2018/11/13/virginias-win-of-amazon-hq2-wasnt-just-based-on.html.

38. CRREDC, *Capital Region Creates: 2019 Progress Report*, 42.

39. Zukin, *Naked City*, 121.

40. Zukin, 4.

41. Zukin, 222–23.

42. Zukin, 223.

43. Data from Mergent Intellect database searches of businesses in Albany, Rensselaer, Saratoga, and Schenectady that rent or own and have an SIC code of either 58 or 79; filtered by minority owned and women owned, 2022.

44. Jill Nagy, "Nafeesa Koslik Brings Cuisine from Her Native Country to 'Nani's Indian Kitchen,'" *Saratoga Business Journal*, December 11, 2020, https://www.saratoga.com/saratogabusinessjournal/2020/12/nafeesa-koslik-brings-cuisine-from-her-native-country-to-nanis-indian-kitchen/.

45. Zukin, *Naked City*, 231–32.

46. U.S. Census Bureau, "Total Population, 2020," *Social Explorer Tables: Census 2020—Preliminary Data*, https://www.socialexplorer.com/data/CENSUS 2020/metadata?ds=SE&table=T002.

47. U.S. Census Bureau, "Total Population, 2020."

48. U.S. Census Bureau, "Means of Transportation to Work for Workers 16 Years and Over, 2019," *Social Explorer Tables: ACS 2019 (1-Year Estimates)*, https://www.socialexplorer.com/data/ACS2019/metadata?ds=SE&table=A09005.

49. U.S. Census Bureau, "Age (Short Version), 2010," *Social Explorer Tables: ACS 2010 (5-Year Estimates)*, https://www.socialexplorer.com/data /ACS2010_5yr/metadata?ds=SE&table=B01001; U.S. Census Bureau, "Household Income (In 2010 Inflation Adjusted Dollars)," *Social Explorer Tables: ACS 2010 (5-Year Estimates)*, https://www.socialexplorer.com/data/ACS2010_5yr /metadata?ds=SE&table=A14001; U.S. Census Bureau, "Age (Short Version), 2019," *Social Explorer Tables: ACS 2019 (5-Year Estimates)*, https://www

.socialexplorer.com/data/ACS2019_5yr/metadata?ds=SE&table=B01001; U.S. Census Bureau, "Household Income (In 2019 Inflation Adjusted Dollars)," *Social Explorer Tables: ACS 2019 (5-Year Estimates)*, https://www.social explorer.com/data/ACS2019_5yr/metadata?ds=SE&table=A14001.

50. U.S. Census Bureau, "Median Gross Rent, 2010," *Social Explorer Tables: ACS 2010 (5-Year Estimates)*, https://www.socialexplorer.com/data/ACS2010_5yr/metadata?ds=SE&table=A18009; U.S. Census Bureau, "Median Gross Rent, 2019," *Social Explorer Tables: ACS 2019 (5-Year Estimates)*, https://www.socialexplorer.com/data/ACS2019_5yr/metadata?ds=SE&table=A18009.

51. Kenneth C. Crowe, "Which Capital Region Communities Grew the Most in New York?," *Times Union* (NY Capital Region), May 26, 2020, https://www.timesunion.com/news/article/Which-Capital-Region-communities-grew-the-most-in-15295810.php.

52. Larry Rulison, "GlobalFoundries Moving Headquarters to Malta," *Times Union* (NY Capital Region), April 26, 2021, https://www.timesunion.com/news/article/Globalfoundries-moving-headquarters-to-Malta-16129166.php.

53. U.S. Census Bureau, "Occupied Housing Units by Year Structure Built, 2019," *Social Explorer Tables: ACS 2019 (5-Year Estimates)*, https://www.socialexplorer.com/data/ACS2019_5yr/metadata?ds=SE&table=A10055; U.S. Census Bureau, "Year Structure Built (Renter-Occupied Housing Units), 2019," *Social Explorer Tables: ACS 2019 (5-Year Estimates)*, https://www.socialexplorer.com/data/ACS2019_5yr/metadata?ds=SE&table=A10059B; U.S. Census Bureau, "Residents Paying More Than 30% or at least 50% of Income on Selected Home Ownership Expenses, 2019," *Social Explorer Tables: ACS 2019 (5-Year Estimates)*, https://www.socialexplorer.com/data/ACS2019_5yr/metadata?ds=SE&table=B10040.

54. U.S. Census Bureau, "White vs. Non-White Homeowners, 2019," *Social Explorer Tables: ACS 2019 (5-Year Estimates)*, https://www.socialexplorer.com/data/ACS2019_5yr/metadata?ds=SE&table=B10060; U.S. Census Bureau, "Residents Paying More Than 30% or At Least 50% of Income on Rent, 2019," *Social Explorer Tables: ACS 2019 (5-Year Estimates)*, https://www.socialexplorer.com/data/ACS2019_5yr/metadata?ds=SE&table=B18002; U.S. Census Bureau, "Residents Paying More Than 30% or at least 50% of Income on Selected Home Ownership Expenses, 2019," *Social Explorer Tables: ACS 2019 (5-Year Estimates)*, https://www.socialexplorer.com/data/ACS2019_5yr/metadata?ds=SE&table=B10040.

55. Leonard Nevarez and Joshua Simons, "Small–City Dualism in the Metro Hinterland: The Racialized 'Brooklynization' of New York's Hudson Valley," *City & Community* 19, no. 1 (March 2020): 16–43, https://doi.org/10.1111/cico.12429.

56. U.S. Census Bureau, *Social Explorer Tables: ACS 2010 (5-Year Estimates)* and *ACS 2019 (5-Year Estimates)*.

57. Office of the New York State Comptroller, *Housing Affordability in New York State* (Albany: Office of the New York State Comptroller, June 2019).

58. Robin Cooper, "What's behind the Continued Investment in Glens Falls," *Albany Business Review*, November 14, 2019, https://www.bizjournals.com/albany/news/2019/11/14/glens-falls-power-breakfast-investment.html.

59. 2000 data from Capital District Regional Planning Commission, *Capital Region Statistical Report* (Albany, NY: CDRPC, September 2015); 2019 data from U.S. Census Bureau, *Social Explorer Tables: ACS 2019 (5-Year Estimates)*.

60. U.S. Census Bureau, *American Community Survey 2014–2018* census tract data.

61. Crowe, "Which Capital Region Communities Grew the Most in New York?"

62. U.S. Census Bureau, "Poverty Status in of Families by Family Type by Presence of Children under 18 Years, 2010," *Social Explorer Tables: ACS 2010 (5-Year Estimates)*, https://www.socialexplorer.com/data/ACS2010_5yr/metadata?ds=SE&table=A13002; U.S. Census Bureau, "Poverty Status in of Families by Family Type by Presence of Children under 18 Years, 2019," *Social Explorer Tables: ACS 2019 (5-Year Estimates)*, https://www.socialexplorer.com/data/ACS2019_5yr/metadata?ds=SE&table=A13002.

63. U.S. Census Bureau, "Median Gross Rent, 2010," *Social Explorer Tables: ACS 2010 (5-Year Estimate)*, https://www.socialexplorer.com/data/ACS2010_5yr/metadata?ds=SE&table=A18009; U.S. Census Bureau, "Median Gross Rent, 2019," *Social Explorer Tables: ACS 2019 (5-Year Estimate)*, https://www.socialexplorer.com/data/ACS2019_5yr/metadata?ds=SE&table=A1800.

64. U.S. Census Bureau, "Median Gross Rent as a Percentage of Household Income in the Past 12 Months (Dollars), 2010," *Social Explorer Tables: ACS 2010 (5-Year Estimates)*, https://www.socialexplorer.com/data/ACS2010_5yr/metadata?ds=SE&table=A18003; U.S. Census Bureau, "Median Gross Rent as a Percentage of Household Income in the Past 12 Months (Dollars), 2019," *Social Explorer Tables: ACS 2019 (5-Year Estimates)*, https://www.socialexplorer.com/data/ACS2019_5yr/metadata?ds=SE&table=A18003.

65. *Social Explorer Tables: ACS 2010 (5-Year Estimates)* and *ACS 2019 (5-Year Estimates)*.

66. *Capital Region Indicators: Benchmarking Progress in New York's Capital Region* (Albany, NY: Capital District Regional Planning Commission, August 2016), https://www.academia.edu/32460027/Capital_Region_Indicators.

67. *Capital Region Indicators.*

68. *Capital Region Indicators.*

69. *Capital Region Indicators.*

70. U.S. Census Bureau, "Gross Rent As a Percentage Of Household Income in the Past 12 Months," *PolicyMap Tables: ACS 2016-2020 (5-Year Estimates)*.

71. Kenneth C. Crowe and Leigh Hornbeck, "Capital Region Sees Coronavirus-Driven Spike in New Residents from New York City," *Times Union*, April 4, 2021, https://www.timesunion.com/news/article/new-york-city-residents-relocate-upstate-16070020.php.

72. Crowe and Hornbeck, "Capital Region Sees Coronavirus-Driven Spike."

73. Eric Willett and Matt Mowell, "COVID-19 Impact on Resident Migration Patterns," CBRE, April 1, 2021, https://www.cbre.com/insights/reports/covid-19-impact-on-migration-patterns.

74. Natasha Vaughn and Aliya Schneider, "Hudson Ranked 1st as Migration from NYC Climbs," HudsonValley360.com, April 22, 2021, https://www

.hudsonvalley360.com/news/columbiacounty/hudson-ranked-1st-as-migration-from-nyc-climbs/article_e3597b8a-bf94-529c-8071-486b36779abd.html.

75. Todd Kehoe, "Real Estate Sales Boom in Lake George, Stay Strong in Albany in 2020," *Albany Business Review*, March 26, 2021, https://www.bizjournals.com/albany/news/2021/03/26/residential-real-estate-albany-lake-george.html.

76. Davies quoted in Kehoe, "Real Estate Sales Boom in Lake George."

77. John Cropley, "Capital Region Housing Sales, Prices Jump 7% in 2020 despite COVID," *Daily Gazette*, January 25, 2021, https://dailygazette.com/2021/01/25/capital-region-housing-sales-prices-jump-7-in-2020-despite-covid/.

78. Taylor Borden, "The Post Office Says 300,000 New Yorkers Have Fled the City—for Places like the Hamptons and Even Honolulu," *Business Insider*, November 18, 2020, https://www.businessinsider.com/where-rich-new-yorkers-fleeing-coronavirus-moved-post-office-2020-11.

79. Interview with Mark Eagan, June 28, 2021,

80. Suzanne Spellen, "A Wave of Renovation Is Removing Troy's Rust Belt Decay to Open the Way for New Urban Economy and Culture," *New York Daily News*, sec. Lifestyle, October 4, 2013, https://www.nydailynews.com/lifestyle/real-estate/urban-renovations-uncover-riches-troy-article-1.1472989.

81. upstatecurious, "I got zero pics of the charming interior of the huge, equally charming beer garden-style outdoor seating area at @thedaleny," Instagram, April 21, 2021, https://www.instagram.com/p/CN8sEt5jhnh/.

82. Josh Ruben, "'Scare Me' Proves There's No Greater Horror Than the Unassuming White Guy," interview by Joseph Longo, October 1, 2020, *MEL Magazine*, https://melmagazine.com/en-us/story/scare-me-josh-ruben-interview.

83. Interview with Caroline Corrigan, December 10, 2020.

84. Zukin, *Naked City*, 45.

85. Jeramey Jannene, "City Hall: Arts Board Wants New City Flag Search," Urban Milwaukee, November 14, 2018, https://urbanmilwaukee.com/2018/11/14/city-hall-arts-board-wants-new-city-flag-search/.

86. Josh Moniz, "Flagged for Content: Rochester Flag Criticism Stirs Debate," *Post Bulletin* (Rochester, MN), September 9, 2015, https://www.postbulletin.com/news/news/local/flagged-for-content-rochester-flag-criticism-stirs-debate/article_ea652115-12aa-5e9b-9544-aa7629e969ce.html.

87. They are called vexillologists.

88. Ted Kaye, "Lessons from the American City Flag Redesign Efforts," *Research and News of the North American Vexillological Association* 4 (December 2018): 18–23.

89. Kaye, "Lessons from the American City Flag Redesign Efforts," 19.

90. John Gurda, "It May Be the People's Flag for Much of Milwaukee, but That Wasn't Good Enough for the Common Council," *Milwaukee Journal Sentinel*, February 6, 2020, https://www.jsonline.com/story/news/solutions/2020/02/06/milwaukee-common-council-ignites-flag-war-over-peoples-flag/4646492002/.

91. Pun absolutely intended.

92. Comment on KOMU-8, "Columbia Seeks Comment on City Flag Design Finalists," Facebook, October 20, 2015, https://www.facebook.com/komu8

/posts/10153605107107557?comment_id=10153605328547557&comment_tracking=%7B%22tn%22%3A%22R%2342%22%7D.

93. In U.S. cities, 22 percent of residents are immigrants compared to 11 percent in suburban counties and 4 percent in rural counties. See Kim Parker, Juliana Menasce Horowitz, Anna Brown, Richard Fry, D'Vera Cohn, and Ruth Igielnik, *What Unites and Divides Urban, Suburban and Rural Communities* (Washington, DC: Pew Research Center, May 22, 2018), https://www.pewresearch.org/social-trends/2018/05/22/demographic-and-economic-trends-in-urban-suburban-and-rural-communities/.

94. Liz Young, "What Is Albany's Brand?," *Albany Business Review*, May 23, 2019, https://www.bizjournals.com/albany/news/2019/05/23/capital-albany-region-brand-attract-investment.html.

95. Young, "What Is Albany's Brand?"

96. Young.

97. Interview with Caroline Corrigan. December 10, 2020.

98. Quotes from Michael Field and Ryan Hanley in "Katie Newcombe Explains How We Grow CAPNY," *Capital Region Business Podcast*, May 7, 2021, https://capitalregionbusiness.com/katie-newcombe-explains-how-we-grow-capny/.

99. Jessica Kelly, "Advice on CapNY's Hot Market, From 3 First-Time Home Buyers," CapNY, February 1, 2021, https://capny.us/2021/02/01/first-time-home-buyer-advice-in-a-hot-market/.

100. Kelly, "Advice on CapNY's Hot Market."

101. Jessica Kelly, "Moving Upstate: Miami Transplant Tony Quezada," CapNY, February 3, 2021, https://gocapny.com/2021/02/03/moving-upstate-miami-transplant-tony-quezada/.

102. Percent Arts, Entertainment, and Recreation Industries employment, 2016-2020, for the City of Miami, FL; Troy, NY; Albany, NY; Schenectady, NY; Saratoga Spring, NY, *PolicyMap* (based on U.S. Census Bureau data), accessed September 16, 2022, https://www.policymap.com. Percent Accommodation and Food Service employment, 2016-2020. for the City of Miami, FL; Troy, NY; Albany, NY; Schenectady, NY; Saratoga Spring, NY, *PolicyMap* (based on U.S. Census Bureau data), accessed September 16, 2022, https://www.policymap.com.

103. Percent of all homes that are likely affordable for a 4-person family earning 100% of AMI between 2016-2020, *PolicyMap* (based on data from U.S. Census Bureau and Department of Housing and Urban Development), accessed September 14, 2022, https://www.policymap.com.

104. Jeff Lautenberger, "If You Sell a House These Days, the Buyer Might Be a Pension Fund; Yield-Chasing Investors Are Snapping Up Single-Family Homes, Competing with Ordinary Americans and Driving up Prices," *Wall Street Journal (Online)*, sec. Markets, April 4, 2021, http://www.proquest.com/docview/2508227481/citation/6B216B7A43BF4CD9PQ/1.

105. Interview with Pat Harris, June 10, 2021.

106. Interview with Pat Harris, June 10, 2021.

107. Maureen Sager, "The Team behind the CapNY Brand," *ACE* (blog), April 8, 2021, https://www.upstatecreative.org/the-team-behind-the-capny-brand/.

108. Rio Riera Arbogast, "5 Companies with Unique Social Missions: CapNY," CapNY, February 17, 2021, https://capny.us/2021/02/17/5-capny-companies-with-unique-social-missions-2/.

109. Interview with Pat Harris, June 10, 2021.

CHAPTER 3

1. Interview with Rocky Ferraro. January 14, 2021.

2. Interview with Caroline Corrigan. December 10, 2020.

3. Interview with Elroy McDaniels, a pseudonym. January 5, 2021.

4. Interview with Megan Brenn-White. July 26, 2021.

5. Interview with Shelby Schneider. June 3, 2021.

6. Interview with Patrick Harris. June 10, 2021.

7. Interview with Taylor Lorenz. August 16, 2021.

8. Interview with Mark Castiglione. June 8, 2021.

9. Gregory Krieg, "How Can Trump Lie So Much and Be 'Authentic' at the Same Time?," CNN, May 5, 2018, https://www.cnn.com/2018/05/05/politics/trumps-lies-authentic-to-his-supporters; John Baldoni, "Is Donald Trump A Role Model For Authenticity?," Forbes, January 2, 2016, https://www.forbes.com/sites/johnbaldoni/2016/01/02/is-donald-trump-a-role-model-for-authenticity/?sh=135dbd9e33bc; Caroline Tanner, "Study Finds Trump Voters Believe Trump Is Authentic, Even If He Appears to Lie," USA Today, May 2, 2018, https://www.usatoday.com/story/news/politics/onpolitics/2018/05/02/trump-supporters-were-more-enthusiastic-their-support-him-candidate-extent-they-justified-trumps-lie/573371002/.

10. See Michel Foucault, Discipline and Punish: The Birth of the Prison, trans. Alan Sheridan (New York: Vintage Books, 2006).

11. Marshall Berman, The Politics of Authenticity: Radical Individualism and the Emergence of Modern Society, new ed. (London; New York: Verso, 2009), xxvii.

12. Berman, The Politics of Authenticity, 17.

13. Berman, 21.

14. Berman, 20–21.

15. Berman, 313.

16. Berman, 313.

17. Berman, 225.

18. Jill Ann Harrison, "Rust Belt Boomerang: The Pull of Place in Moving Back to a Legacy City," City & Community 16, no. 3 (2017): 263–83.

19. Harrison, "Rust Belt Boomerang," 2.

20. Interview with Mark Eagan June 28, 2021.

21. David Frum, "Every Culture Appropriates," Atlantic, May 8, 2018, https://www.theatlantic.com/ideas/archive/2018/05/cultural-appropriation/559802/.

22. Cathy Young, "To the New Culture Cops, Everything Is Appropriation," Washington Post, April 21, 2015, https://www.washingtonpost.com/posteverything/wp/2015/08/21/to-the-new-culture-cops-everything-is-appropriation/.

23. bell hooks, *Black Looks: Race and Representation* (Boston: South End Press, 1992, 39).

24. bell hooks, "Beyoncé's Lemonade Is Capitalist Money-Making at Its Best," sec. Music, *Guardian*, May 11, 2016, https://www.theguardian.com /music/2016/may/11/capitalism-of-beyonce-lemonade-album.

25. Berman, *The Politics of Authenticity*, 312. Emphasis in the original.

26. The three types are adapted from Ning Wang, "Rethinking Authenticity in Tourism Experience," *Annals of Tourism Research* 26, no. 2 (1999): 349–70.

27. See *Pawn Stars*, season 11, episode 7, "The Smoking Gun." Aired January 25, 2015 on History Channel (A&E Networks).

28. Wang, "Rethinking Authenticity in Tourism Experience," 355.

29. If you want to go down this rabbit hole, I suggest you start with Shuja Haider, "Postmodernism, Explained and Explained and Explained Again," The Outline, November 12, 2019, https://theoutline.com/post/8250/postmodern-philosophy-trump.

30. Fredric Jameson, *The Cultural Turn: Selected Writings on the Postmodern 1983–1998*. (London: Verso, 2009).

31. Susan Berfield and Lindsey Rupp, "The Aging of Abercrombie & Fitch," *Bloomberg*, January 22, 2015, https://www.bloomberg.com/news/features/2015-01-22/the-aging-of-abercrombie-fitch-i58ltcqx.

32. Wang, "Rethinking Authenticity in Tourism Experience," 351.

33. June Deery, *Reality TV*, Key Concepts in Media and Cultural Studies (Cambridge, UK; Malden, MA: Polity Press, 2015), 49.

34. Deery, *Reality TV*, 50.

35. Deery, 51.

36. Berman, *The Politics of Authenticity*, 313–14.

37. Beth Coleman, *Hello Avatar: Rise of the Networked Generation* (Cambridge, MA: MIT Press, 2011).

38. Louis Wirth, "Urbanism as a Way of Life," *Urban Life: Readings in the Anthropology of the City* 44, no. 1 (1938), 12.

39. Wirth, "Urbanism as a Way of Life," 23.

40. Henri Lefebvre, *The Urban Revolution* (Minneapolis: University of Minnesota Press, 2003).

41. Internet researcher Nathan Jurgenson once wrote, "This same line exists in every book i read," followed by a photo of a passage from an unnamed book that reads, "The internet did not create this phenomenon. But it was perfectly designed to accelerate this phenomenon," Twitter, December 30, 2020, https:// twitter.com/nathanjurgenson/status/1344342269906755584?s=20.

42. Manuel Castells, *The Power of Identity*, 2nd ed., Information Age, Economy, Society, and Culture (Malden, MA: Blackwell, 2004), 11.

43. Castells, *The Power of Identity*, 9.

44. Castells, 8.

45. Castells, 420.

46. Evgeny Morozov, *To Save Everything, Click Here: The Folly of Technological Solutionism* (New York: PublicAffairs, 2013), 347.

47. Quoted in Morozov, *To Save Everything, Click Here*, 315.

48. Russell Brandom, "Facebook Is Changing the Way It Enforces Its Real Name Policy," The Verge, December 15, 2015, https://www.theverge.com/2015/12/15/10215936/facebook-real-name-policy-changes-appeal-process.

49. Morozov, *To Save Everything, Click Here*, 317.

50. Andrew Potter, *The Authenticity Hoax: Why the "Real" Things We Seek Don't Make Us Happy* (New York: Harper Perennial, 2011), 162.

51. Crystal Abidin, "Layers of Identity," *Real Life*, April 16, 2018, https://reallifemag.com/layers-of-identity/.

52. Abidin, "Layers of Identity."

53. CapNY, homepage, accessed July 28, 2021, https://gocapny.com/.

54. CapNY, "Ask Us About Life in CapNY," accessed July 28, 2021, https://capny.us/ask-us-about-life-in-capny/.

55. Interview with Katie Newcombe. June 28, 2021.

CHAPTER 4

1. Sharon Zukin, *Naked City: The Death and Life of Authentic Urban Places* (Oxford: Oxford University Press, 2011), 28.

2. Sharon Zukin, *Loft Living: Culture and Capital in Urban Change*, 25th anniversary ed. (New Brunswick, NJ: Rutgers University Press, 2014), 59.

3. Zukin, *Loft Living*, 58.

4. Zukin, *Loft Living*, 68.

5. A.M. Gittlitz, "For a People's Beetlejuice," *A.M.'s Newsletter* (blog), October 30, 2020, https://gittlitz.substack.com/p/bio-exorcism-and-class-war.

6. John R. Logan and Harvey L. Molotch, *Urban Fortunes: The Political Economy of Place* (Berkeley: University of California Press, 2007), 81.

7. Logan and Molotch, *Urban Fortunes*, 83.

8. Logan and Molotch, 62.

9. Many cities the size of those in the Capital Region are led by people who legislate as a part-time job and have no staff. Logan and Molotch, 153.

10. Logan and Molotch, xxiv.

11. Joe Shaw, "Platform Real Estate: Theory and Practice of New Urban Real Estate Markets," *Urban Geography* 41, no. 8 (September 13, 2020): 1037–64, https://doi.org/10.1080/02723638.2018.1524653.

12. Jathan Sadowski, "The Internet of Landlords: Digital Platforms and New Mechanisms of Rentier Capitalism," *Antipode* 52, no. 2 (2020): 562–80, https://doi.org/10.1111/anti.12595.

13. Sadowski, "The Internet of Landlords," 564.

14. Shaw, "Platform Real Estate," 1053.

15. Shaw, 1048.

16. Shaw, 1049.

17. David Harvey, "The Art of Rent: Globalisation, Monopoly and the Commodification of Culture," *Socialist Register* 38 (2002), 94, https://socialistregister.com/index.php/srv/article/view/5778.

18. Harvey, "The Art of Rent," 94.

19. Harvey, 95.

20. According to its website, a third of its 19-million-euro budget goes to "communication, reputation building and protection of the Champagne AOC." "Legal Resources of the Comité Champagne and Financial Resources of the Comité Champagne," accessed July 2, 2021, https://www.champagne.fr/en/comite-champagne/about-us/legal-and-financial-resources.

21. Karl Marx, *Grundrisse* (London: Penguin Classics, 1993), 539.

22. Interview with Katie Newcombe, June 28, 2021

23. Harvey, "The Art of Rent," 95.

24. Harvey, 96.

25. Harvey, 101.

26. Capital Region Economic Development Council, *Capital Region Creates: 2019 Progress Report* (Albany, NY: CREDC, 2019), 49, https://regionalcouncils.ny.gov/sites/default/files/2019-10/2019CapitalRegionProgressReport.pdf.

27. Capital Region Economic Development Council, *Capital Region Economic Development Council 2015 Progress Report: The Tech Valley in Focus* (Albany, NY: CREDC, September 21, 2015).

28. Harvey, "The Art of Rent," 101.

29. Mark Robarge, "Sanctuary City Supporters, Foes Clash Outside Troy City Council Meeting," *The Record*, June 2, 2017, https://www.troyrecord.com/news/sanctuary-city-supporters-foes-clash-outside-troy-city-council-meeting/article_7d36b085-41ac-5902-b2d4-abc700050723.html. Despite the atrocious coverage in this article, you can't deny the lede photo where my friend and comrade Adam is being put in a chokehold by someone carrying an American flag.

30. His reasoning, in case you're interested, was the following: "The term 'sanctuary city' has no legal meaning. It is an imprecise term that can and often does refer to a wide array of state and local policies on immigration enforcement. Lacking a precise meaning it tends to create confusion as well as an unsubstantiated set of expectations." Kenneth C. Crowe, "Troy Mayor Vetoes Sanctuary City Resolution," sec. News, *Times Union*, July 12, 2019, https://www.timesunion.com/news/article/Troy-mayor-vetoes-sanctuary-city-resolution-14092316.php.

31. Sarah Kershaw, "For Schenectady, A Guyanese Strategy; Mayor Goes All Out to Encourage a Wave of Hardworking Immigrants," sec. New York, *New York Times*, July 26, 2002, https://www.nytimes.com/2002/07/26/nyregion/for-schenectady-guyanese-strategy-mayor-goes-all-encourage-wave-hardworking.html.

32. See David Graeber, *Bullshit Jobs* (New York: Simon & Schuster, 2019).

33. CapNY, "Cities and Destinations," accessed July 28, 2021, https://gocapny.com/__citiesandtowns/.

34. Zukin, *Naked City*, 27.

35. Sarah Banet-Weiser, *Authentic™: Politics and Ambivalence in a Brand Culture*, Critical Cultural Communication (New York: New York University Press, 2012), 110.

36. Mark Fisher, *Capitalist Realism: Is There No Alternative?* (Winchester: Zero Books, 2009), 9.

37. See David Banks, "Castle in the Cloud," *Real Life,* July 29, 2021, https://reallifemag.com/castle-in-the-cloud/; David A. Banks, "Where Do You Live?," *Eflux Architecture,* Software as Architecture, August 14, 2020, https://www.e-flux.com/architecture/software/337954/where-do-you-live/; and David A. Banks, "Against We," *Commune Magazine,* October 2019, https://communemag.com/against-we/.

38. David Banks, "Subscriber City," *Real Life,* October 26, 2020, https://reallifemag.com/subscriber-city/.

39. Farm land is increasingly concentrated, and there less of it. See Sarah K. Lowder, Jakob Skoet, and Terri Raney, "The Number, Size, and Distribution of Farms, Smallholder Farms, and Family Farms Worldwide," *World Development* 87 (November 1, 2016): 16–29, https://doi.org/10.1016/j.worlddev.2015.10.041.

40. Patrick Clarck, "Mega Landlords Are Snapping Up Zillow Homes before the Public Can See Them," *Bloomberg,* May 21, 2021, https://www.bloomberg.com/news/articles/2021-05-21/mega-landlords-are-snapping-up-zillow-homes-before-the-public-can-see-them.

CHAPTER 5

1. Tricia Garcia, dir., "Harlottown," *King of the Hill,* season 10, episode 4, November 20, 2005.

2. "REDC FAQs," accessed June 16, 2020, https://regionalcouncils.ny.gov/redc-faqs.

3. New York State, Regional Economic Development Councils, accessed June 14, 2021. https://regionalcouncils.ny.gov/.

4. That prize went to the Central New York region, centered around Syracuse, which spent it on the New York State Fair Grounds; the headquarters for TCGplayer, Inc., which runs an online marketplace for Pokémon and Magic the Gathering Cards; and four new greenhouses for the company Green Empire Farms. See LocalSYR, "What Ever Happened to the $500 Million Awarded to Central New York?," *WSYR* (blog), December 11, 2019, https://www.localsyr.com/news/local-news/what-ever-happened-to-the-500-million-awarded-to-central-new-york/.

5. Capital Region Economic Development Council (CREDC), *Capital Region Economic Development Council Strategic Plan,* November 14, 2011, 7, https://regionalcouncils.ny.gov/sites/default/files/2017-12/CREDCStrategicPlan2011_online_version.pdf.

6. CREDC, *Capital Region Economic Development Council Strategic Plan,* 8.

7. CREDC, *Capital 20.20: Advancing the Region through Focused Investment,* October 5, 2015, 6, https://esd.ny.gov/sites/default/files/CapitalRegionURI.pdf.

8. Jimmy Vielkind, "$50M Is Back of the Pack," sec. Local News, *Times Union,* December 19, 2012, https://www.timesunion.com/local/article/50M-is-back-of-the-pack-4131247.php.

9. Jimmy Vielkind, "Abruptly, Capital Region Council Co-Chair Resigns," *Times Union*, October 4, 2012, https://blog.timesunion.com/capitol/archives /158994/abruptly-capital-region-council-co-chair-resigns/.

10. "About," Adirondack Film Commission, accessed June 14, 2021, https:// filmadk.org/about/.

11. Kathleen Phalen-Tomaselli, "Washington County Tourism Social Media Numbers Come under Scrutiny," *Glens Falls Post-Star*, January 25, 2020, https:// poststar.com/news/local/washington-county-tourism-social-media-numbers-come-under-scrutiny/article_do32f916-a2ec-5002-9713-109fobe691d1.html.

12. Interview with Mark Eagan, June 28, 2021.

13. Regional Economic Development Councils (REDC), "Center for Economic Growth Working Capital," accessed August 3, 2021, https://regional-councils.ny.gov/cfa/project/16876.

14. REDC, "Center for Economic Growth Working Capital."

15. Interview with Katie Newcombe, June 28, 2021.

16. James Skoufis, *Final Investigative Report: Public Authorities in New York State* (Albany, NY: New York State Senate, December 16, 2019), https:// www.nysenate.gov/sites/default/files/article/attachment/public_authorities_ investigative_report_0.pdf.

17. These figures come from searching for "Cuomo" and filtering by "news /article" and "press release" on https://regionalcouncils.ny.gov/news, accessed August 26, 2021.

18. *Spatial fix* is a term used by David Harvey to describe the process of transforming a place to reinvest capital that may otherwise become devalued. See David Harvey, *The Limits to Capital* (London: Verso, 2018), 415.

19. Peter K. Eisinger, *The Rise of the Entrepreneurial State: State and Local Economic Development Policy in the United States*, La Follette Public Policy Series (Madison: University of Wisconsin Press, 1988), 341.

20. Christopher Walker, *Community Development Corporations and Their Changing Support Systems* (Washington DC: The Urban Institute, December 2002), https://www.urban.org/sites/default/files/publication/60731/410638-Community-Development-Corporations-and-their-Changing-Support-Systems. PDF, quoted in Lorraine E. Garkovich, "A Historical View of Community Development," in *Introduction to Community Development: Theory, Practice, and Service-Learning*, ed. Jerry W. Robinson Jr. and Gary Paul Green (Los Angeles: SAGE Publications, 2010), 34.

21. Garkovich, "A Historical View of Community Development," 18–45.

22. See Eisinger, *The Rise of the Entrepreneurial State*, ch. 2.

23. Robert A. Caro, *The Power Broker: Robert Moses and the Fall of New York* (New York: Knopf, 1974).

24. James Skoufis, *Final Investigative Report: Public Authorities in New York State*.

25. Industrial Development Agency Directory and Reports, accessed September 16, 2022, https://www.abo.ny.gov/paw/paw_weblistingIDA.html.

26. Ann Maloney, *Annual Report on Public Authorities in New York State* (Albany, NY: Authorities Budget Office, July 1, 2022), https://www.abo.ny.gov /reports/annualreports/ABO2022AnnualReport.pdf.

27. Schenectady Metroplex Development Authority, "City of Schenectady Industrial Development Agency," accessed August 3, 2021, https://www.schenectadymetroplex.com/city-of-schenectady-industrial-development-agency/.

28. John R. Logan and Harvey Luskin Molotch, *Urban Fortunes: The Political Economy of Place*, 20th anniversary ed. (Berkeley: University of California Press, 2010).

29. Alan G. Hevesi, *Industrial Development Agencies in New York State: Background, Issues and Recommendations* (New York: Office of the State Comptroller, May 2006), https://www.osc.state.ny.us/files/local-government/publications/pdf/idabackground.pdf.

30. Office of the New York State Comptroller, "IDA Reform," accessed August 4, 2021. https://www.osc.state.ny.us/legislation/ida-reform.

31. Skoufis, *Final Investigative Report: Public Authorities in New York State*, 67.

32. "Mazzone Hospitality's Gatta Named Chair of Scotia BID," *Albany Business Review*, August 14, 2012, https://www.bizjournals.com/albany/news/2012/08/14/scotia-bid-names-names-board-chair.html.

33. Center for Economic Growth, "What We Do," accessed August 4, 2021, https://www.ceg.org/meet-ceg/what-we-do/.

34. Quoted in Mike De Socio, "Albany Region Resources for Small Business Owners Struggling with Coronavirus," *Albany Business Review*, May 27, 2020, https://www.bizjournals.com/albany/news/2020/03/27/albany-local-resource-guide-small-business.html.

35. Center for Economic Growth, "Center for Economic Growth and Upstate Alliance for the Creative Economy Announce Merger," April 15, 2019, https://www.ceg.org/articles/center-economic-growth-upstate-alliance-creative-economy-announce-merger/.

36. Michael DeMasi, "Former Editor to Head Troy Business Improvement District," *Albany Business Review*, January 21, 2014, https://www.bizjournals.com/albany/morning_call/2014/01/former-editor-to-head-troy-business.html.

37. Michael DeMasi, "Troy Merchants, in Pursuit of BID, Hire Downtown Promoter," *Albany Business Review*, March 31, 2008, https://www.bizjournals.com/albany/stories/2008/03/31/story8.html.

38. Bloor West Village, "History of the Bloor West Village BIA," accessed August 27, 2021, https://www.bloorwestvillagebia.com/History. See also Katharine N. Rankin, Kuni Kamizaki, and Heather McLean, "Toronto's Changing Neighborhoods: Gentrification of Shopping Streets," in *Global Cities, Local Streets: Everyday Diversity from New York to Shanghai*, edited by Sharon Zukin, Philip Kasinitz, and Xiangming Chen (New York: Routledge, Taylor & Francis Group, 2016), 140–69.

39. Michael DeMasi, "Albany Allowing Restaurants to Continue Sidewalk Dining This Winter," *Albany Business Review*, October 30, 2020, https://www.bizjournals.com/albany/news/2020/10/30/albany-patio-heaters-extended-sidewalk-permits.html.

40. Mike De Socio, "Lark Street Study Aims for Safer, More Walkable Neighborhood," *Albany Business Review*, November 15, 2019, https://www

.bizjournals.com/albany/news/2019/11/15/lark-street-improvement-study-safety-walkability.html.

41. Michael DeMasi, "Downtown Troy BID Offers Free Workshop on Social Media," *Albany Business Review*, October 11, 2012, https://www.bizjournals.com/albany/morning_call/2012/10/downtown-troy-bid-offers-free-workshop.html.

42. Quoted in Michael DeMasi, "Downtown Troy Business Owners Oppose Methadone Clinic Expansion," *Albany Business Review*, June 10, 2015, https://www.bizjournals.com/albany/blog/health-care/2015/06/downtown-troy-business-owners-oppose-methadone.html.

43. Jordan Carleo-Evangelist, "'Ghost Tickets' Had Repercussions," *Times Union*, December 27, 2009, https://www.timesunion.com/local/article/Ghost-tickets-had-repercussions-560678.php.

44. Philip Schwartz, "10 Minutes With: Elizabeth Young," *Albany Business Review*, April 12, 2013, https://www.bizjournals.com/albany/print-edition/2013/04/12/10-minutes-with-elizabeth-young.html.

45. Amy Siverson, "Business Improvement District Helps Keep Lark St. Hopping," *Albany Business Review*, March 12, 2001, https://www.bizjournals.com/albany/stories/2001/03/12/focus2.html.

46. Michael DeMasi, "Albany, New York Social Media Campaign #capture ALB Will Bring Red Picture Frames to Downtown," *Albany Business Review*, May 29, 2015, https://www.bizjournals.com/albany/news/2015/05/29/big-red-picture-frames-coming-to-downtown-albany.html.

47. Michael DeMasi, "Uncle Sam Statues Draw Curious to Downtown Troy Slideshow (Video)," *Albany Business Review*, May 7, 2013, https://www.bizjournals.com/albany/news/2013/05/06/uncle-sam-statues-boost-business-in.html.

48. Julie Napoli, Sonia Dickinson-Delaporte, and Michael B. Beverland, "The Brand Authenticity Continuum: Strategic Approaches for Building Value," *Journal of Marketing Management* 32, no. 13–14 (September 2016): 1201–29, https://doi.org/10.1080/0267257X.2016.1145722, 1202.

49. Napoli, Dickinson-Delaporte, and Beverland, "The Brand Authenticity Continuum."

50. Napoli, Dickinson-Delaporte, and Beverland, 1206.

51. Napoli, Dickinson-Delaporte, and Beverland, 1217.

52. Sarah Banet-Weiser, *Authentic™: The Politics of Ambivalence in a Brand Culture* (New York: NYU Press, 2012), 100.

53. Banet-Weiser, *Authentic™*, 213.

54. Interview with Katie Newcombe, June 28, 2021.

55. Interview with Mark Eagan, June 28, 2021.

56. Crystal Abidin, "Layers of Identity," *Real Life*, April 16, 2018, https://reallifemag.com/layers-of-identity/.

57. *The Young and the Restless: How Portland Competes for Talent* (Portland, OR, and Memphis, TN: Impresa, Inc. and Coletta & Company, 2004), https://prosperportland.us/wp-content/uploads/2016/07/The-Young-and-the-Restless-How-Portland-Competes-for-Talent.pdf, 60.

58. Jamie Peck, "Struggling with the Creative Class," *International Journal of Urban and Regional Research* 29, no. 4 (December 1, 2005): 740–70, https://doi.org/10.1111/j.1468-2427.2005.00620.x., 760.

59. Interview with Megan Brenn-White, July 26, 2021.

60. Tracy Ziemer, "Seeking Friends or Businesses in the Hudson Valley? There's Now an App for That," *Times Union*, March 17, 2021, https://www.timesunion.com/hudsonvalley/news/article/Upstate-Curious-app-launches-in-Hudson-Valley-16027075.php.

61. Inness, "Home," accessed July 29, 2021, https://inness.co/.

62. Interview with Megan Brenn-White, July 26, 2021.

63. Interview with Brenn-White.

64. Interview with Brenn-White.

65. Quoted in Ziemer, "Seeking Friends or Businesses in the Hudson Valley?"

66. Abidin, "Layers of Identity."

67. Interview with Elroy McDaniels (a pseudonym), January 5, 2021

68. Interview with McDaniels.

69. I'm paraphrasing this bit from page 12 of Jean Baudrillard's *Simulacra and Simulation* (Ann Arbor: University of Michigan Press, 1994): "Disneyland is presented as imaginary in order to make us believe that the rest is real, whereas all of Los Angeles and the America that surrounds it are no longer real, but belong to the hyperreal order and to the order of simulation."

70. Zoe Hurley, "Imagined Affordances of Instagram and the Fantastical Authenticity of Female Gulf-Arab Social Media Influencers," *Social Media + Society* 5, no. 1 (January 1, 2019), https://doi.org/10.1177/2056305118819241, 11.

71. For more on Lorenz's career trajectory, see Taylor Lorenz, "The Other Side with Photogrammetry: How Taylor Lorenz Went behind the Camera with Some of LA's Most Illustrious Influencers," interview by Charlise Koch, Storybench, April 8, 2021, https://www.storybench.org/the-other-side-with-photogrammetry-how-taylor-lorenz-went-behind-the-camera-with-some-of-las-most-illustrious-influencers/.

72. Marisa Kashino, "This Social Media Influencer Gets Paid to Live in Luxury Buildings," *Washingtonian*, April 2, 2018, https://www.washingtonian.com/2018/04/02/social-media-influencer-gets-paid-live-luxury-buildings/.

73. Allie Jones, "The New Frontier in Celebrity Spon-Con: Tavi Gevinson Advertises Her Own Address," *The Cut*, March 15, 2017, https://www.thecut.com/2017/03/celebrity-sponcon-tavi-gevinson-advertises-her-own-address.html.

74. Kate Lindsay, "Alison Roman Is Reportedly Pivoting (Back) to Restaurants," *NoFilter*, October 26, 2020, https://influence.co/nofilter/alison-roman-restaurant-table-on-ten.

75. Alana Massey, "Alana Massey," accessed September 2, 2021. http://alanamassey.com.

76. June Deery, *Reality TV*, Key Concepts in Media and Cultural Studies (Cambridge, UK; Malden, MA: Polity Press, 2015), 30.

77. Deery, *Reality TV*, 45.

78. In an interview with François L'Yvonnet, Baudrillard admits to having used imaginary quotations: "The funniest being the one that stands as an epigraph to a chapter in *Simulacre et Simulation* falsely attributed to Ecclesiastes. . . . Nobody spotted it!" Jean Baudrillard, *Fragments: Conversations with François L'Yvonnet*, trans. Chris Turner (London: Routledge, 2004), 11.

CHAPTER 6

1. "Trappist Westvleteren—Our Beers," n.d., accessed October 30, 2020, https://www.trappistwestvleteren.be/en.

2. Mark Fisher, *Capitalist Realism: Is There No Alternative?* (Winchester, UK: Zero Books, 2009).

3. Gary P. Green and Anna Haines, *Asset Building and Community Development*, 4th ed. (Los Angeles: SAGE, 2016).

4. Ted Howard, Lillian Kuri, and India Pierce Lee, "The Evergreen Cooperative Initiative of Cleveland, Ohio" (Cleveland: The Cleveland Foundation, September 29, 2010), 3, https://community-wealth.org/sites/clone.community-wealth.org/files/downloads/paper-howard-et-al.pdf.

5. Stacey A. Sutton, "Cooperative Cities: Municipal Support for Worker Cooperatives in the United States," *Journal of Urban Affairs* 41, no. 8 (November 17, 2019): 1–22, https://doi.org/10.1080/07352166.2019.1584531, 12.

6. Sutton, "Cooperative Cities," 12.

7. Finger Lakes Regional Economic Development Council, *Annual Report and Recommended Priority Projects: Year 8, 2018* (Rochester, NY: Finger Lakes REDC, 2018).

8. Katie Washington, "Interview with OWN Rochester," by Kevin Gustafson and Larry Fenster, *All Things Co-op* podcast, September 22, 2020. https://www.youtube.com/watch?v=f24i_oaWVfo.

9. Washington, "Interview with OWN Rochester."

10. "An Exit Option for Business Owners, With No Pandemic Penalty," Evergreen Cooperatives, June 9, 2020, http://www.evgoh.com/2020/06/09/an-exit-option-for-business-owners-with-no-pandemic-penalty/.

11. Sutton, "Cooperative Cities," 18.

12. Barry Hirsch and David Macpherson, "IV. Metropolitan Area," 2021, Union Membership and Coverage Database from the CPS, http://unionstats.com/.

13. Sean Collins, "'We're Fighting for Our Community, for Our Patients': Interview with Michael Fitzsimmons of NYSNA at AMC," *Strikewave*, December 16, 2020, https://www.thestrikewave.com/interviews/nysna-amc-interview-with-michael-fitzsimmons.

14. See Bethany Bump, "AG: Albany Med Violated Human Trafficking Law, Must Repay Filipino Nurses," sec. News, *Times Union*, June 17, 2021, https://www.timesunion.com/news/article/AG-Albany-Med-violated-human-trafficking-law-16254812.php.

15. Loretta Pyles and David Banks, "Chancellor Johnson Isn't Fighting for SUNY: Our Union Will," *Strikewave*, December 11, 2019, https://www.thestrikewave.com/original-content/uup-will-fight-for-suny-against-austerity.

16. Hirsch and Macpherson, Union Membership and Coverage Database, http://unionstats.com.

17. "Selected Economic Highlights for 2008" (Baton Rouge: Louisiana Economic Development, March 13, 2009), https://www.opportunitylouisiana.com /docs/default-source/Performance-Reporting/selected-economic-highlights /selected_economic_highlights_for_2008.pdf?sfvrsn=e5a6d405_4.

18. See Thomas A. Reiner and Robert H. Wilson, "Planning and Decision-Making in the Soviet City: Rent, Land, and Urban Form," in *The Socialist City: Spatial Structure in Soviet and East European Cities*, ed. Richard Anthony French and F. E. Ian Hamilton (Chichester; New York: Wiley, 1979), 49–72.

19. Walter Benjamin, "The Work of Art in the Age of Mechanical Reproduction," in *Illuminations: Essays and Reflections* (Boston: Mariner Books, 2019), 193.

20. David Harvey, "The Art of Rent: Globalisation, Monopoly and the Commodification of Culture," *Socialist Register* 38 (2002): 108, https:// socialistregister.com/index.php/srv/article/view/5778.

21. Harvey, "The Art of Rent," 109.

22. Sharon Zukin, *Naked City: The Death and Life of Authentic Urban Places* (Oxford: Oxford University Press, 2011), 244.

23. Gunn Enli and Linda Therese Rosenberg, "Trust in the Age of Social Media: Populist Politicians Seem More Authentic," *Social Media + Society* 4, no. 1 (January 1, 2018): 9, https://doi.org/10.1177/2056305118764430.

Index